Law, Governance and Technology Series

Volume 75

The *Law, Governance and Technology Series* is intended to attract manuscripts arising from an interdisciplinary approach in law, artificial intelligence and information technologies. The idea is to bridge the gap between research in IT law and IT-applications for lawyers developing a unifying techno-legal perspective. The series will welcome proposals that have a fairly specific focus on problems or projects that will lead to innovative research charting the course for new interdisciplinary developments in law, legal theory, and law and society research as well as in computer technologies, artificial intelligence and cognitive sciences. In broad strokes, manuscripts for this series may be mainly located in the fields of the Internet law (data protection, intellectual property, Internet rights, etc.), Computational models of the legal contents and legal reasoning, Legal Information Retrieval, Electronic Data Discovery, Collaborative Tools (e.g. Online Dispute Resolution platforms), Metadata and XML Technologies (for Semantic Web Services), Technologies in Courtrooms and Judicial Offices (E-Court), Technologies for Governments and Administrations (E-Government), Legal Multimedia, and Legal Electronic Institutions (Multi-Agent Systems and Artificial Societies).

Lídia Ballesta Martí

The Communication to the Public of Musical Works Online in the European Union's Legislation

Striving for a Fair Balance

Springer

Lídia Ballesta Martí
Department of Public Law and Legal History Studies
Autonomous University of Barcelona
Cerdanyola del Vallès, Spain

ISSN 2352-1902 ISSN 2352-1910 (electronic)
Law, Governance and Technology Series
ISBN 978-3-031-94131-3 ISBN 978-3-031-94132-0 (eBook)
https://doi.org/10.1007/978-3-031-94132-0

This Springer imprint is published by the registered company Springer Nature Switzerland AG
The registered company address is: Gewerbestrasse 11, 6330 Cham, Switzerland

Thanks to my mentors and my partner for believing in me, and for their support and inspiration.

To my father and mother, with eternal gratitude and love.

Competing Interests The author has no competing interests to declare that are relevant to the content of this manuscript.

List of Abbreviations

Art.	Article
BC	Berne Convention
CDSM/CDSMD	Directive 796/2019 on the Copyright on the Digital Single Market
CJEU	Court of Justice of the European Union
CMO	Collective Management Organisation
Commission	European Commission
Coreper	Committee of Permanent Representatives of the Council
Council	Council of the European Union
CtoP	Communication to the Public
DSB	Dispute Settlement Body
DSU	Dispute Settlement Understanding
ECJ	European Court of Justice
EFTA	European Free Trade Association
EP	European Parliament
EU	European Union
GATT	General Agreement on Tariffs and Trade
IA	Impact Assessment
InfoSoc	Directive 29/2001 on the Information Society
IP	Intellectual Property
MA	Make available (right)
MS	Member States
OCSSPs	Online Content Sharing Service Providers
p.	Page/pages
para.	Paragraph
RBIr	Regulation Brussels I (recast)
RC	Rome Convention
RIIR	Rome II Regulation
TFEU	Treaty of Functioning of the European Union
TRIPS	

	Trade-Related Aspects of Intellectual Property Rights (agreement)
TUE	Treaty of the European Union
UCC	Universal Copyright Convention
US/USA	United States of America
WCT	WIPO Copyright Treaty
WIPO	World Intellectual Property Office
WPPT	WIPO Performances and Phonograms Treaty
WTO	World Trade Organisation

Contents

Part I International Legal Framework of the Communication to the Public Right in Musical Works

1 Defining Concepts of Copyright and Communication to the Public Right Through the Applicable International Legal Framework 3
1.1 First Generation of Conventions: From Berne to Rome 4
1.1.1 The Object: Musical Work v Performances Phonograms and Broadcasts 11
1.1.2 The Subjects: The Rightsholders 18
1.1.3 The Right of Public Performance and Communication to the Public 23
1.2 Early "Internet" Treaties: The TRIPs Agreement and the WIPO Internet Treaties (WCT & WPPT) 29
1.3 TRIPs Agreement and the WTO 30
1.3.1 CtoP and the WTO Dispute Settlement System: The Dispute WT/DS160 Against the Section 110(5) of the US Copyright Act 34
1.4 WIPO Internet Treaties: From Public Performance to the Making Available 39
1.5 Overview: The Limits of the Multilateral Legal Framework on Copyright 44
References 45

Part II The Right of Communication to the Public of Musical Works Online Under EU Copyright Legislation and Case-Law

2 Fundamentals of the EU Copyright Law 51
2.1 EU Objectives and Principals: Single Market, Culture and Human Rights 51
2.2 EU Competence on Copyright; Principle of Conferral and Copyright Legal Bases 53

2.3 The Exercise of the EU Competence on Copyright 58
2.3.1 The EU Copyright Acquis 59
2.3.2 Principles of Subsidiarity and Proportionality in the EU Copyright Legislation 64
2.4 Overview: Adequacy of the Legal Basis and Legal Instruments to Advocate for a Unitary Copyright System 69
References 71

3 The Right of Communication to the Public of Musical Works Online in the EU Copyright Law 73
3.1 The (Non)Conceptualisation of Right of Communication to the Public in the EU Legislation: Article 3 of the InfoSoc Directive Shortcomings 75
3.1.1 Communication to the Public and Making Available 79
3.1.2 Secondary Acts of Communication and the Non-Exhaustion Principle 83
3.2 The CJEU Configuration of the Communication to the Public Right in Musical Works Online: An Approach Through Dynamic Criteria 86
3.2.1 Which Acts Constitute a 'Communication'? 91
3.2.2 Who Is the 'Public'? 98
References 103

Part III Liability and Enforcement of Infringements of Communication to the Public Right in Online Music

4 The Directive 2019/790 on Copyright in the Digital Single Market . . 107
4.1 CtoP of Online Music Works Under Article17 CDSM Directive: A New Liability Regime or a redefinition of CtoP? 113
4.2 The New Liability System for CtoP: OCSSPs' Liability and Exemptions 119
4.3 The compatibility of Article 17 with the EU Charter of Fundamental Rights: An Attempt for Annulment 128
4.4 The CDSM Directive and the Role of Stakeholders in the Music Field 132
4.5 Overview: Rightsholders as Beneficiaries of the Copyright Legislation, CDSM Directive and Fundamental Rights Balancing 141
References 142

5 Enforcement of Communication to the Public Right 145
5.1 Determining Jurisdiction 151
5.2 Determining Applicable Law 160

5.3 Overview: Need for a Renewal of International Enforcement Rules for Online Infringements 165
References 166

6 A Proposal for a "Streaming Levy" for Communication to the Public Acts of Musical Works Online: Striving for a Fair Balance 167
6.1 Final Overview: Striving for a Fair Balance 172
References 173

Legislation 175

Case Law 179

Institutional Documents 181

Part I
International Legal Framework of the Communication to the Public Right in Musical Works

Having a clear, internationally accepted legal definition of the communication to the public (CtoP) right of musical works is not easy, especially in the constantly changing scenario for the music industry. Furthermore, it is also complex to define the object of protection and subjects of such rights. Therefore, before any analysis, it is essential to categorise music and copyright concepts and become familiar with the terms to avoid misconceptions.

In the context of music copyright, the communication to the public (CtoP) right is defined as the act of communication by performing or making available a copyright-protected musical work to an undefined group of people out of the communicator's private sphere. Such communication may occur through live performances of the musical work or by playing a phonogram, irrespective of the medium used. Communicating a phonogram entails acts like broadcasting or performing the phonogram in a space open to the public, as well as communicating the phonogram by any other wire or wireless means, which also includes the act of making phonograms available to an uncertain public by giving them access to those sound files on the Internet.

Most legal frameworks recognize communication to the public as an exclusive economic copyright within performing rights, granting rightsholders the authority to permit or prohibit public performances of their works and to receive financial compensation for their public use or exploitation.

On the other hand, concerning copyright, it is essential to clarify that there are two different conceptions of it: one provided by the *common law* systems and the other provided by the *civil law*.

Copyright in the *common law* system emerged from the Statute of Queen Anne in 1710. The document gave authors the right to authorise the printing of their works; that is, the right to copy. In the common law system, the central element of protection is the work itself, as the object, rather than the subjects as creators and their relationship with their work. The work is conceived as a product, and its protection by such a copyright system is based on economic rights to grant the production of creative works.

The civil law system of copyright comes mainly from the French Revolution conception of "droits d'auteur" as a "natural right" of the subject who creates an artistic object, so these systems also recognised moral rights, apart from economic ones. This conception is focused on the link between the author and the work as part of their intellect. The right of authors is a personal right based on the idea of protecting creativity as an expression of the idea of the subject. That copyright[1] concept refers to authors' rights in their intellectual creations. As in civil law systems, copyright is a right *"ad personam"*; any other right that someone different from the author may have in an artistic creation is referred to as related rights (also named neighbouring rights).[2]

[1] It stands *for derechos de autor, diritto d'autore, droits d'auteur or Urheberrechte.*

[2] That stands for *derechos conexos/ diritti connessi/ droits voisins/ verwandte Schutzrechte*. The term *related rights* is used in this study with such a meaning.

Chapter 1
Defining Concepts of Copyright and Communication to the Public Right Through the Applicable International Legal Framework

The Internet and technological advancements have fundamentally altered how music is consumed and communicated to the public. While music has become globally accessible, copyright law remains territorial and is often constrained by outdated multilateral harmonization instruments. It means that many different legislations rule on copyright. Therefore, there is not a univocal definition of CtoP to be sufficiently accurate to remain valid throughout the globe because of the non-self-executing nature of the existing international rules on this topic. Indeed, the multilateral international treaties that constitute the current international copyright legal framework can be divided into two main generations of treaties: the first-generation conventions (up to 1970') and the early Internet generation treaties (concluded during the second half of the 1990s'), both from the twentieth century and both requiring internal normative development.

The first-generation treaties -that with their review and modifications in 1971 are still valid today- include: The Convention for the Protection of Literary and Artistic Works (Berne Convention, 1886),[1] The Universal Copyright Convention (UCC, 1952)[2] and The Convention for the Protection of Performers, Producers of Phonograms and Broadcasting Organizations (Rome Convention, 1961).[3]

After the 1971 amendments to the international copyright legislation, the need to protect other certain related rights appeared, and two new conventions were concluded. The last two conventions of the first generation are:

---

[1] Berne Convention for the Protection of Literary and Artistic Works. Done at Berne on 9 September 1886. (Last revised; amended on September 28, 1979).

[2] Universal Copyright Convention. Adopted at Geneva on September 6, 1952. (Last revised at Paris on July 24, 1971).

[3] International Convention for the Protection of Performers, Producers of Phonograms and Broadcasting Organisations. Done at Rome on October 26, 1961.

L. Ballesta Martí, *The Communication to the Public of Musical Works Online in the European Union's Legislation*, Law, Governance and Technology Series 75,
https://doi.org/10.1007/978-3-031-94132-0_1

The Convention for the Protection of Producers of Phonograms Against Unauthorized Duplication of Their Phonograms (Geneva or Phonograms Convention, 1971)[4] and
The Convention Relating to the Distribution of Programme-Carrying Signals Transmitted by Satellite (Brussels or Satellites Convention, 1974).[5]

The second generation of treaties -also known as the early Internet generation of treaties- arrived to adapt the international copyright legislation to the challenges of technology and the Internet. This group includes: The WIPO Copyright Treaty (WCT)[6] and the WIPO Performances and Phonograms Treaty (WPPT),[7] both concluded in 1996 and known as the WIPO Internet Treaties.

The WTO Agreement on Trade-Related Aspects of Intellectual Property Rights (TRIPs)[8] because although it only covers those aspects of the copyright directly linked to trade, it directly affects the economic rights of copyright and related rights.

The first generation of copyright conventions provided the earliest definitions of the objects of protection and the subjects owning the corresponding rights derived from such protection. Meanwhile, the second generation of treaties adapted rights granted under previous treaties to the new scenarios for the objects of protection faced by the rightsholders.

The following paragraphs will study the definition and evolution of objects, subjects and CtoP right through these international conventions.

1.1 First Generation of Conventions: From Berne to Rome

The first multilateral agreement on copyright is the Convention for the Protection of Literary and Artistic Works signed in Berne on 9 September 1886. Also known as the Berne Convention, it is one of the 26 treaties administrated by the WIPO nowadays.[9]

The agreement was revised at Paris in 1896 and at Berlin in 1908, completed at Berne in 1914, revised at Rome in 1928, Brussels in 1948, Stockholm in 1967 and Paris in 1971. Its last amendment was in 1979.

[4]Convention for the Protection of Producers of Phonograms Against Unauthorized Duplication of Their Phonograms, adopted at Geneva on October 29, 1971.

[5]Brussels Convention Relating to the Distribution of Programme-Carrying Signals Transmitted by Satellite, Done at Brussels on May 21, 1974.

[6]WIPO Copyright Treaty (WCT), adopted in Geneva on December 20, 1996.

[7]WIPO Performances and Phonograms Treaty (WPPT), adopted in Geneva on December 20, 1996.

[8]WTO, Agreement on Trade-Related Aspects of Intellectual Property Rights, adoptet in Marrakesh on April 15, 1994.

[9]See https://www.wipo.int/treaties/en/.

The Berne Convention conclusion was promoted by the International Literary and Artistic Association and sponsored by the Swiss Government.[10] After three diplomatic conferences celebrated in Berne, the Convention for the Protection of Literary and Artistic Works was adopted by eight countries: Belgium, France, Germany, Great Britain, Italy, Spain, Switzerland and Tunisia.

This treaty aimed to achieve a multilateral agreement with worldwide application and a consistent legal-philosophical approach. Despite being based on the principle of national treatment, the Berne Convention settled a minimum level of protection that must be granted among the parties. With that objective, the convention not only set up the rules to protect the authors who created or published work in another member country but also established the Berne Union in the very first Article of the Convention,[11] which can be considered the embryo of an International Organization to protect the authors worldwide.[12] "The constitution of a "Union" means that a permanent link among countries was created.[13] As a structure to achieve its aim, the Berne Convention established in Article 16 of the original 1886 text an International office, namely "Bureau of the International Union for the Protection of Literary and Artistic Works", placed under the "*high authority of the highest government authority of the Swiss Confederation*".[14] The attributions of the Bureau were not mentioned in the convention's text. Still, it provided the countries of the Union with powers to set up the Bureau's attributions by common agreement. Furthermore, all the Union member countries committed to supporting the Bureau's cost. In 1967, the Stockholm Act replaced the *International Bureau of the Berne Union* with the *International Bureau of the World Intellectual Property Organization (WIPO*[15]*)*. It was not

---

[10]For a further historical approach to the Berne Convention, see Ricketson and Ginsburg (2015), pp. 3–36.

[11]Original text of Article 1 of the Berne Convention in 1886, and after the Rome conference of revision in 1928, still remain the same nowadays. This article states:

> The contracting countries constitute a Union for the protection of the rights of authors in their literary and artistic works". The words "contracting countries" were replaced by the words "the countries to which this Convention applies

[12]According to Sobrino Heredia (2010) the origin of the modern International Organisations as we know today can be dated between 1815 and 1914 with the proliferation of international conferences and the establishment of permanent institutional structures such as the Berne Union.

[13]Bogsch (1986).

[14]Original text of Article 16 of the Berne Convention in 1886:

> [1] An international office shall be established under the name "Bureau of the International Union for the Protection of Literary and Artistic Works."
>
> [2] This Bureau, the cost of which shall be supported by the Administrations of all the countries of the Union, shall be placed under the high authority of the High Administration of the Swiss Confederation and shall work under its direction. Its functions shall be determined in common agreement between the countries of the Union.

[15]Officially called the "International Bureau of Intellectual Property".

until the said revision Act that the Assembly of the Berne Union and the Executive Committee of the Berne Union were established as organs of that structure.[16]

Therefore, 1967 Stockholm Act introduced institutional changes, and its revision of the Berne Convention intended to respond to the technological advancements achieved in those decades but also to the needs of the then newly independent developing countries organised under the non-aligned movement, which, in a coherent with their proposals of a new international economic order, claimed to have access to the works with educational purposes.[17]

However, the clauses regarding the developing countries introduced in the Stockholm Act never got into force. They had to wait until the review Conference in Paris in 1971 to ensure the universal effect of the Convention and the incorporation of those special provisions relating to developing countries in an Annex that now forms an integral part of the Convention. Since then, the Berne Convention has remained unchanged despite the constantly changing context of its application scope. Not only that, but it has increased in the number of states parties.[18]

Regarding its content, the protection of works and the rights of their authors is intended to be achieved through three basic principles: the principle of "national treatment," the principle of "automatic" protection and the principle of "independence" of protection.

The principle of "national treatment" means that works the author of which is a national of a Contracting State or works first published in such a State must be given the same protection in each of the other Contracting States as granted to the works of its own nationals. This is a "non-discrimination" rule among authors of the Member States; A Member State may not grant foreign authors less protection than it grants its own.

The "automatic protection" principle[19] through the abolition of formalities conditioning protection. That implies the protection must not be conditional upon compliance with any formality; the rights accorded under the Convention do not require anything else than points of attachment of author nationality or place of first publication, without any requirement of State endorsement.

The "principle of the independence" of protection states that protection of a work is independent of protection given to it in the work's country of origin.

[16] Stockholm Act, relating to the revision of the Berne Convention Protocol Regarding Developing Countries, revised at Stockholm on July 14, 1967.

[17] One of the principles of the New International Economic Order included strengthening international assistance to promote industrialisation in developing countries through, in particular, the provisioning of sufficient financial resources and opportunities for the transfer of appropriate techniques and technologies. About the position of the new states and their movement, see Falk (1996).

[18] See the Status States Party of the Berne Convention, updated on August 1, 2023, available at https://www.wipo.int/export/sites/www/treaties/en/docs/pdf/berne.pdf.

[19] The "*automatic protection*" and "*independence*" principles were introduced by the 1908 Berlin revision of the Berne Convention.

These three principles imply that authors' rights in a work created (or first publication) are automatically protected within the countries of the Berne Union without regard as to whether the country of origin would protect the work.

As can be seen, the Berne Convention was conceived with a euro-centrical copyright approach based on civil law systems and the *"droits d' auteur"* tradition. After the Brussels revision in 1948, although some common law systems participated, those countries did not have an essential influence on developing the Convention reform.

On the other hand, the United States and most Latin American states, as well as other developing countries, did not embrace the previously approved version of the text of the Berne Convention and consequently did not adopt the Convention in an early stage.[20] Instead, those countries had already established two conventions between themselves: the Buenos Aires Convention in 1910[21] and the Washington Convention in 1946.[22]

With the aim to avoid this duplicity and fragmentation regimes, therefore, aiming to achieve an international copyright system and universally widespread copyright protection of literary, scientific and artistic works, the Universal Copyright Convention (UCC)[23] was signed in Geneva in 1952, under UNESCO's auspices.[24] The Universal Copyright Convention, administrated by UNESCO, was signed[25] by 36 countries, and in a few months, four other countries subsequently added their signatures.

The UCC introduced requirements of form for the copyright protection, as opposed to the principle of automatic protection stated in the Berne Convention. Such formalities were compatible with the system applied under the national law of many signatory countries, for example, the USA. Among those formalities, one relevant UCC achievement was introducing the copyright notice through the "©" symbol.[26]

The UCC also responded to the developing countries' need for international copyright protection without fulfilling the Berne Convention's higher requirements. That is why it is possible to say that the UCC was, at a time, the main international instrument regarding international copyright relations of the countries that, for any reason, did not join the Berne Union, as it offered a combination of national

[20] For Berne Convention Member States and their accession date see: Contracting Parties of the Berne Convention. In: Wipo Lex. https://wipolex.wipo.int/en/treaties/ShowResults?search_what=C&treaty_id=15.

[21] Buenos Aires Convention on Literary and Artistic Copyright, signed in Buenos Aires on 11 August, 1910.

[22] Inter-American Convention on the rights of the author in literary, scientific and artistic works. Concluded at Washington on 22 June 1946.

[23] Universal Copyright Convention.

[24] For an historical point of view on UCC see: Dubin (1954), pp. 89–119.

[25] For UCC signatories and member states and their accession date visit WIPO Lex website: https://wipolex.wipo.int/en/treaties/parties/208.

[26] Article III UCC (1952 Text Version.

treatment and minimum protection at a somewhat lower level than that of the Berne Convention.[27]

Most of the Berne Union countries also adopted the UCC. Both texts are complementary to each other, while both conventions contain provisions regulating the relation between them. Furthermore, the UCC first text already introduced provisions[28] stating that such a new convention shall not affect the provisions of the Berne Convention in any way, which takes priority over the UCC when applicable among countries of the Berne Union. Also, according to the declaration annexed to that Article, those works originating in a developed Berne Union country that has withdrawn from the Berne Union after 1951 shall not be protected under the UCC in the countries of the Berne Union; as the Appendix declaration relating to Article XVII clarifies.[29] Regarding this Article, Dr. Silke von Levinsky considers a scenario more theoretical than practical. She reflects "that a developing country which is a Member of the Berne Union and a Contracting State to the UCC would in the future withdraw from the Berne Union and follow the procedure under letter (b) of the Appendix Declaration relating to Article XVII UCC (Paris text); in this case, as an

---

[27] Blomqvist J (2021) Universal Copyright Convention—RIP - The IPKat [Guest post]. In: IP Kat. https://ipkitten.blogspot.com/2021/12/guest-post-universal-copyright.html.

[28] Article XVII and Appendix Declaration Relating to Articles XVII, UCC (1952 Text Version)., available at https://en.unesco.org/about-us/legal-affairs/universal-copyright-convention-appendix-declaration-relating-Article-xvii-and.

[29] Article XVII of the UCC:

> 1. This Convention shall not in any way affect the provisions of the Berne Convention for the Protection of Literary and Artistic Works or membership in the Union created by that Convention.
>
> 2. In application of the foregoing paragraph, a Declaration has been annexed to the present Article. This Declaration is an integral part of this Convention for the States bound by the Berne Convention on 1 January 1951, or which have or may become bound to it at a later date. The signature of this Convention by such States shall also constitute signature of the said Declaration, and ratification, acceptance or accession by such States shall include the Declaration as well as the Convention.

The Appendix declaration relating to Article XVII of the UCC states as follows:

> The States which are members of the International Union for the Protection of Literary and Artistic Works, and which are signatories to the Universal Copyright Convention,
>
> Desiring to reinforce their mutual relations on the basis of the said Union and to avoid any conflict which might result from the co-existence of the Convention of Berne and the Universal Convention,
>
> Have, by common agreement, accepted the terms of the following declaration:
>
> a) Works which, according to the Berne Convention, have as their country of origin a country which has withdrawn from the International Union created by the said Convention, after 1 January 1951, shall not be protected by the Universal Copyright Convention in the countries of the Berne Union;
>
> b) The Universal Copyright Convention shall not be applicable to the relationships among countries of the Berne Union insofar as it relates to the protection of works having as their country of origin, within the meaning of the Berne Convention, a country of the International Union created by the said Convention.

exception from the letter (a), the UCC would apply to such developing country in its relations with other countries that are both parties to the UCC and the Berne Union".[30]

Although the current text of the Berne Convention does not explicitly mention the UCC, it provides in its Article XX that countries of the Union may "enter into special agreements among themselves, in so far as such agreements grant to authors more extensive rights than those granted by the Convention, or contain other provisions not contrary to this Convention. The provisions of existing agreements which satisfy these conditions shall remain applicable."[31]

Accordingly, the Berne Convention does not exclude Berne Union countries from joining the UCC or any other treaty; it simply does not recognise a lower protection level than the granted by the Berne Convention to apply in the relations between Berne Union countries.

Both the Universal Copyright Convention and the Berne Convention were revised at a Paris conference in 1971 to take into consideration the special needs of developing countries, especially regarding liberalised regulations for translations, reproductions, public performances, but exclusively for educational and research purposes. However, despite the 1971 reform of the Berne Convention, most developing countries chose to join only the UCC. In 1980, there were 25 countries which were part of the UCC but not of the Berne Convention, namely Colombia, Cuba, Ecuador, El Salvador, Ghana, Guatemala, Kenya, Nigeria, and the United States, among others. By the early 1980s, the number of countries party to the Berne Convention was 71, while for the UCC was 73. But Since 2006, no country has joined the UCC; meanwhile, one of its first Member States, Cambodia, has recently joined the Berne convention. The number of States Parties of the Berne Convention on first August 2023 is 181.[32]

This change of preferences between the two legal frameworks may be because UCC seems to become obsolete, probably because it does not offer a rule like the principle of retrospective protection stated in the Berne Convention. Its Article 18 says:

This Convention shall apply to all works which, at the moment of its coming into force, have not yet fallen into the public domain in the country of origin through the expiry of the term of protection.

Accordingly, the Berne Convention gives automatic international protection to the existing works protected by the country of origin when becoming a state part of the convention.

Neither of the conventions introduced any protection of performers, producers and broadcasting organisation's rights in any of their revisions. It was not until 1961 that the related rights of performers, producers, and broadcasting organisations were

[30] von Lewinski (2006), p. 5.

[31] Article XX of the Universal Copyright Convention.

[32] See updated data on the WIPO official site available at https://www.wipo.int/export/sites/www/treaties/en/docs/pdf/berne.pdf.

internationally recognised and protected in one convention: The Convention for the Protection of Performers, Producers of Phonograms and Broadcasting Organizations,[33] also named the Rome Convention. This treaty was adopted under the aegis of the Berne Secretariat (as the predecessor of the current WIPO), the International Labour Organization (ILO) and UNESCO[34] in Rome on 26 October 1961. These three organisations are also jointly responsible for the administration of the Convention and constitute the Secretariat of the Intergovernmental Committee set up in the text. The Intergovernmental Committee is the governing and deliberative body concerning the Convention, as it does not provide for the institution of a Union.

The Rome Convention, for the first time, internationally recognised and regulated the rights of those subjects, different from the author, who made the execution, fixation, and transmission of certain artistic works. Thus, the Rome Convention does not regulate copyright but related rights. By the time this treaty was adopted, few countries had national rules protecting the rights of performers, producers and broadcasters.[35] The convention aimed to grant a minimum of recognition and protection of those beneficiaries' rights, who become eligible as they take part in the creation process by performing, recording or broadcasting the copyright-protected music works. The protection of those subjects' rights was not claimed until new inventions like the gramophone, cinematography and radio widely spread at the beginning of the twentieth century. The role of artists, producers and broadcasters became essential to publicise authors' works. On the other hand, such technification and the popularisation of sound recordings lead to a higher unemployment rate among performers. As Ficsor says:

> The disc became the enemy of the performer, taking away his chance of work; in this, by increasing the consumption of recordings, broadcasting also helped.[36]

This situation remains one of the main concerns, but it has been worsened by the Internet and streaming industry. As many artists struggled for fair remuneration, back in 1961, performers and producers demanded the right to exercise some control over the many uses for their performances and recordings and receive compensation for those uses.

Based on the principles of national treatment, as done in Berne, the Rome Convention introduced minimum obligations towards the member countries to protect performers, producers and broadcasting organisations' rights regarding their performances, phonograms and broadcast, respectively. The Rome Convention established just a minimum protection, like authorising certain users of the works and compensation for such uses, setting a minimum protection period of 20 years

[33] International Convention for the Protection of Performers, Producers of Phonograms and Broadcasting Organisations. Done at Rome on October 26, 1961.

[34] For a further historical approach, see Masouye and Bogsch (1981). pp. 8–14.

[35] The United States of America has never been part of the Rome Convention. For a complete list of Contracting parties see 'WIPO Administred Treaties - Rome Convention'. https://www.wipo.int/wipolex/en/treaties/ShowResults?search_what=C&treaty_id=17.

[36] Ficsor (2003).

since the performance, the phonogram or the broadcast was released. The Rome Convention has never been revised since 1961. But, just 10 years after its approval, a new convention appeared regarding the protection of producers of phonograms. It was in 1971 when the Geneva Convention for the Protection of Producers of phonograms was adopted against unauthorised duplication of their phonograms.[37] The technological changes during the decade of the 1970s and 1980s in the twentieth century, specifically the appearance of recording devices available for the current public—namely tape recorders or cassettes—gave the public the possibility to make copies cheaply. Those unauthorised copies were not only for private use but also for illegal distribution. In order to reduce the piracy of phonograms and protect producers' rights, the Contracting States of the Geneva Convention agreed to establish rules against making unauthorised copies, the importation and the distribution to the public of such duplicates. This convention is also administered by WIPO jointly with the ILO and UNESCO.

Finally, mentioning The Convention Relating to the Distribution of Programme-Carrying Signals Transmitted by Satellite is also necessary, signed in Brussels in 1974.[38] Following the same philosophy, the Rome Convention. The Brussels Satellites Convention provides the obligation for its contracting States to take measures against unauthorised distribution on or from its territory of any programme-carrying signal transmitted by satellite.

As these first-generation conventions show, the difference between copyright and related rights is basically found in the protected objects and the rights' subjects, especially in the context of music copyright's very own traits. For this reason, the following sections examine objects and subjects of copyright and related rights and the configuration of the CtoP right as they are presented and configured in the first generation of conventions.

1.1.1 The Object: Musical Work v Performances Phonograms and Broadcasts

Copyright law, as a property right, has an object to protect: the artistic works. Therefore, in the field of music, the copyright object is the musical work.

Defining a musical work is not easy since there are different trends in philosophy and musicology about the conception of a musical work or its existence.[39] Among them, some contemporary theories in musicology recall the realist theory of types

[37] Convention for the Protection of Producers of Phonograms Against Unauthorized Duplication of Their Phonograms, adopted at Geneva on October 29, 1971.

[38] Brussels Convention Relating to the Distribution of Programme-Carrying Signals Transmitted by Satellite, Done at Brussels on May 21, 1974.

[39] For further discussion on this topic see: Butt (2015) or Goehr (2003), available at https://oxford.universitypressscholarship.com/view/10.1093/0198235410.001.0001/acprof-9780198235415.

and tokens, first developed in the semiotic field by Ch.S. Peirce to achieve a definition of *musical work* in this train of thought. Stanović[40] assesses different theories based on the dichotomy of *types-tokens* to classify musical works as abstract entities named *types*. At the same time, those *types* are known through *tokens*, which are the concrete performances and/or sound recordings of a type. Thus, a musical work as a type may be encountered in or through its various tokens. In other words, one musical work may come in the form of many different and unique performances or phonograms and their digitisations.[41] The conceptualisation of musical works as types allows us to classify and include new forms of *tokens* that technology is bringing about, like digitisations of phonograms, new sound files directly embodied in digital format or even new forms of assets like Non-Fungible Tokens (NFT).[42]

Another approach is given by R. Arnold, who distinguishes between *content* or message and *signal* or medium. When talking about music, the content corresponds to a musical work, which is an intangible asset produced by the intellect and creativity of music artists and takes the form of musical composition. Whereas the musical composition itself is immaterial, it is usually embodied in different signals or mediums, which are phonograms or sound recordings.

On the other hand, Barron[43] recognises the achievements of the role of copyright law doctrine in forging the musical work concept. Thus, copyright law protects the object through a property right: the musical work. However, Barron explains how this legal notion of musical work achieved by copyright law also derives from an aesthetic conception of the musical work that emerged from the field of musical practice, theory and criticism around the XIX century. In her study, Barron's arguments, when discussing different ideas that influenced the conception of musical work as an immaterial object, cite Goehr's. Both agree on the idea that a musical work should be wholly and accurately represented in the form of a score; that this score should be complied with perfectly in performance', recognising the independent existence of musical works from their performances and likewise from their sound recordings.

That copyright law conception applied to *musical works* already appears in the Berne Convention in its 1886 version of the text,

The definition of the *works protected* term in the Berne Act 1886 concluded with the following general residual formulation: 'in fact, every production whatsoever in

[40] Stanovic (2018), pp. 125–144.

[41] Digitization meaning the process of changing data into a digital form that can be easily read and processed by a computer. - According to Oxford's Dictionary, https://www.oxfordlearnersdictionaries.com/definition/english/digitization.

[42] NFTs are based in cryptocurrencies technology and use crypto transactions, which are secure, instant and with no intermediaries. NFTs contain certificates of authenticity in concert tickets, limited-edition experiences, digital content, merchandise, and music. For further information see *An Introductory Guide to NFTs in the Music Industry at* https://www.mi.edu/in-the-know/introductory-guide-nfts-music-industry/, *Copyright & NFTs of Digital Artworks* at https://ipkitten.blogspot.com/2021/03/guest-post-copyright-nfts-of-digital.html.

[43] Barron (2006), pp. 101 at 106.

the literary, scientific, or artistic domain which can be published by any mode of impression or reproduction'. As Ginsburg and Ricketson mention,[44] this definition was reshaped in the Berlin Act 1908,[45] with the general formulation '*... such as*' that introduces an inclusive list of examples. The subsequent revisions maintained that general formulation but have expanded this list of examples.

The current text of the Berne Convention determines the object of protection in Article 2(1). There, it defines what shall be considered copyright-protectable work, stating that 'literary and artistic works shall include every production in the literary scientific and artistic domain, whatever may be the mode or form of its expression...'[46] This statement is followed by the aforementioned exhaustive list of examples of acts that shall be considered copyright-protectable work. Regarding music, this catalogue includes as musical works the 'musical compositions with or without words'.[47] Although this first paragraph of the Article does not explicitly state the requirement of originality of artistic works to be considered as such, Article 2 (3) states that 'arrangements of music ... shall be protected as original works without prejudice to the copyright in the original works. The requirement of originality[48] can be excerpted from that statement when referring to copyright in original works, meaning musical compositions, as a separate object from the arrangement of music, constituting a new object of copyright protection. Thus, the convention protects original musical works by means of copyright and recognises copyright protection on the variations made on those original musical works, independent of such works' copyright. The unique arrangements made on a former original musical work constitute a new musical work, becoming a new object of protection.

It is also interesting to note that, according to the definition given by the Berne Convention, copyright protectable works in the music creation process refer only to the content, this is musical works, as per Arnold's[49] classification- or to types, according to Stanović's[50]-, but not to signals or tokens. That means that signals or tokens, namely performances, sound recording and digitisations, are outside the scope of the Convention.

If we stick to the legal definition given by Article 2(1) of the Berne Convention, the conception of musical work does not reach the signal but only the content. However, Article 2(2) leaves to the Member States of the Berne Union the ability to prescribe whether musical works need to be 'fixed in some material form' (e.g. phonograms) to be copyright protectable or not. That is, if the existence of a

---

[44] Ricketson and Ginsburg (2015), p. 17.

[45] Berlin Act 1908, 13 November 1908, available at https://wipolex.wipo.int/en/text/278699.

[46] Article 2(1) Berne Convention.

[47] TRIPs Agreement.

[48] The originality criteria on musical works is covered, in this book when assessing CJEU case law in Chap. 3, Sect. 3.2. For an approach on topic see: Margoni (2016), p. 85; Waelde (2015), p. 23.

[49] Arnold (2011), p. 272.

[50] Stanovic (2018), p. 129.

signal is an additional requirement for the content to be considered an object of copyright protection.

Fixing musical works in a sound recording involves embedding the content on a signal, the musical composition to a phonogram. This materialisation of the incorporeal artistic creation of a music composition into tangible and/or audible assets exceeds just the author's action. In this process, other artists and professionals—performers, producers and publishers- interfere in creating a new and substantial *musical object* different from the author's intellectual creation or the performances and phonograms. These new objects, like musical arrangements, constitute a new object, but in this case, the Berne Convention does not recognise them as new musical works. Those new musical objects shall be protected by related rights but not by copyright. The Berne Convention explicitly excludes the publishing of music from its scope of protection when Article 3 states the criteria of eligibility for protection. In the third paragraph of such provision, it defines "published works" as those 'works published with the consent of their authors, whatever may be the means of manufacture of the copies, provided that the availability of such copies has been such as to satisfy the reasonable requirements of the public, having regard to the nature of the work'.[51] Following that, it explicitly enounces that the performance of musical works, the communication by wire or the broadcasting of works shall not constitute publication, according to the Convention. Nothing is said about phonograms, but it must be understood that if a performance of a musical work does not constitute publication, the recording of the performance of such work itself neither does it.

Therefore, despite indirectly recognising the importance of the signal to support content, the Berne Convention does not offer protection to signals itself but just to the content, excluding performances and phonograms from copyright protection. Such exclusion was basically because the conception of copyright that prevails in the Berne Convention, as was mentioned, comes from the European conceptualisation of copyright as *droits auteur* used in countries with civil law systems.[52]

Another reason might be that it was not until the twentieth century that recorded music began to spread widely; it was by that time when the need to protect the phonograms, as new *musical objects,* appeared and consequently also new rights and rightsholders. However, even though, as we saw, the Berne Convention has been revised several times,[53] phonograms and performances have never been included in the Convention as objects of copyright protection, despite the application of common law tradition countries.

---

[51] Article 3(3), Berne Convention.

[52] Ficsor (2003), pp. 8–10.

[53] Berne Convention for the Protection of Literary and Artistic Works of September 9, 1886, completed at Paris on May 4, 1896, at Berlin on November 13, 1908, completed at Berne on March 20, 1914, revised at Rome on June 2, 1928, at Brussels on June 26, 1948, at Stockholm on July 14, 1967, and at Paris on July 24, 1971, and amended on September 28, 1979.

On the other hand, the Universal Copyright Convention Article I refers to the undertaking of Contracting States to provide protection.

> of the rights of authors and other copyright proprietors in literary, scientific and artistic works, including writings, musical, dramatic and cinematographic works, and paintings, engravings and sculpture.[54]

The reference to the object of protection needs to be taken from this provision, as there is no other provision in the UCC containing a definition or list of works protected nor enumerating the protected rights. So, it is something that was left under national legislation criteria. As Dubin[55] wrote in 1954 when the UCC was discussed, it was felt that the rights and works should include those given to authors by the States; thus, an enumeration of such rights was rejected as it might have been read as a limited list. Consequently, UCC refers to the object when mentioning its protection of the "rights of authors and other copyright proprietors in literary, scientific and artistic works" in Article I.

Another interesting aspect to note is that the Berne Convention for the Protection of Literary and Artistic Works clearly defines in its title the object of protection, and it is later, in its preamble, where mentions the protection of the subjects' rights; that is "*the rights of authors in their literary and artistic works*".

Conversely, the negotiations of the International Convention for the Protection of Performers, Producers of Phonograms and Broadcasting Organisations[56] chose to mention the subjects on is title. No reference to object is either in the title not in the preamble. Instead, it does refer to subjects' rights as protecting "*the rights of performers, producers of phonograms and broadcasting organisations*". Having said that, however, the Rome Convention does not refer to objects in the title nor the preamble; there is parallelism between the opening formulas of the two conventions.[57]

In the Rome Convention's first Article, when recognising the protection of performers, producers and broadcasters 'rights, it states that such protection does not affect *the copyright on artistic works recognised by the Berne Convention.*[58] That clearly shows that subjects and objects of protection diverge from those in the Berne Convention, consequently covering new rights which are also recognised as rights related to copyright but different from it. Thus, the Rome Convention recognised certain related rights regarding specified objects despite not containing any explicit reference to "objects" in a single Article. For example, in Article 3, the convention defines some concepts to determine the scope of protection. It clarifies the significance of two objects, phonograms and broadcastings, but not performances. Rome convention text also references objects in Articles 4, 5 and 6 when

[54] Article I, UCC, 1952. The text of this Article has never been amended.

[55] Dubin (1954), pp. 101–102.

[56] Shortened to Rome Convention, done at Rome on October 26, 1961.

[57] Masouye and Bogsch (1981), p. 141.

[58] Article 1, Rome Convention.

referring to them as points of attachment for the different subjects to have their rights protected by the convention, even though no definition is given.

For this treaty, “phonogram” is any “exclusively aural fixation of sounds of a performance or other sounds” (Article 3 (b)). That is to say, when an audible sound is fixed or embodied, it is protected by the convention. Phonogram refers exclusively to the recording of sounds, just the audio, excluding the protection of sound synchronised with images or just images with no sound. Protection is given to the fixation of whatever is the origin of the sound, not referring to the fixation of music or sounds of performances exclusively, but also including nature sounds or sounds created by technological means. Such refers to another object that is not defined: performance.

Paragraph (j) of Article 3 defines broadcasting as the transmission by wireless means for public reception of sounds (i.e. radio) or images and sounds (i.e. television).

When this provision refers to “wireless means,” it excludes any transmission of sounds or phonograms to the public by connecting a sound player to loudspeakers, as it does not cover cable transmissions. Moreover, it excludes any transmission to a single person or a defined small group of people. Masouye and Bogsch point out that when shaping the Rome Convention, the 1961 Rome Conference “was of the opinion that only transmission by Hertzian waves or other wireless means should constitute broadcasting”.[59]

But in the music field, the generic concept of “musical works” is used to define the object of copyright. Therefore, seeking fora difference while finding a general concept of protected objects for related rights could be named *musical objects,* which represent or embody *musical works*. Such musical objects protected by related rights are performances of musical works, phonograms -as fixation of the performance of musical works or other sounds-and broadcastings- meaning the transmission of a performance or a phonogram of a musical work. In other words, the Rome Convention recognises protection based on signals, whereas the Berne Convention does it on the content.

In the autumn of 1985, after the 23rd General Conference of UNESCO and the WIPO’s 15th series of meetings, the Directors-General of UNESCO and WIPO convened a Committee of Governmental Experts on Dramatic, Choreographic and Musical Works to discuss copyright and conceptual issues related to dramatic, choreographic and musical works.[60] The aim was to contrive a set of interpretative “principles” and comments on the international copyright legislation concepts to afford clarification and guidance to domestic legislators. The Experts Committee meeting took place at UNESCO headquarters in Paris from 11 to 15 May 1987 and congregated experts from 41 states and observers from 15 intergovernmental and

[59] Masouye and Bogsch (1981), p. 142.

[60] UNESCO, WIPO Report of the Committee of Governmental Experts on the Principles Relating to the Protection of Copyright and the Rights of Performers in Respect of Dramatic, Choreographic and Musical Works, 1987.

international non-governmental organisations. Although the Principles discussed and forged by the Committee are not binding on any state, as long as they are not part of any copyright treaties, such principles highlighted the issues of copyright conceptualisation. As early as 1987, those "principles" created international awareness of the challenges of copyright caused by technological developments, which are still, and will be, challenging copyright law. Among those principles, we can find definitions of the different objects of protection; for example, according to principle MW,1 'Musical works' mean all kinds of original combinations of sounds (compositions) with or without text (lyrics or libretto). That principle excludes dramatic and choreographic works with music from the "musical work" concept, as music is considered just like a part of another protected work in those cases. The second paragraph of that principle specifies that musical works are the object of copyright law general rules. Finally, the principle clarifies that no material fixation is needed to obtain protection on musical works. Although music works protection may be restricted to those works that are fixed in a material form (including scores and phonograms), the Committee recommends avoiding such requirement of fixation to obtain protection for musical works. All these things considered, we can state that the object of protection of copyright are musical compositions, with or without lyrics, conceived as immaterial content derived from a music artist's intellectual creation, named musical works, which can be embodied and/or represented in different signals or music objects becoming protected objects of related rights, such as phonograms, performances or broadcastings.

To summarise, Fig. 1.1 shows the object of copyright and the objects corresponding to related rights. The object of copyright is the musical works.

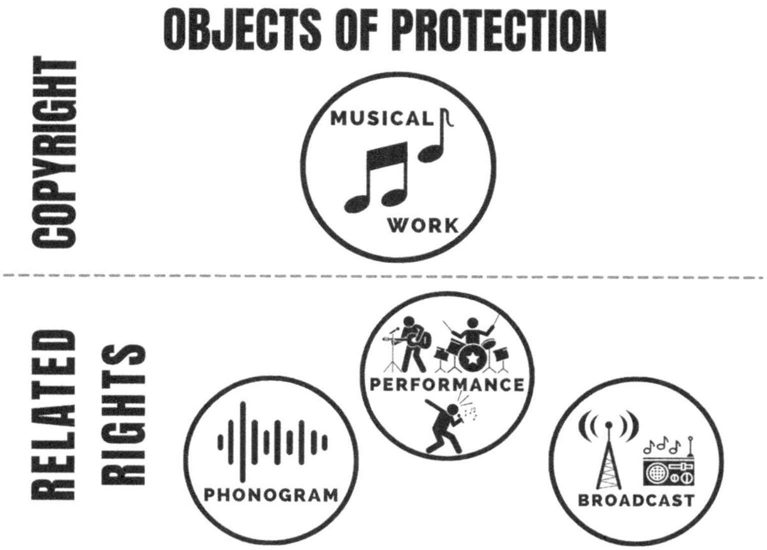

Fig. 1.1 Objects of Copyright and Related Rights. *Source*: Author's elaboration

While the object of related rights may be either the performances, the phonograms—including sound recordings and digitisations- of such musical works or even the broadcasting of those performances and phonograms.

1.1.2 The Subjects: The Rightsholders

Since musical work is defined as the object of protection of the copyright law, determining the subject is to figure out the person who entitles rights to that object. Subjects are the persons whose legal interest is protected either by copyright or by any of the related rights. Someone becomes a rightsholder because a person is entitled to copyright or related rights as part of the creative process. Also, a person or entity can become a rightsholder despite not taking part in the creative process by obtaining ownership to exploit those rights—either by inheritance or under the agreement. Therefore, in music, copyright subjects are those whose intellectual activity and creativity generate a musical composition -with or without lyrics- or whoever buys those rights to the copyright subject. That means authors, including songwriters and lyricists, are copyright owners. Frequently, there is no unique copyright owner on one musical work because many subjects usually participate in the creation process. This is the case, for example, of co-authorship of musical works created by various music band members or a song written by a composer and a lyricist, both known as songwriters. The Berne Convention mentions the "author" as the subject of copyright in Article 1 when stating the Establishment of a Union for the protection of authors' rights in their literary and artistic works. No further description of who should be considered as the author is found in the text by means of the convention. The UCC also refers to subjects in its first Article when describing its aim as "to provide for the adequate and effective protection of the rights of authors and other copyright proprietors in literary, scientific and artistic works". This formulation might lead to confusion if thinking that such reference to "other copyright proprietors rights" refers to someone different from the author who holds any other right rather than copyright, namely related or neighbouring rights. That conception cannot be valid as the UCC was concerned with common law "copyright" rather than the civil law definition of "droits des auteurs" reflected in the Berne Convention. When mentioning "other copyright proprietors," it means anyone who entitles copyright because of an author's transfer of such property right to them, either wholly or partly, whether it is *inter vivos* or *mortis causa.*

On the other hand, subjects concerning related rights are already cited in the title of the Rome Convention and in Article 2, which specifies the protection given by the Convention under the principle of National Treatment. The subsequent Article 3 defines two related rights subjects: performers and phonogram producers. The subject's definition is based on the action taken on the object, as the person who performs or fixes it.

The meaning given by the Rome Convention to "*performers*" includes:

> "actors, singers, musicians, dancers, and other persons who act, sing, deliver, declaim, play in, or otherwise perform literary or artistic works"[61]

According to that, specifically in the music field, the definition of the subject as a performer stands for the person who takes part in the performance of a musical work, namely musicians, singers and any music performing artist. Regarding the "producer of phonograms" meaning, the Rome convention defines it as:

> "the person who, or the legal entity which, first fixes the sounds of a performance or other sounds".

The same definition is given by Article 1 of the Convention for the Protection of Producers of Phonograms.[62] Hence, the subject is the person or entity making the sound recording process possible. Finally, although there is no definition of "broadcasting organisation" in Article 3 of the Rome Convention, it can be easily deducted from the definition given in Article 3 (f) when it describes "broadcasting" as the transmission by wireless means for public reception of sounds or images and sounds; so, a broadcasting organisation it the one that runs such transmission. Therefore, subjects of related rights are the ones who own or are entitled to rights on each signal or *token* as an object of protection of related rights. That is, the ones who own rights in their performances, sound recordings or broadcasting acts of other related rights' objects, namely performers, phonogram producers and broadcasting companies, as shown in Fig. 1.2.

This definition of the subjects responds to a conception based on the copyright law's classic distribution of roles creators-executors, an idea depicted by international treaties. But the difference between creators and performers is sometimes not so simple when talking about music. Different subjects participate in the entire process of creating a music piece, from the composition of the musical work to its performance, life or recording sessions, as well as the arrangements. That is why the distribution of roles and rights has been challenged in some literature. Based on Arnold's[63] distinction above on content and signal, Aguilar[64] questions the validity of the law's distinction between composition and performance. Consequently, she challenges the distinction between authors and performers as the dichotomy of creator-executor. For instance, in a jam session, whether it is recorded or not, shall performers also be considered authors of those unique improvised music pieces? Besides, contributions made by certain performing artists when performing a musical work, live or in a recording session, sometimes are so significant that they turn the original musical composition into a unique or different musical piece. Should such contributions be considered as joint authorship, as long as they are an important part of the creative process of the musical work? And, consequently, should those

---

[61] Article 2 of the Rome Convention.

[62] Article 1 of the Geneva Convention.

[63] Arnold (2011).

[64] Aguilar (2018), p. 778.

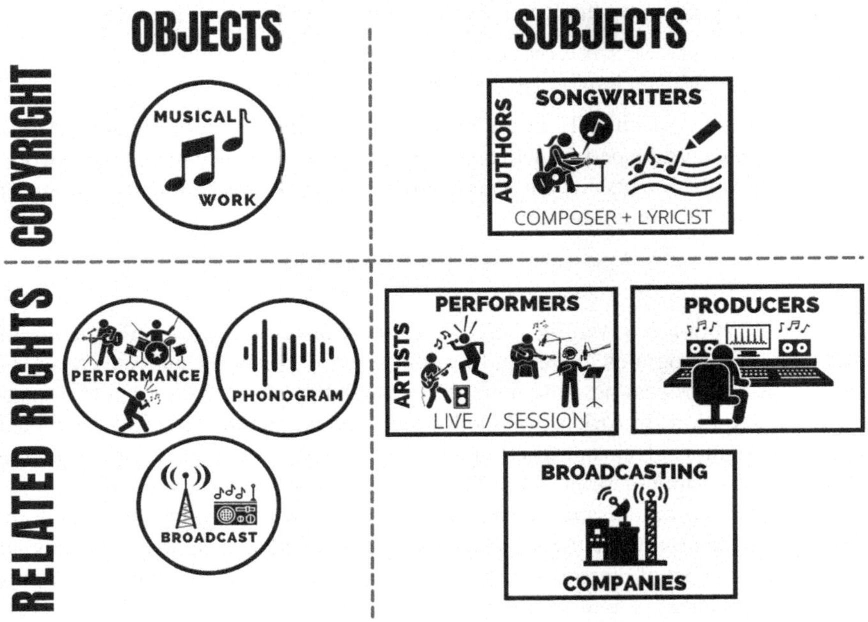

Fig. 1.2 Objects and subjects of copyright and related rights. *Source*: Author's elaboration

performers have part of the copyright on the musical work or hold their part as related rights?

These are not easy questions to answer, and neither the international treaties nor most national laws offer a clear solution.

Having said that, principle MW5 of the Principles Relating to the Protection of Copyright and the Rights of Performers[65] interprets those questions related to improvisations and aleatoric musical works. The criteria for protecting musical improvisations is based on originality since it depends on "the level of their dependence on pre-existing works". The dependence on a pre-existing musical work should provide new protection for improvisations as adaptations of previous works. The more independent improvisations from any existing work should obtain protection as new independent works, provided they are of an original nature. This principle allows that the additional condition of their fixation may be required to grant protection of such improvisations. Still, there is no criteria to grade the minimum level of originality needed for an independent protection.

For its part, principle MW6 provides a definition for the named "Aleatoric musical works". It includes protection for performers' contributions, either as

[65] UNESCO, WIPO Report of the Committee of Governmental Experts on the Principles Relating to the Protection of Copyright and the Rights of Performers in Respect of Dramatic, Choreographic and Musical Works, 1987.

adaptation work or as contributions to an existing work, providing performers protection as a joint authorship of the work. Aleatoric musical works are defined as:

> compositions where the composers leave room to the creative contributions of performers authorising and inviting them to make certain choices (concerning the intensity, duration and other elements of sound or melodic units, the repetition or combination of some parts of the work, etc.) or finalising the works in certain respects based on parameters and instructions given by the composer.[66]

In any case, the main requirement for obtaining copyright protection is linked to the object, not the subject. Therefore, the existence of a musical work and the requirement of a certain level of "originality" is what creation must be considered a new protectable work. Charlotte Waede approaches that there is no clear space in the legal protection of certain and new forms of music making. Although the standard of "originality" has evolved due to the CJEU case law,[67] originality is the key point to those questions".

A similar situation happens to phonogram producers when they make music arrangements. However, protection for music arrangements is regulated in Article 2 (3) of the Berne Convention. According to that provision,[68] arrangements of music have to be protected as original works. But the question is if this protection should be just under the scope of the related rights or may be protected by copyright. Although neither performers nor phonogram producers are entitled, they are not strictly authors. The interpretation of Article 2 (3) of the Convention provides a positive answer for the "authorship" of producers for their arrangements, which are considered new works. To clarify that provision, Principle MW4[69] indicates that adaptations and arrangements of musical works and the translations of their lyrics are protected by copyright if they fulfil the originality requirement. That new copyright of the arrangement would exist without prejudice to the copyright in the original works. Moreover, the provision seems to claim full respect for the adaptor's copyright in the adaptation - arrangement or translation- even though it has been with the authorisation of the original work's author.

As the interpretative principles were developed in 1987, and by then, the use of synthesisers and computers in musical creations was widely spread, clarification for the protection of works electronically produced was already approached. Principle MW3 recognise as copyright subjects those "persons who produced the creative element without which the resulting works would not be entitled to copyright protection". Consequently, this introduces new copyright subjects in this field,

---

[66] UNESCO and WIPO, *Report of the Committee of Governmental Experts on the Principles Relating to the Protection of Copyright and the Rights of Performers in Respect of Dramatic, Choreographic and Musical Works 1987*. See principle MW6.

[67] CEJU Case law is reviewed in Chap. 3, Sect. 3.2.

[68] Article 2 (3) of the Berne Convention.

[69] UNESCO, WIPO Report of the Committee of Governmental Experts on the Principles Relating to the Protection of Copyright and the Rights of Performers in Respect of Dramatic, Choreographic and Musical Works, 1987.

such as producers, programmers, sound engineers, etc., who are recognised as authors or co-authors as long as their contribution to the work provides significant creativity elements. Therefore, this creative contribution should also be understood as an element of originality" if it is so significant to provide independence from the original work, making it recognisable as a new musical work. This is the case of remixes that add a base beats to an origin. Still, it does not necessarily create new work entitled to receive independent copyright protection and, consequently, authorship for the remixer.[70]

Arrangements, adaptation and remixes are common nowadays, especially in electronic music. A clear example of this is the song *Tu Vuò Fa' L'Americano* (title in English*: We no speak Americano),* created by Renato Carusone[71] (composition) and Nicola Salerno (lyric) in 1956. The authorship of this song is registered under Salerno and Carusone's names.[72] Since their creation, many performers have done different versions of this song,[73] but none of them, apart from Carusone,[74] holds any copyright on the song, as they are not considered authors. In 2010, the duo *Yolanda Be Cool,*[75] and producer Duncan Maclennan (aka *DCUP)* introduced new arrangements and sampled the song. This version was registered as a new musical work, and its authorship is shared by Salerno, Carusone, Matthew Handley, Andrew Stanley and Duncan Maclennan.

Finally, arrangements or contributions made by musicians when performing musical works in recording sessions are rarely considered co-authorship despite sometimes providing uniqueness to the song. Likewise, performers' contributions to those creative processes can only be protected by related rights, not copyright.

[70] Professor Yahong Li proposes to add remix as a protectable subject matter; that is create a right to remix and grant protection to remixers. See Li (2020).

[71] Renato Carusone is the real name of the artist known as his stage name Renato Carosone. (See the site of the *Discogrefia nazionale della canzone italiana del Istituto Centrale per i Beni Sonori ed Audiovisivi* http://discografia.dds.it/scheda_artista.php?ida=1533) He is registered as an author in the SIAE with his real name Renato Casusone.

[72] See the registration of the song *We speak no Americano* at BMI's repertoire database Sonview. https://repertoire.bmi.com/Search/Search?SearchForm.View_Count=50&SearchForm.Main_Search=Title&SearchForm.Main_Search_Text=We+no+speak+americano&SearchForm.Sub_Search=Please+Select&SearchForm.Search_Type=all.

The first work refers to Carusone's original work. The second one, registered as a new work with the same title but with different ISWC, refers to Handley, Stanley and Maclennan's version including their authorship jointly to Carusone's and Salerno's.

[73] Performed by artists like Sophia Loren in 196 1 or Rocco Hunt in 2016, among may others. See the phonograms registrations in SCF Catalogue at https://catalogo.scfitalia.it/.

[74] See the original version by Carusone in https://www.youtube.com/watch?v=BqlJwMFtMCs&list=RDBqlJwMFtMCs&start_radio=1.

[75] Yolanda Be Cool is an Australian duo formed by Matthew Handley and Andrew Stanley who collaborated with the Producer DCUP- stage name for Duncan Maclennan - to produced the version "We speak no Americano" which become a hit in 2010 https://www.youtube.com/watch?v=7E9Ed9DUQoQ.

1.1.3 The Right of Public Performance and Communication to the Public

For a wide definition of the communication to the public right, we can base it on the one given by Prof. Delia Lipszig.[76] She writes that:

> Public communication of a work' means any act by which a number of persons may be given access to all or part of it in its original or transformed form, by means other than the distribution of copies.

This definition is wide enough to include in its acts of public performance and communication of phonograms. Following the idea of Lipszig, the right of public communication covers all forms of communication: direct communication ('live performances'), indirect communication (by using fixations of a musical work such as phonograms), as well as communication through other mediums of transmission (such as broadcasting, satellite or internet communication).

Many different actions may be considered as acts communicating a musical work to the public. The different acts of public communication show that the 'author's right also covers every activity which permits the work to reach an audience different from that to which the original communication was directed.[77]

Following Lipszig's approach, all public communication acts can be categorised as follows. Public performance is a way of direct communication, namely *stage* or 'live' performances, meaning the communication of the musical work to the public through the live performance of the music executors, which requires the presence of the performers before an audience, which is also physically present.

Communication to the public is an indirect way to communicate the musical works by the transmission of fixation of such works in a place accessible to the public which is fiscally present. The transmission may be made by playing the fixation on material support (devices like music players and loudspeakers) or through communicating a broadcast to the public simultaneously with the presence of the public where the transition occurs. Finally, the last type of public communication is broadcasting, which is the transmission of either a fixed musical work or the retransmission of a live performance. It is indirect communication, even if it's the transmission of a live event because the public is not present at the same place. However, it can be transmitted simultaneously as the performance is happening. A musical work, being an immaterial entity, cannot be communicated to the public itself. To communicate a musical work, either a performance or a phonogram is needed; consequently, the latter would also be communicated. Therefore, the object of communication to the public is both musical works and their signals, despite the fact they refer to performances or music recordings. As Fig. 1.3 shows, musical works will be communicated to the public through their signals such as performances, phonograms of sound recording digitisations and the broadcast of any of

---

[76] Lipszyc (1999), p. 10.

[77] Lipszyc (1999), p. 189.

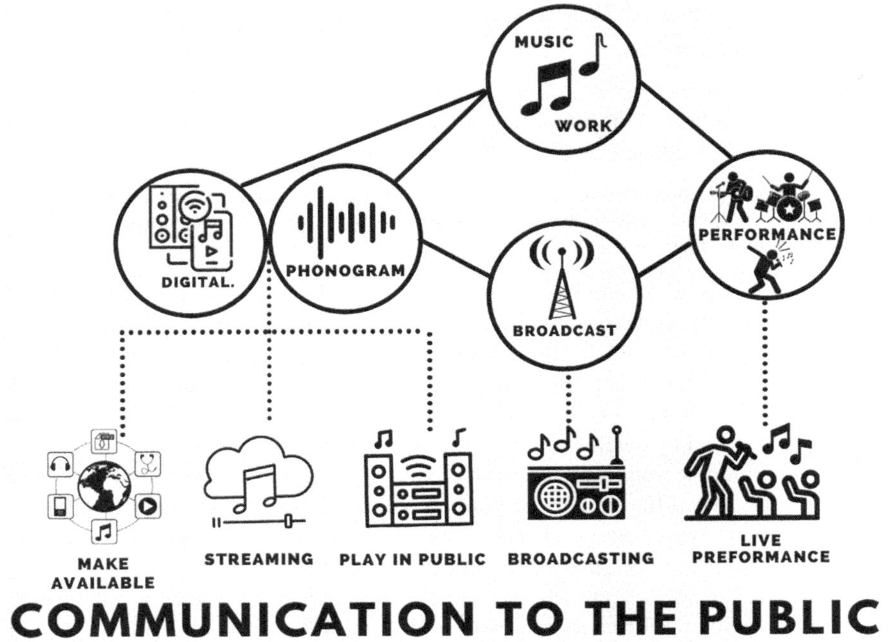

Fig. 1.3 Objects of Comunication to the Public. *Source*: Author's elaboration

them. However, when talking about the subjects, rights owners may be songwriters, performers (artists and musicians), producers, publishers, record labels and even broadcasting entities.

On the one hand, on the kind object and, on the other hand, on the type of act of communication to the public that is realised. The different actions considered as CtoP acts will be assessed in Chap. 4 later in this book.

Figure 1.4 summarises the relation between object and subjects and their role in the creation process, representing a share of the communication to the public right. The figure also includes the role that publishers and record labels play. Despite not being natural subjects of the CtoP right, both are entitled as part of the copyright or related rights because of exploitation agreements signed with songwriters, performers or producers. Songwriters create musical works, and they are often linked to a music publisher who is in charge of investing in the creation process as well as managing the copyright and the revenues of it. Songwriters' musical works are communicated either by live performance or through a phonogram, sound recording or digitally. Usually, publishers are also in charge of contacting producers or record labels to embody the musical work in a phonograph and artists and performers to play it. Usually, publishers' functions are run by record labels themselves.

While publishers are more directly linked to authors, record labels are more directly linked to performers and producers. Traditionally, record labels' main roles were, on the one hand, to find music artists, develop and promote them, and

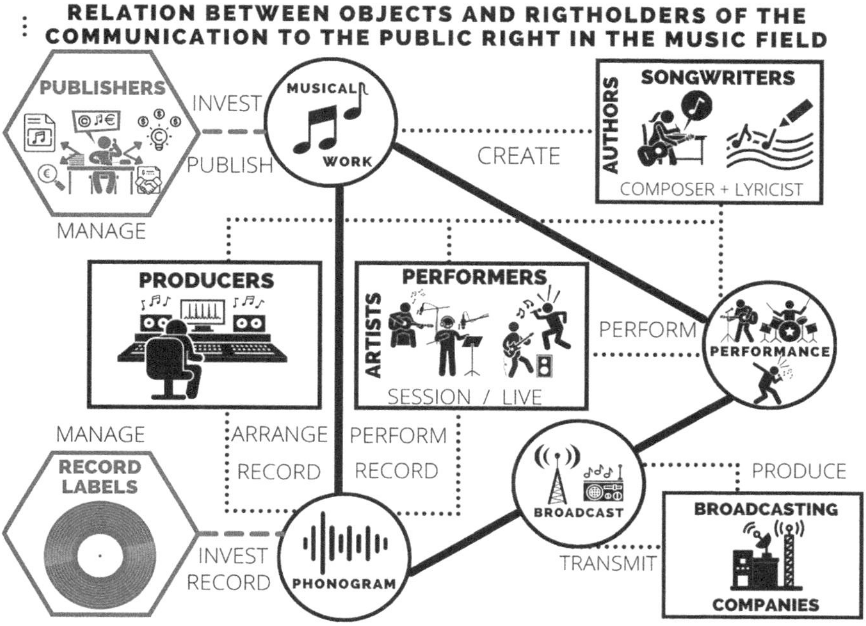

Fig. 1.4 Relation between objects and right holders of the communication to the public right in the music field. *Source*: Author's elaboration

on the other hand, to hire a producer to arrange and record the music promote and distribute it. This is known as A&R (which stands for artist and repertoire). The record labels' compensation was primarily based on the income generated from the exploitation of physical copies of phonograms, specifically mechanical rights and performing rights. Mechanical rights include royalties from reproduction rights—i.e., making copies of the recording—as well as earnings from the distribution of those copies. This means that record labels' income comes, on one hand, from a percentage of the revenues generated by the sale of copies and, on the other hand, from revenues derived from the communication to the public of the phonograms they created and invested in.

Since the beginning of the twenty-first century, the music and recording industry has undergone significant changes, and today, physical copies of phonograms are rarely distributed. However, mechanical rights now apply to streams and downloads of digital copies of phonograms. These rights are not exclusively paid for recordings but also for the embedded musical works. This means that revenue from mechanical rights is distributed among record labels, authors, and publishers.

Record labels now offer artists multiple-rights deals, commonly known as deals "360." Such deals mean that record labels are responsible not only for A&R (Artist and Repertoire) but also for managing and investing in marketing, synchronization partnerships, digital global promotion, tours, concerts, and even publishing.[78] All this means new incomes apart from the traditional ones. In exchange for those services, record labels receive revenues derived from communication to the public right of the artist for both sound recording and live performances. Consequently, through exploitation agreements with authors, publishers hold part of the copyright; meanwhile, record labels own part of the related rights, per the contracts signed with performing artists and producers working for them. Since record labels assumed publishers' functions, they also hold part of the copyright share. When broadcasting organisations retransmit a performance or a play a phonogram, the copyright and related rights owners are entitled to receive their corresponding part of the communication to the public revenues. Besides, the broadcasting company owns the right to claim revenues for the rebroadcasting or the communication to the public of their broadcast run by a third party.

Moving on to how communication to the public is defined in the first generation of Conventions, the 1886 text of the Berne Convention already recognised the public performance of musical works as a part of the economic rights of authors in Article 9.[79]

Nowadays, the current text of the Berne Convention in Article 11[80] recognises the exclusive right of authors to authorise not only the public performance of their works by any means or process but also any communication to the public of the performance of their works. Besides Article 11*bis, recognised* authors' exclusive right of authorising communication to the public:

(i) *the broadcasting of their works or the communication thereof to the public by any other means of wireless diffusion of signs, sounds or images;*
(ii) *any communication to the public by wire or by rebroadcasting of the broadcast of the work when this communication is made by an organisation other than the original one;*
(iii) *the public communication by loudspeaker or any other analogous instrument transmitting, by signs, sounds or images, the broadcast of the work.*[81]

Even though communication to the public seems to be regulated twice, in Articles 11 and 11bis, it is not, as the meaning of "communication to the public" differs in each Article. For a proper interpretation of those provisions, it is essential to refer to Ficsor's[82] explanation made in the 2003 WIPO Guide to the Copyright and related rights. According to the guide, Article 11 (1 refers to (i) public performance and

[78] For further information see *Ifpi - The Role of a Record Company*, available at https://powering-the-music-ecosystem.ifpi.org/ (last visited 2 June 2021]*The Value of a Label - IFPI GLOBAL MUSIC REPORT 2019* (219 AD], available at https://powering-the-music-ecosystem.ifpi.org/download/GMR_The_Value_of_a_Label.pdf.

[79] See *Berne Convention First Original Text in* 1886, *'Convention de Berne Pour La Protection Des Œuvres Littéraires et Artistiques,'* available at https://wipolex.wipo.int/en/text/278701.

[80] Berne Convention, Article 11 as amended on 24 July 1971.

[81] Berne Convention, Article 11 bis.

[82] Ficsor (2003).

(ii) communication of the performance. Here, there is a difference between the act of performing a work in the presence of the public (i) and the (ii) communication of a work (or its performance or recital) to a public being at a place other than from where the communication is made.[83] However, such communication refers to any communication to the public other than broadcasting and related communications, as communication by broadcasting is covered by Article 11bis. This communication requires neither the presence of the public nor their attention, as it is sufficient that the performance is made in a place open to the public or communicated to the public in the sense of making the performance available to the public.[84]

Moving to Article 11bis contains the right of authors or other rightsholders to authorise three different acts: (i) the broadcasting of their works by wireless means, (ii) the communication to the public by wire, or rebroadcasting of the broadcast, run by someone different from the original broadcaster, and (iii) the public communication of the broadcast by loudspeaker or similar.

The first act is broadcasting, which has to be understood under the Berne Convention as the "communication of works to the public by wireless means". But broadcasting is only one kind of communication to the public by means of wireless diffusion. Accordingly, there are many other possible kinds of communication to the public through wireless diffusion.[85] Paragraph (1)(ii) of Article 11 clarifies that the act of communication needs to be made by an organisation other than the original one, which means that authors or other rightsholders have a right separate from the right to authorise the original act of broadcasting,[86] as it constitutes a new or secondary communication to the public of the broadcast of a work, not the work itself. Thus, this provision refers to two ways of the communication to the public broadcasting: by wire or by wireless means; the latest is also named rebroadcasting. Having said that, it is important to remember that despite referring to broadcasting actions, the Berne Convention only protects the rights of authors, not of the broadcasters, which will be protected under the Rome Convention.

Eleonora Rosati, based on WIPO's guide,[87] summarises the interpretation of Article 11bis(1)(iii) as that the use of the term 'public communication' instead of 'communication to the public' means that this act does not involve the transmission of the work to another place: it is an act carried out in a place where the public is or may be present, and, in that sense, it is similar to public performance and public recitation.[88]

The second paragraph of Article 11bis leaves the Union countries hands the task of regulating the conditions for exercising such right of authorisation in their jurisdiction. But that paragraph also puts two limits to domestic legislators; the

---

[83] Ibid. BC-11.7.

[84] Ibid. BC-11.10.

[85] Ibid. BC-11bis.6.

[86] Rosati (2020).

[87] Ficsor (2003).

[88] Rosati (2020), p. 6.

conditions cannot be prejudicial to the moral rights of authors, nor to their right to obtain equitable remuneration.

Finally, the last paragraph, 11bis (3), excludes the possibility of making copies other than the ephemeral recording needed for the broadcasting itself.

Referring to the Universal Convention, its first 1952 text did not include any provision recognising authors' right to public performance or any other form of communication to the public of musical works. In its Article VI bis, it was not until the 1971 Paris Review Conference that the UCC grants the "basic rights ensuring the author's economic interest." Such provision includes recognising the exclusive authors' right to authorise the public performance and broadcasting their works, as Berne did. Those two conventions state the right that authors have to authorise the communication to the public of their work and receive fair economic compensation for them. However, they do not explain which acts or under which conditions should be considered as CtoP. CtoP is also granted in the Rome Convention[89] as one of the related rights that performers, phonogram producers and broadcasters enjoy.

Article 7.1. (a)[90] grants performers the "possibility of preventing" the broadcasting and the communication to the public of their performance without their consent. This provision sets up a minimum of protection granting just the "possibility of preventing" but not the *right to authorise or prevent,* as given to producers or broadcasters. Such Article also limits this performer's possibility of authorising broadcasting or the public communication to those performances that have not been fixed. If the performance used to broadcast or for public communication is made from a fixation, Article 7 excludes the performer's possibility to prevent such communication or broadcasting. However, Article 12[91] grants performers and/or phonogram producers the right to receive a single equitable remuneration from the person or entity that uses a phonogram published for commercial purposes or a copy of it directly for broadcasting or any communication to the public. This right on secondary uses of phonograms embodying a performance is granted not only for the performer but also for the producers of the phonograms. Rome convention allows the possibility to grant that remuneration right to one of the categories of subjects: performers, producers, or to both of them.

The right to such a single equitable remuneration is only applicable if phonograms published for commercial purposes are used in such a way. If phonograms are used in broadcasting, they must be directly used, excluding rebroadcasting.[92]

Article 13 (d) of the Rome Convention sets a narrow scope of the broadcasters' rights by limiting their exclusive right to communication cases to the public in places accessible to the public against payment of an entrance fee. Nowadays, this situation

[89] Rome Convention.

[90] Rome Convention, Art. 7.1(a).

[91] Rome Convention Art. 12.

[92] Ficsor (2003). RC-12.4.

of rebroadcasting against payment is nearly obsolete.[93] As Professor *Tatiana Synodinou* points out,[94] the Rome Convention dates to 1961, the early years of television when just a few had private television devices, and the communication to the public of broadcasts in public places against the payment of an entrance fee was usual.

Therefore, the scope of CtoP rights in the earliest treaties covers the right of authors to authorise public performance and the communication to the public or broadcasting of their music works, as well as to receive moral respect and equitable remuneration for that. The CtoP right scope also reaches performers' possibility of banning the communication to the public or broadcasting their unfixed performances and receiving economic compensation for the secondary uses of their fixed performances. This possibility to receive remuneration for the use of phonograms is extended to performers and producers, while broadcasting organisations only keep the right, as mentioned above, on broadcasts to authorise their communication to the public when an entrance fee is required.

1.2 Early "Internet" Treaties: The TRIPs Agreement and the WIPO Internet Treaties (WCT & WPPT)

Since the last revision of first-generation treaties in 1971, new technological developments have been taking place. The first wave of technological changes was during the 1970s and 1980s. New systems like compact cassette systems facilitating "home taping" satellite broadcasting, cable television or video technology interfered somehow with music distribution and its communication to the public. Such changes also interfered with the copyright legislation, as the international treaties seemed to fail to protect creators' rights in front of those technological challenges. Instead of advocating for updating the international legislation, either by a revision or by adopting new international norms, the international copyright community chose the option of setting guiding principles to governments on how to face those challenges. This strategy, named by Sam Ricketson[95] in 1986 as "guided development", was based mainly on the interpretation of existing international norms. However, this guidance strategy was insufficient by the end of the 1980s despite its impact on domestic copyright legislation development.[96] Domestic copyright legislation development leads to many definitions of copyright elements, namely categories of works, rights, and exceptions. That situation and the lack of harmonised copyright international

[93] An example of this almost obsolete situations of rebroadcasting against payment is when a club, bar o other facilities charge the public with an entrance fee and display, for instance, sport events to the public in their facilities.

[94] Synodinou (2017), p. 2.

[95] Ricketson (1986), p. 35.

[96] Ficsor (2003), p. 10.

rules result in numerous conflicts about applying the principle of national treatment. Furthermore, none of the first-generation copyright conventions contained any sanctioning system nor specific enforcement procedures. Thus, in case of violations of obligations under those conventions, the only possibility for dispute resolution was bringing the case to the International Court of Justice. Not having international copyright law enforcement standards was inefficient in ensuring the convention's compliance by its members. Moreover, there was no international instrument to redress the emerging and fast-growing piracy problem. This practice was jeopardising the grant of reproduction rights and threatening the global system of copyright protection and related rights.

To deal with this problem, WIPO started by setting up committees of experts to update the international legislation; those committees were working on a "protocol" to the Berne Convention and, in parallel, on a new instrument to update the international norms on the rights of performers and producers of phonograms, as the latter were the most affected by the piracy hazard. At the same time, a process of rebuilding the international trade order was taking place. Thus, the Governments concerned preferred to engage in a discussion within TRIPS negotiations in the Uruguay Round while WIPO works were decelerating. The TRIPs Agreement was more complex and with a wider scope, including all intellectual property rights. It aimed to be integrated into what later became the World Trade Organization.

1.3 TRIPs Agreement and the WTO

Negotiations on the trade-related aspects of the intellectual property rights (TRIPs) agreement within the Uruguay Round negotiations of the General Agreement on Tariffs and Trade (GATT) started in September 1986. The final text was adopted in April 1994, along with the other agreements linked as Annex 1C to the Marrakesh Agreement Establishing the World Trade Organization (WTO).[97]

The WTO Agreement on Trade-Related Intellectual Property Rights (referred to as TRIPs) sets the minimum standard that the members of WTO must provide for the protection of Intellectual Property rights, including copyright. Substantive copyright protection standards are laid down in Section 1, Part II of the TRIPs (Articles 9 to 14), named the "standards concerning the availability, scope and use" of copyright and related rights.[98] TRIPs sets a minimum standard of protection while incorporating the obligations existing in the Berne and Rome Conventions, as well as a safeguard clause in favour of the Berne and Rome Conventions: Article 2.2

[97] WTO, Agreement on Trade-Related Aspects of Intellectual Property Rights, Apr. 15, 1994, Marrakesh Agreement Establishing the World Trade Organization, Annex 1C, 1869, (1994). Marrakesh.

[98] Ibid. Articles 9 to 14.

states that nothing in Parts I to IV of the Agreement shall derogate from existing obligations that Members may have to each other under the intellectual property existing conventions, namely the Berne and the Rome Conventions, among others. That means widening the protection focus from "authors" to "rightsholders", including authors and any other person entitled to related rights.

In relation to the principle of national treatment, the TRIPS Agreement on Articles 1.3, 3 and 4(b) also appeals to the Berne and Rome Conventions. Furthermore, those Articles apply *mutatis mutandis*, the criteria of eligibility, and the exceptions to national treatment provided for in the Rome Convention.

Despite not providing any enforcement mechanism, the Berne Convention provided adequate basic copyright protection standards. Hence, the TRIPS Agreement did not bring about significant changes in the existing substantive norms on copyright and related rights. Indeed, the substantive provisions of the Berne and Rome conventions are incorporated in the TRIPS Agreement by reference. Article 9.1 refers explicitly to the Berne Convention and states that: "Members shall comply with the substantive provisions 1 to 21 of the Berne Convention (1971) and the Appendix thereto".

In the case of the Rome Convention, although some Articles are explicitly mentioned in the Agreement, many other provisions are included without specific reference.[99]

Therefore, in general terms, the level of protection required in TRIPS corresponds to the level provided by the Berne and Rome conventions, with one major exception. Article 9.1 on TRIPS introduces an exception for the Berne Convention provisions on moral rights, conferred by its Article 6bis, and the rights derived therefrom.

In essence, Member States part in TRIPs agreed to be bound by all the obligations presented in the previous Berne and Rome conventions, with the exception of moral rights, whether they were part of them or not. Furthermore, the Member States are not permitted to make any reservations from the minimum obligations set on those agreements.

As mentioned, TRIPS's contribution to copyright substantial provisions is minimal, and no re-interpretation of the Berne Convention protected rights is given. As assessed by Nikita Malevanny,[100] there was an attempt to provide a definition of "public", according to which public communication rights would explicitly encompass on-demand uses, but it did not succeed.

The TRIPS introduced only two substantial improvements, both referring to phonograms: first, the recognition of rental rights, with certain conditions and exceptions, for certain categories of works, phonograms among them; and second, the extension of the minimum term of protection for the rights of performers and

[99] Some of this provisions are Articles 1(2), 2(2), 3(1), 4(b) and 14(6). See *The TRIPS Agreement and the Conventions referred to in it*. Available at https://www.wto.org/english/tratop_e/trips_e/ta_docs_e/1_tripsandconventions_e.pdf.

[100] Malevanny (2019), p. 7.

producers of phonograms to 50 years, instead of the 20 years term provided in the Rome Convention.

Since the TRIPS Agreement is based on the Berne Convention for the protection of authors' rights, likewise, the protection of performers and phonogram producers is based on the provisions of the Rome Convention. Article 14(1) TRIPS[101] grants performers just a "possibility of preventing" certain acts "in respect of a fixation of their performance on a phonogram". This formula does not give full exclusive rights, allowing performers the possibility of preventing "the fixation of their unfixed performance and the reproduction of such fixation" and the non-authorized "broadcasting by wireless means and the communication to the public of their live performance."

Malevanny,[102] in his assessment of the reproduction right, points out Article 14 (1) ambiguity about the communication to the public. The discussion lays on whether the formulation "the fixation of their unfixed performance and the reproduction of such fixation" refers to "the fixation of their unfixed performance" (position of some scholars like Correa,[103] Morgan[104] Ricketson and Ginsburg[105]) or to "a fixation of their performance on a phonogram" (theory advocated by Gervais[106]).

But such a problem can't be extrapolated to the communication to the public. The main issue is in the second part of the Article: if the possibility of prohibition is limited to the communication of only *live* performances. The word "live" in this provision excludes the communication to the public of any phonograms or sound recordings made in the studio. However, the communication to the public of live performances that have previously been fixed is not so clear. Therefore, this provision of the TRIPS may mirror to Article 7(1) of the Rome Convention, which states that performers have *the possibility of preventing:*

> the broadcasting and the communication to the public, without their consent, of their performance, except where the performance used in the broadcasting, or the public communication is itself already a broadcast performance or is made from a fixation.[107]

---

[101] Art. 14(1) TRIPS:

> In respect of a fixation of their performance on a phonogram, performers shall have the possibility of preventing the following acts when undertaken without their authorization: the fixation of their unfixed performance and the reproduction of such fixation. Performers shall also have the possibility of preventing the following acts when undertaken without their authorization: the broadcasting by wireless means.

[102] Malevanny (2019), p. 28.

[103] Correa (2020), p. 159.

[104] Morgan (2002), p. 167.

[105] Ricketson and Ginsburg (2022), pp. 19–28.

[106] Gervais (2021), p. 174.

[107] Rome Convention, Article 7(1).

If ignoring the reference to broadcasting and focusing just on the reference to the public communication, the sentence in the Rome convention has to be read as performers may prevent the communication to the public of their performance without their consent except where the performance used in the public communication is itself is made from a fixation.

The provision seems to exclude the public communication of any sound recording from the performer's possibility of authorisation. Hence, the provision's part related to the communication to the public is redundant as live broadcasting is the only way to communicate a live performance without using a fixation (phonogram)g. Such provisions could be understood as they refer to performers' possibility of prohibition of broadcasting and any act of communication to the public only of their live performances, which need to be fixed in a signal, at least temporarily, to make such communication or broadcasting possible.

Since Article 14(1) of the TRIPS is based on Rome Convention Article 7(1), the previous interpretation cannot be considered valid if taking into account the meaning given to that Article in the Guide to the Rome Convention published by WIPO.[108] The document, published in 1981, explains that there was an attempt to use the term "live" to refer to the performances in the final text of the RC. Still, such expression was rejected, not only for the different meanings that the term "life" has from the word "*direct*" in French and the different connotations that I may have in other countries, but also because a "direct" performance for the performer may not be "direct" for the public. That is why the Rome Convention did not adopt the expression "live" that was finally taken up in the TRIPS Agreement text. Therefore, to allow both texts to be compatible, the parallelism of both allows us to extrapolate the interpretation given to the RC Article 7(1) to the TRIPS provision. According to the aforementioned guide consent "is required for broadcasting and communication to the public of a "*live*" performance, provided no broadcasting or recording of this performance has intervened".[109] That is, performers' rights are limited to the possibility of authorising the public's communication of their performances that have not already been fixed or broadcast. Therefore, performers' exclusive right to authorise their performances is linked to their simple decision to appear or not on the stage or in the studio. Once performances are fixed, the right that allows performers to retain control over their performances vanishes, and as such, an exclusive right is granted to the authors in their work. Not recognising the minimum of such exclusive rights to performers moves them to a secondary role in the creation process, and their protection in the international conventions seems to become merely representative. Article 14 of the TRIPs Agreement also recognises only the exclusive right of reproduction to phonogram producers, but nothing is mentioned about communication to the public. The only indirect reference can be found in Article 14(2), which states their right to authorise or prohibit their phonograms' direct or indirect reproduction.

---

[108] Masouye and Bogsch (1981).

[109] Ibid, p. 37.

Broadcasting organisations have their rights stated in Article 14(3) of the TRIPS. They have the right to authorise or prohibit undertaken without the fixation, the reproduction of fixations, and the rebroadcasting by wireless means of broadcasts. Regarding communication to the public, such a provision only recognises the rights of broadcasting organisations on their broadcasts. Instead of using a general formulation, the specification of television broadcast can be interpreted as implicitly excluding the public communication of radio broadcasts and podcasts from the scope of control of the original broadcasting organisation. According to that meaning, radio stations are not allowed to prohibit the public communication of their radio broadcasts communicated without their permission, despite communicating by using an unauthorised fixation of the broadcast or not. Another interpretation of that last part of Article 14(3) TRIPS could be understanding the term "television broadcasts" as an example rather than an exclusivity; therefore, that provision should also be applied to any broadcast by analogy.

Finally, the TRIPS Agreement in Article14(6) refers directly to the Rome Convention provisions to establish any conditions, limitations, exceptions, and reservations to the related rights. Likewise, it calls on the *mutatis mutandis* application of Article 18 of the Berne Convention regarding the application in time of conventional obligations to the rights of performers and producers of phonograms.

1.3.1 CtoP and the WTO Dispute Settlement System: The Dispute WT/DS160 Against the Section 110(5) of the US Copyright Act

What seemed to be more significant of the TRIPS agreement for copyright purposes was that it contained a mechanism for state-to-state enforcement of the international rules by incorporating the WTO dispute resolution process. The fifth part of the TRIPS Agreement[110] is dedicated to "Dispute Prevention and Settlement". While Article 63 refers to the publicity and transparency of Member States' laws, rules, rulings and procedures, Article 64 refers to the dispute settlement system. Article 64 provides that Articles XXII and XXIII of GATT 1994 will apply to consultations and settling disputes under TRIPS, as elaborated and applied by the Dispute Settlement Understanding[111] (DSU).

Following the DSU procedures,[112] up to date, only ten disputes related to copyright have been brought before the WTO Dispute Settlement Body (DSB)'

[110] Articles 63 and 64 TRIPS Agreement.

[111] World Trade Organization, Annex 2 of the WTO Agreement - Dispute Settlement Understanding on rules and procedures governing the settlement of disputes (DSU) (15 April 1994).

[112] The DSU provides rules and procedures for consultations and the settlement of disputes between members concerning their rights and obligations under certain WTO agreements, listed in Appendix 1 of the DSU. Available at https://www.wto.org/english/tratop_e/dispu_e/dsu_e.htm#25¡.

and most of them just reached the consultation stage. Only two (DS160 and DS362) have moved to a panel stage,[113] and the Dispute Settlement Body adopted a ruling accordingly.[114] None of them was the object of a review by the Appellate Body.

The dispute *(DS160) US—Section 110(5) of the United States Copyright Act* refers to the exceptions and limitations to the communication to the public exclusive rights of copyright holders. Such a case is the only case in which the respondent (US) paid the complainant (EU - European Communities by that time) € 1.2 million per year during 3 years as compensation for its continuing non-compliance with the ruling by the panel.[115] But this case is relevant not only because of the very exceptional economic compensation measure for future economic harm but mainly for the importance that an international organ within a dispute settlement clarified the scope of the "minor exceptions" doctrine, thereby establishing an international benchmark.[116] The Panel, in that case, concluded as an initial matter that (i) there is a "minor exceptions" doctrine that applies to Berne Convention Article 11bis and 113, and (ii) the doctrine has been incorporated into the TRIPS Agreement.[117]

The minor exceptions doctrine is articulated in TRIPs Art 13. It allows Member States to confine limitations and exceptions to the exclusive rights as long as those limitations or exceptions do not conflict with a normal exploitation of the work nor unreasonably prejudice the legitimate interests of the right holders.[118]

The complaint came from the European Communities on 26 January 1999 against the US amendment of Section 110(5) of the US Copyright Act introduced by the "Fairness in Music Licensing Act"[119] enacted on 27 October 1998. The amendment introduced a new limitation to rightsholders' exclusive right of communication to the public of musical works and recordings: the "Business exemption" in Article 110(5) (B).

CtoP right in the music field is granted by the US legislation in Article 106 (4), (5) and (6) of the Copyright Act as a public performance right. Such Article recognises, and so did it before the 1998 amendment, the exclusive rights of musical works copyright owners, among others, to authorise and to perform the copyrighted work publicly[120]; to display the copyrighted work publicly[121]; and in the case of

[113]Data up to the date of writing this book.

[114]The two cases are: *United States—Section 110(5) of US Copyright Act of 26 January 1999 (DS160)* and *China — Measures Affecting the Protection and Enforcement of Intellectual Property Rights (DS362).*

[115]Van Den Bossche (2022), p. 8.

[116]Babu (2017), p. 137.

[117]WTO, *One-page summary of key findings of the dispute DS160: United States — Section 110 (5) of US Copyright Act.*

[118]TRIPS Agreement., Article 13.

[119]Code 17 U.S. (1998) Fairness in Music Licensing Act, Pub. United States, United States.

[120]TRIPS Agreement, Article 106(4).

[121](1947) 17 Title U.S.Code - U.S. Copyright Act. United States, United States. Article 106(5).

sound recordings, to perform the copyrighted work publicly by means of digital audio transmission.[122]

Therefore, since 1978, the Copyright Act has authorised restaurants, bars and retail stores using "homestyle" audio and video equipment to play broadcast music without paying license fees,[123] being a limitation of the CtoP exclusive right.

The Copyright Act "Homestyle Exemption" is stated in Article 110(5)(A).[124] But the "Fairness in Music Licensing Act" of 1998 introduced a new limitation by adding another paragraph on that Article, §110(5)(B), what was known as the "Business exception". This amendment was promoted by restaurant, bar and small business associations, who lobbied Congress to exempt all "secondary uses[125] of broadcast music."',[126] with the direct opposition of the copyright management organisations or performing rights organisations ("PROs") -as they are named in US[127]-, who issue licenses on behalf of American and foreign music authors and publishers. While "Homestyle Exemption" allows small businesses to play radio music for customers in their establishments without infringing rightsholders communication to the public right as long as they play it through home-like equipment, the new "Business exemption" on §110 did focus on the source of music playing, plus the building size and/or the number of loudspeakers used.[128] The provision also stated the music must be "originated by a radio or television broadcast station licensed as such by the Federal Communications Commission, or, if an audiovisual transmission, by a cable system or satellite carrier".

Although it seems to be a very limited exemption, it allowed most small and medium businesses to play music and consequently to communicate to the public

---

[122]Ibid. Article 106(6).

[123]Helfer (2000), p. 95.

[124]17 U.S. Code, Copyright Act, §110(5)(A).

> §110—Limitations on exclusive rights: Exemption of certain performances and displays
>
> Notwithstanding the provisions of sect. 106, the following are not infringements of copyright (…)
>
> (5)(A) except as provided in subparagraph (B), communication of a transmission embodying a performance or display of a work by the public reception of the transmission on a single receiving apparatus of a kind commonly used in private homes.

[125]Secondary uses are those actions where a third party uses a work that has already been broadcasted or distributed to the public. That may constitute an act of communication to the public, such as when a business displays music by turning on the radio, television, etc. to make the music or program be heard by the public within its establishment.

[126]Helfer (2000), p. 96.

[127]Main PROs acting were the American Society of Composers, Authors and Publishers ("ASCAP"), Broadcast Music, Inc. ("BMI") and the Society of European Stage Authors and Composers ("SESAC").

[128]*See* U.S. Code, Copyright Act, §110(5)(B). To invoke the exemption, businesses must meet the square footage requirement (less than 3750 gross square feet for food or drinking service establishments and less than 2.000 for other activities), but bigger locations can become exempt if they use a limited number of loudspeakers to project the music. (less than six loudspeakers, of which a maximum of 4 of them can be located in any 1 room or adjoining outdoor space).

without obtaining a license. It turned to prejudice the rightsholders' legitimate interests, representing an important economic loss for them.

On the same day the amendment entered into force, 26 January 1999, the European Communities (EC, from now on) requested consultations[129] with the United States under Article 4 of the "DSU" and Article 64.1 of the TRIPs Agreement, challenging the US new exemptions as incompatible with the obligations undertaken under Article 9.1 of the TRIPs Agreement together with Articles 11(1)(ii) and 11bis(1)(iii) of the Berne Convention (1971). EC understood those exemptions could not be justified under the Berne Convention or the TRIPs Agreement. On the other hand, the US argued that the TRIPs Agreement and the Berne Convention allowed States to place minor limitations on the exclusive rights of copyright owners. Hence, the exemptions were justifiable, according to such limitation.

The EC estimated the annual losses to European rights holders because of the US Article 110(5) exemption to $53.65 million.[130] The amount was far from the less than $500,000 yearly loss estimated by the US.

The US argument that Article110(5) of the Copyright Act constitutes a minor exemption needs to be compatible with the standards of the international legislation; therefore, the exemptions need to meet the requirements set in Article 13[131] of the TRIPs Agreement; (i) confined to certain special cases; (ii) do not conflict with a normal exploitation of the work; and (iii) do not unreasonably prejudice the legitimate interests of the right holder.[132]

The Panel clarified that the three criteria, under Article 13, must be met cumulatively by states when introducing limitations or exceptions to exclusive rights.[133] Based on these criteria, the Panel found that the "Homestyle exemption" in Article 110(5)(A) met the requirements of Article 13, and, therefore, it was compatible with Berne Convention Article 11bis(1)(ii) and (iii). The Panel considered that the exemption was confined to "certain special cases" as it was well-defined and limited in scope and reach (13–18% of establishments covered). Furthermore, the Panel concluded that the "Homestyle exemption" did not conflict with a normal exploitation of the work, as there was little nor caused unreasonable prejudice to the legitimate interests of the right holders in light of its narrow scope. There was no evidence showing that the right holders, if given opportunities, would exercise their direct licensing rights.

However, regarding the "Business exemption", the Panel found that it did not meet any of the requirements of Article 13. The exemption in Article 110(5)

---

[129] WTO, United States - Section 110(5) of the US Copyright Act: Report of the Panel (2000).

[130] Babu (2017), p. 137.

[131] For an exhaustive iterpretation of Article 13 of theTRIPS Agreement see the WTO Analytical Index—TRIPS Agreement Article 13, avialable at https://www.wto.org/english/res_e/publications_e/ai17_e/trips_art13_jur.pdf.

[132] Babu (2017), pp. 143–147.

[133] WTO, *One-page summary of key findings of the dispute DS160: United States — Section 110 (5) of US Copyright Act.*

(B) could not qualify as a "certain special case" under Article 13, as its scope in respect of potential users covered 70 per cent of eating and drinking establishments and 45 per cent of retail establishments, which are the main types of establishments intended to be covered by Article 11bis(1)(iii). Moreover, the exemption "conflicts with a normal exploitation of the work," as the Panel argued, the exemption deprived the right holders of musical works of compensation, as appropriate, for the use of their work from broadcasts of radio and television and (iii) in light of statistics demonstrating that 45 to 73 per cent of the relevant establishments fell within the business exemption, the US could not proof that the business exemption did not unreasonably prejudice the legitimate interests of the right holder. Thus, the business exemption was found inconsistent with Article Berne Convention Article 11bis(1)(iii) and 11(1)(ii) and Article 13 TRIPS. The DSB adopted the panel report on 27 July 2000, and the US informed the Dispute Settlement Body of its intention to respect its WTO obligations.[134] On October 23, 2000, the EC requested arbitration to determine the period for the US to implement the panel's recommendation. It was determined that the deadline for implementation should be 27 July 2001. On 23 July 2001, the US and the EC requested arbitration to determine the level of nullification or impairment of benefits to the EC as a result of section 110(5) (B). In this case, the arbitrators determined that the value of the benefits lost to the EC was $1.1 million per year. However, the US and the EC were engaged in discussions to find a mutually acceptable dispute resolution. On 23 June 2003, the US and the EC notified the WTO of a mutually satisfactory temporary arrangement regarding the dispute. Pursuant to this arrangement, the US paid $3.3 million to the EU to a fund established to finance activities of general interest to music copyright holders, in particular awareness-raising campaigns at the national and international level and activities to combat piracy in the digital network. The arrangement covered a three-year period, which ended on 21 December 2004. By the date of this work, the US has not amended section 110(5)(B). As has been regularly notified by the U.-S. Administration until their last Status Report on 19 May 2022: "The U.-S. Administration will work closely with the U.S. Congress and will continue to confer with the European Union to reach a mutually satisfactory resolution of this matter."

The main question is why the EU has done nothing to claim for the loss generated from 2004 until 2022 due to the "business exemption" in section 110(5) of the US Copyright Act, which has not been amended and is still in force.

A possible response to that might be that since 2004, the way to play music has changed, not only in business establishments. However, nearly all businesses still use background music in their locations; most do not tune in to the radio or the TV but use music streaming services or other formats. The text on section 110(5)(B) of the US Copyright Act states the music must be "originated by a radio or television broadcast station licensed as such by the Federal Communications Commission, or,

[134] Section 110(5) of US Copyright Act | United States Trade Representative. https://ustr.gov/issue-areas/enforcement/dispute-settlement-proceedings/united-states—-section-1105-us-copyright-ac.

if an audio-visual transmission, by a cable system or satellite carrier", which leaves out its scope most of the internet music streaming services. Such streaming services are not broadcast stations because they are neither licensed by the Federal Communications Commission nor broadcast stations by their nature. Without entering the nature of streaming services, a topic that will be assessed later in this book, it can be pointed out that streaming services and online radio stations are not broadcasting stations as required by the business exemption. As Taylor McGraw[135] wrote in 2018, "There is no litigation (in the US) addressing this issue, leaving the relevant parties without a precedent to guide their interpretation of the statute".

In conclusion, the impact that the business exemption can nowadays have on the communication to the public right and on the interests of its right holders is not as it was back in 1999. Thus, the EU efforts on copyright protection are not in the US exemptions anymore, but on other current issues, like content sharing, platforms and new business models.

1.4 WIPO Internet Treaties: From Public Performance to the Making Available

On 20 December 1996, the WIPO Copyright Treaty[136] (WCT) and the WIPO Performances and Phonograms Treaty[137] (WPPT), collectively known as the WIPO Internet Treaties, were agreed. Both treaties were auspices and are administered by WIPO. As pointed out above, WIPO preparatory works were slowed down by the interest of States in concluding the TRIPs Agreement. During the final stage of the WCT and the WPPT negotiations and works, the TRIPS Agreement was adopted and entered into force. That fact quickened the works and negotiation of the WofO Committees working on the new Internet Treaties. The TRIPs provisions have already resolved a few topics pending discussion, so no negotiations were needed for all those issues. The solution was to include the corresponding relevant TRIPS provisions in the new treaties.[138] Such issues referred to the protection of computer programs and databases, the right of rental, and the term of protection of rights in performances and in phonograms.

The preamble of the WCT and the WPPT recognise the profound impact of the development and convergence of information and communication technologies on the creation and use of literary and artistic works".[139] Moreover, both preambles identify that the changes are not only because of technological developments but

[135] Mcgraw (2018), p. 282.

[136] WIPO Copyright Treaty (WCT), adopted in Geneva on December 20, 1996. WIPO, Geneva.

[137] WIPO Performances and Phonograms Treaty (WPPT), adopted in Geneva on December 20, 1996. WIPO, Geneva.

[138] Ficsor (2003). CT-1.2.

[139] WCT Preamble. See also WPPT, Preamble.

also because of the economic, social and cultural evolution. Therefore, introducing new international rules and clarifying existing ones was needed to provide adequate solutions to s. In the final paragraph of their preamble, both treaties stress maintaining a balance between the significant public interest and the rights of authors, performers, and producers of phonograms, respectively.

From the Berne and the Rome Conventions, the status relation of the WCT and the WPPT is that the Internet Treaties are special agreements of the general regime. Article 20[140] in the Berne Convention allows such special agreements among Countries of the Union.

> in so far as such agreements grant authors more extensive rights than those granted by the Convention, or contain other provisions not contrary to this Convention (…).

The Rome Convention includes an analogous provision in Article 22.[141]

In their first Articles, both treaties declare their relationship with the existing Treaties, namely Berne and Rome. After announcing the special agreement nature, Article 1 of the WCT states that the WCT "*shall not have any connection with treaties other than the Berne Convention, nor shall it prejudice any rights and obligations under any other treaties.*" This seems a pretty settled sentence to state that the WTC shall have a connection only with the Berne Convention and shall not prejudice any other treaty. However, using the negative statement in the first part of that sentence was intended to announce no connection between the WCT and the TRIPs Agreement.[142] The analogous provision in WCT is found in paragraphs (1) and (3) of Article 1.[143] Likewise, paragraph (1) announces the relationship with the Rome Convention, while paragraph (3) refers to "other treaties". It is expected to find reference to the Rome Convention in the WPPT, as it is its analogous WIPO treaty *ratione materiae*. However, instead of referring to other treaties, WPPT Article 1 paragraph (2) clarifies that the protection granted under the WPPT does not affect the protection of copyright in literary and artistic works, nor can the WPPT provisions may be interpreted in prejudice of the copyright protection rules.

The WCT, in paragraphs (2) and (4), clarify and reinforces the relation of the Treaty with the Berne Convention by stating that not only does the WTC not derogate the Berne Convention,[144] but also adds an obligation to the WTC Contracting Parties to comply with Articles 1 to 21 and the Appendix of the Berne Convention.[145]

However, there is no administrative relationship between the WCT and the Berne Convention. Thus, being a member of the Berne Union is not a condition of

[140] WCT, Article 20.

[141] WPPT, Article 22.

[142] Ficsor (2003). CT-1.3.

[143] WPPT, Article 1.

[144] WCT, Article 1(2).

[145] WCT, Article 1(4).

accession to the WCT. Any WIPO Member State may become a party of the WCT, as stated in Article 17.[146] Furthermore, Article 17(2) recognises the possibility of intergovernmental organisations becoming part of the treaty after a previous positive decision of the WCT Assembly,[147] as long as they fulfil the requirements of having sufficient competence and binding instruments among their members. The third paragraph acknowledges that the European Communities have the ability to join the WIPO Internet treaties, as the requirements in paragraph two were declared before the Diplomatic Conference that adopted the WCT. Similarly, this was done for the WPPT under Article 26.[148] As the European Union is an international organisation with its legal system, its membership in these treaties demonstrates a commitment to uphold the framework outlined in them when developing and interpreting the European copyright legislation.

Moving to the regulation of the CtoP right in the internet treaties, the WTC made an important step in configuring the concept by updating the meaning to the new ways of communication that technology offers. Article 8 summarises and reasserts the Berne Convention provisions[149] on public performance and CtoP rights and recognises authors' exclusive right of authorizing any communication to the public of their works at the time that offers a definition or clarification of the concept. It states that it recognises authors' exclusive right of authorising *"any communication to the public by wire or wireless means, including the making available to the public of their works in such a way that members of the public may access these works from a place and at a time individually chosen by them*". As Professor Tatyana Aplin[150] points out, Article 8 of the WCT does not refer to Article 11bis(1)(iii) of the Berne Convention. Related to music, Article 8 refers to Articles 11(1)(ii), 11bis(1)(i) and (ii), Berne Convention, which deals only with communication to the public and not communication in public. Accordingly, Aplin also states that "all means of communicating a work in public" are excluded from the scope of Article 8 WCT. However, such a statement is inaccurate, as Article 11bis(1)(iii) refers to the public communication of *broadcasts of works,* not the public communication of works. In essence, Article 8 of the WCT not only supplemented the Berne Convention but also introduced the concept of 'making available to the public'.[151] This new approach to communication to the public right includes the authors' right to authorise the making available of their works to the public. Therefore, it fills the gap brought about by the Internet and digital technologies, which introduced the streaming. Music streaming is separated into two distinct categories: interactive and non-interactive streaming services. In Non-interactive streaming services, the content is

[146] WCT, Article 17.

[147] WCT, Article 15.

[148] WPPT, art. 26.

[149] Berne Convention, Articles 11(1)(ii), 11bis(1)(i) and (ii), regarding musical works and broadcasting; 11ter (1)(i) referring Literary works; and 14(1)(i) and 14bis(1)(i) for audiovisual works.

[150] Aplin (2011), p. 217.

[151] Rosati (2020), p. 6.

pre-determined based on a few limited choices the user inputs, such as a genre of music or artist name; they offer a alike traditional radio experience for the user (p.ex. Online or Internet radio, which are often for free or ad-based). Whereas interactive streaming is characterised by the capability of users to select works to be delivered to their computers or other devices and control what content to play and when; they offer an on-demand experience, like selecting a CD and playing the desired track (p. ex. Spotify, Deezer, Youtube, etc.).[152]

Some national legislations characterise or assimilate the non-interactive streaming to broadcasting as a non-copy-related right and the interactive streaming as an act of distributing copies, as a (physical) copy-related right. However, the streaming service platforms do not provide users with a copy of the work or offer a shortage of users. Article 8 WCT brought what Ficsor names the "umbrella solution."; the treaty extends the applicability of the right of communication to the public to all categories of works and then clarifies that that right also covers transmissions in interactive systems, described in a neutral, legal-characterization-free manner, in the sense that it does not refer either to distribution or communication to the public of works and objects of related rights.[153] Article 8 WCT includes making a work perceptible to the public other than by distributing or displaying physical copies.[154]

Besides, the WTC contains an agreed statement concerning Article 8 that may turn quite obvious as it declares that it has to be understood that "the mere provision of physical facilities for enabling or making a communication does not in itself amount to communication within the meaning of this Treaty or the Berne Convention. That clarifies the no liability of providers of material necessary to carry out an act of communication. Finally, the second part of the agreed statement reminds us that "nothing in Article 8 precludes a Contracting Party from applying Article 11bis (2)".

Regarding related rights, the WPPT regulates the communication to the public and makes available rights in three different provisions as the Treaty is divided into different chapters.[155] After Chapter I on "General Provisions", Chapter II (Articles 5 to 10) and Chapter III (Articles 11 to 14) refer to the rights of the two different subjects whose rights are protected by the WPPT: Performers and Phonogram Producers, correspondingly. Article 10, under the title *The Right of Making Available of Fixed Performances*, grants performers the exclusive right of authorising "the making available to the public of their performances fixed in phonograms, by wire or wireless means, in such a way that members of the public may access them from a place and at a time individually chosen by them." The provision language is the same

[152] Mcgraw, (2018), p. 283.

[153] Ficsor (2003), at CT-8.11.

[154] Executive Committee of the ALAI, Report and Opinion on the making available and communication to the public in the internet environment—focus on linking techniques on the Internet (2013).

[155] Chapter I: General Provisions; Chapter II: Rights of Performers; Chapter III: Rights of Producers of Phonograms; Chapter IV: Common Provisions; Chapter V: Administrative and Final Clauses.

used in Article 8 WCT, but with no reference to the communication to the public, just mentioning the making available right. Likewise, Article 14 WPPT uses the same text than Article 10, *mutatis mutandis,* to grant the making available right of Phonogram Producers.

Article 15 recognises the right of remuneration of both performers and phonogram producers for broadcasting and communication to the public of their phonograms published for commercial purposes, regardless of whether they are for direct or indirect use. Therefore, Article 15 of the WPPT only provides a right to remuneration for broadcasting and other forms of communication to the public, different from making it available. The lack of recognition of exclusive rights of performers and phonogram producers is due to the fact that, with respect to related rights, many countries were not ready to grant exclusive rights for such acts. That is why the two rights appear as separated in WPPT: in Articles 10 and 14, on the one hand, and in Article 15, on the other.[156]

Moreover, the second paragraph in Article 15 transfers the same provision in the second part of the text of Article 12 of the Rome convention, allowing domestic legislations to decide who is entitled to receive such equitable remuneration, either the performer, the phonogram producer or both by share. However, Article 12 of the Rome Convention only applies if the use for broadcasting or any communication to the public is made "directly". At the same time, the WPPT explicitly recognises the right of remuneration for indirect uses, that is, secondary uses, such as playing background music in stores.

The concern or lack of recognition by some countries of exclusive rights for those communication acts, regarding related rights was clearly reflected in the third paragraph of Article 15, as it allows the State party the possibility to apply equitable remuneration as provided only in respect of certain uses, or to limit their application in some other way, or directly not apply these provisions at all. Article 15(3) provides that any Contracting Party willing to declare the possibility of equitable remuneration in a limited manner is allowed to do so by notification deposited with the Director General of WIPO.[157] Apart from the possibilities in other paragraphs of Article 15, the fourth paragraph introduces a mechanism to warrant the equitable remuneration to Performers and producers of unpublished phonograms that have been made available to the public. Article 15(4) considers the presumption that such phonograms had been published for commercial purposes.[158] This means that as a result of uploading a phonogram on a website and making it available in such a way, the phonogram is to be regarded as if it had been published for commercial purposes, regardless of whether there is a commercial purpose behind the act.

No revision or amendment has been introduced to any international treaties analysed here, but there is still a pending subject regarding the protection of

[156] Ficsor (2003). PPT-10.4.

[157] WPPT, Article 15(3).

[158] WPPT, Article15(4).

broadcasting organisations' rights. Although those rights are protected under the Rome Convention, they were not updated by the WIPO Internet Treaties. The 42nd session of the World Intellectual Property Organization's (WIPO) Standing Committee on Copyright and Related Rights (SCCR) took place from 9 to 13 May 2022 in Geneva. *Broadcast Treaty* was one of the main items on the agenda. The issue has been under discussion since the late 1990s. On 4 March 2022, the *Revised Draft Text for the WIPO Broadcasting Organizations Treaty* was published; thus, discussions on protecting broadcasting organisations against unauthorised retransmission and related uses were centred around the proposal, but the session concluded with no further advance on the negotiations.

1.5 Overview: The Limits of the Multilateral Legal Framework on Copyright

One of the most essential rights for the music industry today is the CtoP right. Due to the complex nature of the music industry and the numerous subjects, objects, and rights linked to copyright and related rights in musical works, regulating the CtoP of musical works has become a challenging task. The complexities become more apparent when copyright and related rights rules have to be applied in digital contexts, leading to their global expansion.

The rapid pace of technological advancements has led to the emergence of new businesses and transformed the music consumption landscape. Yet, the sluggish decision-making process of international regulations makes it challenging to keep up with these changes. After examining the key provisions of international copyright treaties that impact the communication to the public right and providing an insightful overview, it has been demonstrated that International Law faces significant challenges to properly regulating such right at the international level. One of the main challenges that International Copyright law faces is owing to the divergent approaches of its two primary legal traditions, Copyright and *Droits d'auteur*. These different approaches pose a significant barrier to achieving uniformity in copyright protection across various jurisdictions. The differences in these approaches often lead to conflict and uncertainty regarding the scope and nature of copyright protection. A consistent and effective international copyright law regime seems impossible unless the different legal traditions achieve a closer approach.

Another important obstacle is the territoriality of copyright and related rights. This legal perspective is being challenged regarding communication to public matters, especially in the music sector. A borderless solution would be optimal in that scenario. Challenging the idea that copyright is limited to a specific geographic territory would mean acknowledging that these rights are linked to the global trade of cultural products. The cultural significance of copyrighted works makes many countries hesitant to leave the regulation of their dissemination and the compensation of the creative industry to international entities. Current International treaties do not provide a global substantive solution that today's copyright needs and such a legal solution seems not to be expected in the medium-short term, even though the WIPO efforts.

In conclusion, from the analysis developed in this chapter it is clear that a global regulation on copyright seems to be an unrealistic goal, The overall general legal framework provided so far by multilateral treaties works just as a basis for building more accurate regional rules and, if there is willingness among the parties, it can even provide mechanisms for dispute resolution. In effect, as has been seen certain disputes, because of the different conceptions of copyright, they can be resolved through a dispute resolution system in international law, like WTO Dispute DS160, which ended with an agreement between the EU and the US on the CtoP rights exceptions introduced by the US Copyright Act. This is an example of how International Law through multilateral agreements can offer a minimum global framework for copyright and related rights; and it even provide the states with dispute resolution mechanisms that help to close the gaps between the different copyright legal traditions and legislations. But, it is also clear that this global framework has to be understood, essentially, as a basis for building more accurate regional rules. Indeed, regional regulations may be a more feasible option because they aim to harmonise the laws of certain Member States with a common copyright legal tradition.

References

Aguilar A (2018) Distributed ownership in music: between authorship and performance. Soc Leg Stud 27:776–798. https://doi.org/10.1177/0964663917734300

Aplin T (2011) 'Reproduction' and 'communication to the public' rights in EU copyright law: FAPL v QC leisure. King's Law J 22:209–219. https://doi.org/10.5235/096157611796769514

Arnold R (2011) Content copyrights and signal copyrights: the case for a rational scheme of protection. Queen Mary J Intellect Prop 1:272–279. https://doi.org/10.4337/qmjip.2011.03.04

Barron A (2006) Copyright law's musical work. Soc Leg Stud 15:101–127. https://doi.org/10.1177/0964663906060985

Bogsch A (1986) The first hundred years of the Berne convention for the protection of literary and artistic works. WIPO Publi. Int Bureau Intelect Property, Geneva

Butt J (2015) What is a 'musical work'? Reflections on the origin of the 'work concept' in western art music. In: Rahmatioan A (ed) Concepts of music and copyright. Edwar Elagar Publishing, Cheltenham, pp 1–22

Correa CM (2020) Trade related aspects of intellectual property rights: a commentary on the TRIPS agreement (Oxford commentaries on international law), 2nd edn. Oxford University Press, London

Dubin JS (1954) Universal copyright convention. Calif Law Rev 42:89–119. https://doi.org/10.1038/171956c0

Falk R (1996) The new states and the international legal order Recueil des Cours. Hague Acad Int Law Recl des cours II:118

Ficsor M (2003) Guide to the copyright and related rights treaties administered by WIPO and glossary of copyright and related rights terms. WIPO, Geneva

Gervais DJ (2021) The TRIPS agreement: drafting history and analysis, 5th edn. Sweet & Maxwell, London

Goehr L (2003) The imaginary Museum of Musical Works. Oxford University Press, Oxford
Helfer L (2000) World music on a U.S. stage: a Berne/TRIPs and economic analysis of the fairness in music licensing act. Bost Univ Law Rev 80
Li Y (2020) The age of remix and copyright law reform 12:113–155. https://doi.org/10.1080/17579961.2020.1727087
Lipszyc D (1999) Copyright and neighbouring rights. United Nations Educational, Paris
Malevanny N (2019) Online music distribution - how much exclusivity is needed? Springer, Berlin
Margoni T (2016) The harmonisation of EU copyright law: the originality standard. In: Global governance of intellectual property in the 21st century: reflecting policy through change. Springer International Publishing, Cham, pp 85–105
Masouye C, Bogsch A (1981) Guide to the Rome convention and to the phonograms convention. World Intellectual Property Organization, Le Petit-Saconnex
Mcgraw T (2018) Music streaming: where Interactive & non-Interactive Services fit under the Homestyle exemption. Wm Mary Bus Law Rev 10
Morgan O (2002) International protection of performers' rights. Hart Publishing, London
Rajesh Babu R (2017) 'Minor exemptions' doctrine in National Copyright law: guidance from the WTO jurisprudence. In: Manoj KS, Mahalwar V (eds) Copyright law in the digital world. Springer, Singapore, pp 133–150
Ricketson S (1986) Berne convention for the protection of literary and artistic works: 1886–1986. Kluver, London
Ricketson S, Ginsburg J (2015) The Berne convention: historical and institutional aspects. In: Gervais DJ (ed) International intellectual property: a handbook of contemporary research. Edward Elgar Publishing Ltd, Cheltenham, pp 3–36
Ricketson S, Ginsburg JC (2022) International copyright and neighbouring rights : the Berne convention and beyond, vol II, 3rd edn. Oxford University Press, London
Rosati E (2020) When does a communication to the public under EU copyright law need to be to a 'New Public'? SSRN Electron J. https://doi.org/10.2139/ssrn.3640493
Sobrino Heredia JM (2010) Las organizaciones internacionales: generalidades. In: Diez de Velasco M (ed) Las organizaciones internacionales, 16th edn. Tecnos
Stanovic A (2018) Musical works, recordings and their digitisations: new philosophical types. Sven Tidskr Musik Swedish J Music Res 99:125–144
Synodinou, T. (2017) The Renckhoff judgment: The CJEU swivels the faces of the Copyright Rubik's Cube (Part I), *Kluwer Copyright Blog*, https://copyrightblog.kluweriplaw.com/2018/09/27/renckhoff-judgment-cjeu-swivels-faces-copyright-rubiks-cube-part/ (2017).
Van Den Bossche P (2022) The TRIPS agreement and WTO dispute settlement: past, present and future. World Trade Institute, Bern
von Lewinski S (2006) The role and future of the universal copyright convention - UNESCO digital library. UNESCO online Copyr Bull II:1–13
Waelde C (2015) Music performed: what is beyond the scores? In: Rahmatian A (ed) Concepts of music and copyright. Edward Elgar Publishing Ltd, Cheltenham, pp 23–49

Part II The Right of Communication to the Public of Musical Works Online Under EU Copyright Legislation and Case-Law

The right of communication to the public is also granted in the EU legislation as one of the exclusive rights covered by copyright and related rights. Initially, the EU first became aware of the importance of copyright as part of the internal market policy because of the exclusivity entitled to distribution rights, as that right could potentially become an obstacle to the internal market. In their early years, copyright was not a matter of interest for the former European Communities. It was not until the late 1980s that copyright came into the focus of the EU Law. Kur, Dreier and Luginbuehl suggest that it might be because of the language barriers and differences between Member States' cultural traditions that cross-border exploitation of copyright-protected work had not have a considerable economic interest for the internal market.[1] The cross-border exploitation of musical works, until the late 20th century, was done mainly in physical format, which means investing in publishing records, tapes or even CDs. Such kind of exploitation is mainly related to reproduction or distribution rights rather than communication to the public. However, music was also exploited in several Member States at the same time, either by live performance or broadcasting, but only the works of a few internationally known artists—and/or authors—had the privilege of being broadcasted or performed in multiple Member States. Therefore, publishing or distributing foreign musical works had no considerable economic interest, as it could be a risky investment due to the language and cultural differences. Interestingly, classical music has no linguistic or cultural boundaries, thus the first case relating to copyright brought before the European Court of Justice in 1971 was the case *C-78/70, Deutsche Gramophon v. Metro SB*,[2] which tackles the distribution of classical music records between Member States. The case referred to the import of classical music records from France into Germany, which had legally been released there by the rightsholder in France, *Deutsche Gramophon*, who sued the German importer. The issue at stake was whether the

---

[1] Kur et al. (2019), p. 290.

[2] CJEU Judgment of 8 June 1971, *Deutsche Gramophon v. Metro SB, C-78/70, ECLI:EU:C:1971:59.*

rightsholder of a copyrighted work could involve its national copyright law in an EU Member State to prevent copyrighted works legally put into the market in another Member State from freely circulating within the EU.[3] That case was the cornerstone not only for recognising copyright as the status of a form of industrial or commercial property but also for spotting the "competence of the Community to regulate the exercise by individuals of copyright and related rights conferred under the law of the Member States".[4] However, the CJEU in the *Deutsche Gramophon* case reminds us that Article 36 of the EEC treaty[5] allows certain prohibitions or restrictions on trade between Member States justified on the grounds of the public protection of industrial and commercial property. The second part of the Article provides such derogations shall not constitute "a means of arbitrary discrimination or a disguised restriction on trade between Member States". The Court takes into consideration how far the exercise of a national right related to copyright, as an intellectual property right, may impede the marketing of products from another Member State. Thus, the exercise of a right related to copyright may fall within the prohibitions laid down in Article 36 of the Treaty. However, the provision only admits those prohibitions which are justified for the purpose of safeguarding rights that constitute the specific subject matter. Finally, the Court declares that if a right related to copyright "is relied upon to prevent the marketing in a Member State of products distributed by the right holder or with his consent on the territory of another Member State on the sole ground that such distribution did not take place on the national territory, such a prohibition, which would legitimise the isolation of national markets, would be repugnant to the essential purpose of the Treaty, which is to unite national markets into a single market. That purpose could not be attained if, under the various legal systems of the Member States, nationals of those States were able to partition the market and bring about arbitrary discrimination or disguised restrictions on trade between the Member States[6]". A part from the restrictions allowed in Article 36 TFEU, the Services Directive[7] in its Article 16 excludes the application of the directive to copyright and related rights. As Professor Rosati approaches, these kinds of restrictions and exclusions attack the proper balance between the need to respect, on the one hand, national rules and, on the other hand, internal market and undistorted competition goals.[8]

Despite the saying "music is a universal language", it is more accurate to refer to Bernard Shaws' quote", Though music is a universal language, it is spoken with all

[3] Kur et al. (2019), p. 244.

[4] Pila and Torremans (2016), p. 250.

[5] Current Article 36 of the TFEU.

[6] CJEU Judgment of 8 June 1971, para. 9–12.

[7] *Directive 2006/123/EC of the European Parliament and of the Council of 12 December 2006 on services in the internal market.* OJ L 376, 27.12.2006, p. 36–68.

[8] Rosati (2021), pp. 7–8.

sorts of accents".[9] In 1971, despite the arrival of communication technologies, copyright law was still based on the principle of territoriality. The international legislation endorsed Such territoriality principle, as the Berne Convention,[10] among other treaties, recognises the principle of national treatment. Therefore, the principle of territoriality in copyright entails that copyright protection of a work is limited, both in scope and in its effects on the state's territory under the laws of which it has been granted.[11] Consequently, if the copyright holder wants to grant its protection in other member States, it needs to seek protection in those States by obtaining a bunch of copyrights, one for each legislation, instead of just a universal or multi-territorial one. Likewise, if users want to exploit a copyrighted work cross-border, they need a specific licence for each state where the work is to be exploited, and it gets more complex when those exploitation rights for different countries have been transferred to different rights holders or collecting societies. Collecting societies, so-called collective rights management organisations (CMOs), grant national licences for their national repertoire and national licences for the repertoire of other societies through bilateral reciprocal agreements. In the case of authors' rights in musical works, the reciprocal agreements are normally limited to the territory in which the collecting society operates. All this hassle represents a challenge to the EU single market as it directly confronts the EU principle of freedom of movement of goods.[12] Such a principle is one of the four pillars of the single market, which is a fundamental of the EU.

In the late 1980s, the European Commission started working on European copyright legislation after other judgements[13] of the CJEU pursued to offset copyright domestic laws and the European Community's ideal of the internal market, as well as highlighting the lack of harmonisation on copyright matters. From that point, the European Commission started building up the *EU copyright legislation* through drafting proposals in the early 1990s to be adopted by the legislative bodies. The first EU legal instrument that regulated copyright issues was the *Council Directive 91/250/EEC of 14 May 1991 on the legal protection of computer programs. It was no longer in* force as it was replaced in 2009.[14] The directive that first regulates the communication to the public right and is still in force is the *Council Directive 93/83/ EEC of 27 September 1993 on coordinating certain copyright rules and rights related to copyright applicable to satellite broadcasting and cable retransmission.*

[9] Bernard Shaw, Volume 1 of 3, (Music review dated December 10, 1890), Start Page 90, Quote Page 91 and 92, Constable and Company Limited, London.

[10] Berne Convention, Article 5.

[11] Dreier (2017).

[12] Principle of freedom of goods is regulated in Article 34 of the TFEU.

[13] *EMI Electrola GmbH v Patricia Im- und Export and others, C-341/87, ECLI:EU:C:1989:30.*

[14] Replaced by Directive 2009/24/EC of the European Parliament and of the Council of 23 April 2009 on the legal protection of computer programs (Codified version) OJ L 111, 5.5.2009, pp. 16–22.

This is one of the 13 directives and two regulations comprising the current EU Copyright acquis.

This part is divided into two chapters. Firstly, it provides an overview of the copyright framework in the EU, including the principles and objectives of the EU, the delegation of EU competence in the copyright field, and how the EU exercises its competence. Secondly, it introduces the EU copyright acquis and explains how these EU legislative actions are aligned with the principles of subsidiarity and proportionality. This chapter also focuses on the EU rules relevant for the communication to the public right, putting special attention on Directive 2001/29/EC (InfoSoc) and the Directive 2019/790/EU (DSMD).

References

Dreier T (2017) Copyright in the times of the internet-overcoming the principle of territoriality within the EU. In: ERA Forum, vol 18, pp 7–19. https://doi.org/10.1007/s12027-017-0462-7

Kur A, Dreier T, Luginbuehl S (2019) European intellectual property law: text, cases and materials, 2nd edn. Edward Elgar Publishing, Cheltenham

Pila J, Torremans P (2016) European intellectual property law. Oxford University Press

Rosati E (2021) Copyright in the digital single market: article-by-article commentary to the provisions of directive 2019/790. Oxford University Press

Chapter 2
Fundamentals of the EU Copyright Law

2.1 EU Objectives and Principals: Single Market, Culture and Human Rights

The Treaty of the European Union (TEU) declares the EU principles and objectives in Article 3. In particular, the first sentence of Article 3.3. defines the internal market as one of the objectives of the EU by stating that "The Union shall establish an internal market". Furthermore, the last sentence of the same Article expresses the compromise of the EU with the culture when declaring the "(EU) shall respect its rich cultural and linguistic diversity, and shall ensure that Europe's cultural heritage is safeguarded and enhanced". The combination of these two statements can be rendered as the *objective of the EU to ensure the safeguard of cultural instruments and their production and promotion within the internal market, as part not only of the European Cultural heritage but also as part of the sustainable development and economic growth of Europe, ensured by scientific and technological advances.*

Therefore, copyright law has a dual dimension: economic and cultural. As early as 1988, the European Commission presented its *Green Paper on Copyright and the Challenge of Technology*, which recognises the dual dimension of copyright as a double value to be protected at the European level by stating that:

> Community must ensure the proper functioning of the common market. To the maximum extent possible, creators and providers of copyright goods and services should be able to treat the Community as a single internal market. This requires the elimination of obstacles and legal differences that substantially disrupt the functioning of the market. Significant differences in the protection available to particular classes of copyright works can clearly fragment the internal market in those works in an undesirable way"[1] [...] "*Intellectual and artistic creativity is a precious asset, the source of Europe's cultural identity and of that of each individual State.* It is a vital source of economic wealth and European influence

[1] Commission of the European Communities, *Green paper on copyright and the challenge of technology: copyright issues requiring immediate action.* (1988). p. 3, para. 1.3.2.

L. Ballesta Martí, *The Communication to the Public of Musical Works Online in the European Union's Legislation*, Law, Governance and Technology Series 75,
https://doi.org/10.1007/978-3-031-94132-0_2

throughout the world. This creativity needs to be protected; it needs to be given a higher status, and it needs to be stimulated.[2]

Under such a complex objective, copyright law has a leading role; copyright law has to contribute to the EU's single market development and growth, as cultural works are also a product in terms of a modern knowledge-based economy.

The European Commission 2008 pointed out the need to promote the free movement of knowledge and innovation as the "Fifth Freedom" in the single market.[3] Additionally, copyright law aims to safeguard that creators and artists continue enriching European society and find the balance between their works and rights and the public interest of culture. Due to the economic background of the EU, it seems that the economic approach of EU copyright law should be more significant than the cultural one. However, the second sentence in the above quotation reflects the spirit of the EU motto, *United in Diversity*. This cultural diversity, which historically has been seen as a secondary element of copyright law, has gradually become a key part of the harmonisation of the EU copyright law.[4] Hence, culture cannot be an obstacle to the single market achievement and growth. Likewise, trade rules cannot be an impediment to cultural development and enjoyment. Trade and culture, as regulated in the same Article 3.3 of the TEU, have to be harmonious rather than incompatible. Following the idea of Professor Rachel Craufurd-Smith,[5] EU economic integration can lead to a more diverse society. The role and value of culture in a society is essential.

Apart from the statute of culture as one of the objectives of the EU, in Article 3 TEU, the Charter of Fundamental Rights of the European Union (CFREU) also provides references to culture, respect for cultural diversity in its Article 22, and protecting the freedom of the arts in Article 13. However, the EU Charter does not safeguard the right to participate in cultural life, except for the brief inclusion of such right as part of the respect of human rights of the elderly in Article 25. Professor Céline Romainville[6] concludes that the CFREU codifies "the protection of cultural interests but develops a very restrictive approach to the right to participate in cultural life". Such the right to participate in cultural life is enshrined in Article 27 of the Universal Declaration of Human Rights (UDHR),[7] which states as follows:

1. Everyone has the right freely to participate in the cultural life of the community, to enjoy the arts and to share in scientific advancement and its benefits.
2. Everyone has the right to the protection of the moral and material interests resulting from any scientific, literary or artistic production of Which He is the author.

---

[2] *Ibid.* p. 6. para. 1.4.4.

[3] European Commission, *Green Paper - Copyright in the Knowledge Economy* (2008), COM(2008) 466 final.

[4] Synodinou (2021), p. 39.

[5] Craufurd-Smith (2004), p. 414, p. 3.

[6] Romainville (2015), p. 159.

[7] United Nations (1948) Universal Declaration of Human Rights | United Nations.

A similar provision is Article 15 (1) (c) of the U.N. Covenant on Economic, Social and Cultural Rights[8] adopted on December 16, 1966, which mentions intellectual property. Still, there is no provision like in the European Convention on Human Rights in 1950. The second paragraph of Article 27 UDHR recognises the "right to the protection" of authors' interests, which is the basic function of copyright. However, we cannot state copyright as a human right despite the abovementioned provisions in the international human rights instruments. Torremans, in his Article,[9] demonstrates that such provisions do not define the substance of copyright in any detail and assesses that copyright and human rights certainly interact. Dessemontet suggests that copyright might enjoy protection as a right of property. Although such a solution seems not to provide further progress for copyright (of authors), it may assist in the protection of those related rights that are premised on financial investment, such as the rights of broadcasting organisations, publishers, and record labels.[10] Accordingly, copyright as part of the right of property is then recognised in Article 17 of the CFEU, particularly in Article 17(2), which clearly states: "Intellectual property shall be protected."

Although the theory that there are not enough arguments for considering copyright as a human right is widely extended, there is no doubt that copyright has a direct impact on human rights, and in reverse. This influence and the interrelation among those rights have to be taken into account by the EU institutions when developing EU copyright law,[11] since human rights are recognised as one of the EU values in Article 2 TEU and as a legal principle governing EU Law in Article 6 TEU.

2.2 EU Competence on Copyright; Principle of Conferral and Copyright Legal Bases

The EU, to accomplish its objectives, is meant to use "the appropriate means commensurate with the competencies which are conferred upon it in the Treaties", as provided in Article 3.6. TEU. From this provision, two EU principles are deemed: the principle of conferral and the principle of proportionality; both principles are referred to in Article 5 TEU. Accordingly, to achieve its objectives, the EU can only act "within the limits of the competencies conferred" by the Member States in the Treaties under the principle of conferral. That is to say that there is a requirement for the EU to fit the matters of its action within any of the competencies conferred in the Treaties. Otherwise, that action cannot be taken, as the corresponding competencies

[8]United Nations (1966) International Covenant on Economic, Social and Cultural Rights.

[9]Torremans (2007), p. 278.

[10]Dessemontet (1998), p. 6.

[11]For an analysis in depth on copyright and Human Rights, see Mahalwar (2017), pp. 151–174, Geiger and Izyumenko (2014), pp. 316–342.

remain with the Member States. When the EU takes an action, such action cannot exceed what is necessary to achieve the objectives of the Treaties, according to the principle of proportionality.

The current Treaties do not contain any direct reference to EU competence in the field of copyright. Considering the dual nature of copyright law, as mentioned above, and following the principle of conferral, it could be argued that the competence of the EU to act in the field of copyright entails more than one power. Hence, the EU, the legal basis for setting up copyright rules, could refer to culture (Article 167 TFEU) and internal market (Article 114 TFEU). However, two interconnected issues arise at this point: on the one hand, the incompatibility between the two competencies, and on the other hand, the possibility of setting more than one legal basis for a single legislative act.

Referring to the first issue, the internal market is a shared competence, while competence on culture is a supporting one,[12] where the EU has limited powers. The European Union had no specific competence in cultural policies until 1992. Hence, the EU's action in cultural matters before that time was only if there was a strong connection with economic interests. Article 167 TFEU confers the EU certain powers in cultural matters, diversity, and the protection of cultural heritage, and paragraph (4) introduces the principle of the integration of cultural considerations in all aspects of EU interventions. However, the EU's competence is limited only to support, coordinate or supplement the actions of the Member States. On the other side, EU competence in the internal market was key to developing the European Communities, present in the Treaties from the beginning. Article 114 TFEU is the general legal basis concerning measures for the harmonisation of Member States' legislation in the internal market. The EU's competence relating to the establishment and functioning of the internal market is a shared competence between the EU and its Member States,[13] which allows both the EU and the Member States to legislate and adopt legally binding acts in an area of shared competence.[14] The internal-market-based competencies are rather flexible compared to culture-based ones, as the EU cannot harmonise national laws in the field of culture. Consequently, the legal basis of Article 114 TFEU[15] has been the main foundation for developing the EU copyright legislation, as the competence of the EU to act in the field of copyright has so far been based on the need to build an internal market, as it has stronger competencies there.[16]

The second issue, regarding the possibility of choosing more than one legal basis for an act, has been solved by the settled case law of the CJEU. The Court of Justice

[12] Article 6 (c) TFEU.

[13] TFEU Article 4(2)(a).

[14] Art. 2 TFEU. The delimitation and exercise of shared competence is further explained in Protocol No. 25 to the Treaties on the exercise of shared competence and in Declaration 18 in relation to the delimitation of competences, annexed to the Treaties.

[15] Formerly Article 95 TCE, and previously Article 66 TCEE.

[16] Ramalho (2014).

Table 2.1 Directives on the Copyright adopted with similar combinations of legal bases

Directives in the Copyright field	Combined legal bases[a]
Directive 93/83/EEC	Article 57(2) and 66 TEEC
Directive 96/9/EC	Article 57(2), 66 and 100a TEC
Directive 2001/29/EC	Article 47(2), 55 and 95 TEC
Directive 2006/115/EC	Article 47(2), 55 and 95 TEC
Directive 2006/116/EC	Article 47(2), 55 and 95 TEC
Directive 2012/28/EU	Article 53(1), 62 and 114 TFEU
Directive 2014/26/EU	Article 50(1), 53(1) and 62 TFEU
Directive 2019/789/EU	Article 53(1), 62 and 114 TFEU
Directive 2019/790/EU	Article 53(1), 62 and 114 TFEU

Source: European Parliament, Opinion of the Legal Service, SJ-0011/19

[a] Article 114 TFEU was formerly Article 95 TEC, and previously corresponded to Article 66 TEEC

settled that "the choice of the legal basis for a Community measure must rest on objective factors amenable to judicial review, which include in particular the aim and content of the measure".[17] Consequently, choosing an incorrect legal basis may lead to the annulment of the act in question.[18] But when it comes to multiple bases that might be applicable, it has to be determined which is the main purpose, and if there is more than one, then determine whether the different legal bases are compatible regarding competence scope and legislative procedures to be applied. In other words, if examination of a measure reveals that it pursues a twofold or multifold purpose which one can be identified as the main or predominant one, whereas the other or others are merely accessorial or incidental, then that act must be based only on the legal basis corresponding to the main or predominant purpose or component.[19] The CJEU admitted more than one legal basis exceptionally when it is established that the act simultaneously pursues several indissociably linked objectives, none being main, secondary or indirect in relation to the other. In such a situation, the act has to be founded on the different corresponding legal bases, provided that they are procedurally compatible.[20]

Accordingly, the legal basis must be determined concerning its own aim and content and not the legal basis used for the adoption of other EU measures that might display similar characteristics in certain cases. Even though Table 2.1 shows that

[17] CJEU Judgment of 26 March 1987, Case C-45/86, Commission v. Council (Generalised Tariff Preferences), ECLI:EU:C:1987:163, para. 5.

[18] Committee on Legal Affairs (2018) Opinion on the legal basis of on the proposal for a directive on copyright in digital single market. Brussels.

[19] CJEU Judgment of 26 March 1987, para. 5.

[20] CJEU Judgment of 11 June 1991, C-300/89, Commission v Council ('Titanium dioxide') ECLI: EU:C:1991:244, para. 17–25.

most of the directives in the copyright field have been adopted on a similar combination of legal bases,[21] as it is examined hereunder.

As previously assessed, developing the EU copyright law has been linked to economic reasons directly connected with the proper functioning of the single market. The legal basis of Article 114 TFEU has been used since the beginning by the EU legislators on the premise of harmonising the different national legislations on copyright as they may constitute an obstacle to the internal market. Member States' different domestic legislations may bring about some rules that prohibit or disguised restrictions on trade between Member States. Based on the principle of territoriality of copyright law, such rules are contrary to the proper development of the internal market. As the CJEU stated, that kind of rule would "legitimise the isolation of national markets, would be repugnant to the essential purpose of the Treaty, which is to unite national markets into a single market. [...] Consequently, it would conflict with the provisions prescribing the free movement of products within the common market [...]".[22] Therefore, Article 114 TFEU is an adequate legal basis if the purpose of the EU is to adopt the measures for the approximation of copyright legislation with the object of the establishment and functioning of the internal market. An explanation of the wide use of Article 114 TFEU in EU copyright law is given by Professor Ana Ramalho when assessing that Article 114 TFEU is a "rather flexible norm, as the substantive choices regarding the content of the legislation are largely left to the EU's discretion".[23] It is because Article 114 TFEU is a functional competence, which means that it is not limited to a particular policy area and allows the EU to legislate in many different policy areas as long as the main objective of the measure is the establishment and functioning of the internal market.

Most copyright directives regulate other elements that can be considered as main objectives, different from the internal market development. Thus, those EU measures need to be supported on the legal basis Article corresponding to its ratione materiae. Therefore, most copyright directives aim to protect the interests of creators and the industry's commercial activity. Most copyrighted works, primarily music, are introduced into the market by companies allowing the exploitation of works. Such activity has to be understood as a "service" within the meaning of Article 57 (b) TFEU, namely an activity of a commercial character which is usually provided for remuneration.[24] As shown in Table 2.1, other legal bases, jointly with Article 114 TFEU, that have been largely used for developing the copyright legislation in the EU are Article 53(1) and 62 TFEU. The CJEU declared that the combination of

[21] Committee on Legal Affairs, Opinion on the legal basis of the proposal for a directive of the European Parliament and of the Council laying down rules on the exercise of copyright and related rights applicable to certain online transmissions of broadcasting organisations and retrans (2019).

[22] CJEU Judgment of 8 June 1971, para. 12–13.

[23] Ramalho (2017), p. 6.

[24] Committee on Legal Affairs, Opinion on the legal basis of on the proposal for a directive on copyright in digital single market.

Article 53(1) TFEU and Article 62 TFEU constitutes the specific legal basis which empowers the Union to adopt directives to ensure the freedom to provide services guaranteed under the Treaties through approximation of the applicable national laws.[25]

Article 53 TFEU is placed under the "Right of Establishment" heading in the TFEU and provides for the adoption of directives to coordinate the provisions laid down by law, regulation, or administrative action in the Member States. Furthermore, Article 62 TFEU under the "Services" heading provides that Article 53 shall apply to the matters covered by that chapter. Article 62 TFEU permits the application of rules stated in Article 53(1) to services, allowing the EU to adopt directives to harmonise or coordinate the different Member States legislations regarding services. However, those Articles refer to the free movement of persons and the free movement of services, which are part of the broader notion of "internal market", and as Ramalho argues, "[Article] 114 absorbs them within its scope".[26] However, the combination of these three Articles has been used as the valid legal basis for developing most and the latest directives on the field of copyright.

There is another potential legal basis for developing the EU copyright legislation, which is Article 118 TFEU. The provision empowers the EU to establish "measures for the creation of European intellectual property rights to provide uniform protection of intellectual property rights"[27] within the EU. Such provision has provided uniform regimes and unitary titles in intellectual property fields like the European Union trademark or the Community design.[28] Accordingly, this legal basis could be an appropriate legal basis to create a European copyright title. This option was considered by the Commission in 2011 when, in its Communication[29] on intellectual property matters, the Commission specified that it "will examine the feasibility of creating an optional "unitary" copyright title on the basis of Article 118 TFEU and its potential impact for the single market, right holders and consumers". The implication of carrying out such a possibility entails copyright unified rules and titles within the EU, that would involve challenging the principle of territoriality that governs copyright law. However, Article 118 TFEU also relies on the internal market as the condition introduces the first sentence of the provision: "[I]n the context of the establishment and functioning of the internal market". Therefore, there must be a link to internal market goals.[30]

---

[25] See CJEU Judgement of 30 May 1989, C-242/87, Commission v Council, ECLI: EU:C:1989: 217.

[26] Ramalho (2017), p. 6.

[27] Article 118 TFEU.

[28] See: *Council Regulation (EC) No 207/2009 of 26 February 2009 on the Community trade mark, OJ L 78, 24.3.2009, p. 1–42.*; and *Council Regulation (EC) No 6/2002 of 12 December 2001 on Community design, OJ L 3, 5.1.2002, p. 1–24.*

[29] European Commission (2011) A Single Market for Intellectual Property Rights Boosting creativity and innovation to provide economic growth, high quality jobs and first class products and services in Europe, COM(2011) 287 final. Commun. COM(2011) 287 Final.

[30] Ramalho (2021), p. 35.

Both legal bases 114 and 118 TFEU refer to the internal market. Also, both require the approval of measures by the ordinary legislative procedure. Even though the implementation of EU copyright rules either by the use of one or the other legal basis entitles significantly different results. Whereas Article 118 TFUE is driven to a unification of rules, Article 114 refers to adopting "measures for the approximation of the provisions". However, the Article does not reveal the level of such approximation. EU can exercise its harmonising competencies at different levels, either by maximum harmonisation or minimum harmonisation techniques.[31] The rate of harmonisation depends on the grade of regulatory leeway left to national legislators when implementing the EU measure. The more room to legislate for Member States, the lower the level of harmonisation achieved within the EU.

When regulating cultural aspects of copyright, EU measures cannot go beyond the mere support of the Member States' action. Otherwise, further measures, like harmonisation, could represent an extra limitation of the EU supporting competence and thus not being compliant with the principle of conferral. Referring to property regimes, the action of the EU cannot interfere in the property regimes which are reserved for national legislations. Article 345 TFEU states that Treaties "shall in no way prejudice the rules in the Member States governing the system of property ownership". Accordingly, copyright in nature is a property right, so national legislations could also claim on that provision reject the EU action if it somehow prejudices the ownership nations' regimes, calling upon the principle of conferral and retaining copyright legislation under their competence. However, as Synodinou highlights, "the application of domestic rules on property ownership that interfere in the internal market has been permitted only if has been deemed necessary for the purpose of the 'specific subject matter' of copyright",[32] a concept that the CJEU has applied to every form of exploration of copyright. In conclusion, the EU is competent to take legislative actions on copyright under the legal basis of Article 114 TFEU, which aims for the harmonisation of legislation in the context of the internal market, as far as those measures do not challenge the principle of conferral since they respect the property and cultural aspects of copyright.

2.3 The Exercise of the EU Competence on Copyright

As previously stated, although there is no specific EU competence on copyright in the Treaties, the EU is competent to adopt measures on copyright matters, and so is the EU. In exercising its competencies, the EU is compelled to respect not only the limits set by the principle of conferral but also the EU action has to be subsidiary, in the sense that no more effective rules can be taken at a lower level. The measures taken by the EU must be proportional to its objectives. By exercising its

[31] Ramalho (2014), pp. 4–6.

[32] Synodinou (2021), p. 4.

competencies, the EU has generated a set of rules known as the EU Copyright Acquis. In the following paragraphs, an overview of the EU copyright acquis is presented, followed by an assessment of the fulfilment of the principles of subsidiarity and proportionality in EU legislative action in the field of copyright.

2.3.1 The EU Copyright Acquis

Since the Council adopted the first Directive regulating copyright matters in 1991, the EU has built up the EU copyright acquis in different stages. Following inspiration from Professor Hugenholtz's[33] approach, the EU development of copyright law harmonisation can be divided into three phases: an initial the 'productive decade' of harmonisation by the first seven directives (1991–2001); a second, 'consolidation and codification decade' (2002–2012); and the last decade of the 'digital copyright reform' (2012–2022).

At the time of the writing of this book, the EU copyright acquis was formed by a bunch of 13 directives and two regulations. The Table 2.2 shows the current acts that are part of the copyright acquis. All these legislative acts regulate matters related to copyright but dealing with different subjects or specific aspects of copyright. As a result of the rise of technology in the 1990s and the increasing number of home personal computers, the EU's first copyright directive was adopted for the protection of computer programs in 1991. This directive was substituted by the *Software* Directive in 2009. In 1992, the Council adopted a Directive[34] harmonising the commercial rental and lending rights and other rights related to copyright in the field of intellectual property. The directive also created a horizontal harmonised framework protecting related rights of performers, phonogram and film producers, and broadcasting organisations at levels beyond the Rome Convention's minimal standards.[35] This directive was substituted in 2006 by a codified version of the current Rental and Lending Directive.[36] Likewise, Council Directive 93/98/EEC, harmonising the term of protection of copyright and certain related rights, was also substituted in 2006 by the codified version in the new 'Term Directive' 2006/116/EC.[37] Term Directives were amended in 2011 by the 'Term Extension Directive',

[33] Hugenholtz (2009), p. 61.

[34] *Council Directive 92/100/EEC of 19 November 1992 on rental right and lending right and on certain rights related to copyright in the field of intellectual property, OJ L 346, 27.11.1992, p. 61–66.*

[35] Hugenholtz (2009), p. 62.

[36] *Directive 2006/115/EC of the European Parliament and of the Council of 12 December 2006 on rental right and lending right and on certain rights related to copyright in the field of intellectual property (codified version), OJ L 376, 27.12.2006, p. 28–35.*

[37] Directive 2006/116/EC of the European Parliament and of the Council of 12 December 2006 on the term of protection of copyright and certain related rights (codified version), OJ L 372, 27.12.2006, p. 12–18.

Table 2.2 The copyright Acquis

Title	Directive short name	Date
Directive 93/83/EEC on the coordination of certain rules concerning copyright and rights related to copyright applicable to satellite broadcasting and cable retransmission	Satellite and Cable / SatCab Directive	9/27/1993
Directive 96/9/EC on the legal protection of databases	Database Directive	3/11/1996
Directive 2001/29/EC on the harmonisation of certain aspects of copyright and related rights in the information society	InfoSoc Directive	5/22/2001
Directive 2001/84/EC on the resale right for the benefit of the author of an original work of art	Resale Directive	9/27/2001
Directive 2004/48/EC on the enforcement of intellectual property right	Enforcement Directive	4/24/2004
Directive 2006/115/EC on rental right and lending right and on certain rights related to copyright in the field of intellectual property	Rental and Lending Directive	12/12/2006
Directive 2006/116/EC on the term of protection of copyright and certain related rights. (Amended in 2011)	'Term Directive'	12/12/2006
Directive 2009/24/EC on the legal protection of computer programs (codified version substituting Directive 91/250/ EEC)	Software Directive	4/23/2009
Directive 2012/28/EU on certain permitted uses of orphan works	Orphan Works Directive	10/25/2012
Directive 2014/26/EU on collective management of copyright and related rights and multi-territorial licensing of rights in musical works for online use in the internal market	'CRM Directive	2/26/2014
Regulation (EU) 2017/1128 on cross-border portability of online content services in the internal market '	Portability Regulation	6/14/2017
Directive (EU) 2017/1564 on certain permitted uses of certain works and other subject matter protected by copyright and related rights for the benefit of persons who are blind, visually impaired or otherwise print-disabled	Marrakech Treaty Directive	9/13/2017
Regulation (EU) 2017/1563 on the cross-border exchange between the Union and third countries of accessible format copies of certain works and other subject matter protected by copyright and related rights for the benefit of persons who are blind, visually impaired or otherwise print-disabled	Marrakech Treaty Regulation	9/13/2017
Directive 2019/790/EU on copyright and related rights in the Digital Single Market	CDSM Directive	4/17/2019
Directive 2019/789/EU on the exercise of copyright and related rights applicable to certain online transmissions of broadcasting organisations and retransmissions of television and radio programmes	Satellite and Cable II / NetCab	4/17/2019

Source: Author's own elaboration. Information sources: European Commission's website and Eur-lex portal

which extended the terms of protection from 50 to 70 years for phonogram producers and performing artists regarding musical sound recordings.

In 1993, another directive was adopted to achieve an internal market for cross-border satellite services, or in other words, cross-border broadcasting services. It was the EU in Directive 93/83/EEC,[38] namely the SatCab Directive, that aimed to grant performers and phonogram producers fair remuneration for the communication to the public of their performances or phonograms via satellite to align the protection with the provisions contained in the first Rental and Lending Directive of 1992.[39]

The Database Directive, approved in 1996, granted the protection of databases by copyright, establishing the *sui generis* right of 'database right', which covers the contents of a database and the investment made for its creation. After more than 5 years of negotiations, the European Parliament and the Council approved the Resale Directive 2001/84/EC[40] which grants the resale right or *droit de suite*[41] of visual artists.

In 2001, the EU adopted the first directive dealing with general matters of copyright, the Copyright Directive,[42] namely the InfoSoc Directive. The InfoSoc Directive became the fundamental instrument governing copyright protection in the EU. It was established to harmonise copyright laws inside the internal market and adapt copyright legislation to technical advancements, particularly to the advent of the digital world. The Directive also aimed to fulfil the commitment to implement the requirements under the WCT and WPPT, signed by the EU in 1996,[43] by means of harmonisation of MS legislations.

During the consolidation and codification decade' (2002–2012), a part of the reforms and codified versions of the early copyright directives mentioned in the previous paragraphs, the EU adopted two directions. First, in 2004, the Directive on the Enforcement of Intellectual Property Rights provided harmonised remedies against copyright infringements. Despite being applicable, the directive is applied without prejudice to the specific enforcement provisions and exceptions in other specific copyright rules, particularly the Directive 2001/29/EC. Eight years later, the

[38] Directive 93/83/EEC of 27 September 1993 on the coordination of certain rules concerning copyright and rights related to copyright applicable to satellite broadcasting and cable retransmission, OJ L 248, 6.10.1993, p. 15–21. Council of the European Communities.

[39] *Council Directive 92/100/EEC*, Recital 25.

[40] *Directive 2001/84/EC of the European Parliament and of the Council of 27 September 2001 on the resale right for the benefit of the author of an original work of art Select. OJ L 272, 13.10.2001, p. 32–36.*

[41] The Resale right or *Droit de suite* allows the author of graphic and plastic works of art to be compensated for further transfers of the work.

[42] Directive (EU) 2019/790 of the European Parliament and of the Council of 17 April 2019 on copyright and related rights in the Digital Single Market and amending Directives 96/9/EC and 2001/29/EC, OJ L 130, 17.5.2019, p. 92–125.

[43] Both Treaties were signed by the Commission on behalf of the EU, in 1996 but not were not ratified until 2009, and entered into force in 2010.

'Orphan Works Directive'[44] was adopted. This directive aims to promote the digitisation of and lawful online access within the EU, to collections of libraries, archives and other organisations with a public interest mission of preservation that contain works that are still protected by copyright but whose authors or other rightsholders are unknown or cannot be contacted to obtain copyright permissions.

The last and current stage of the EU copyright harmonisation is marked by the expansion of the digital era and the idea of realising a Digital Single Market. The objective of achieving a Digital Single Market was included in the 2015 European Commission working program.[45] The current Commission (2019–2024) is engaged with the strategy for *Shaping Europe's digital future*, which sets the goals for the *Digital Decade* up to 2030.[46] The Directive on Collective Management of Copyright and related rights and multi-territorial licensing of rights in musical works for online use in the internal market ("CRM Directive") was adopted in February 2014. Although its adoption was already during the 'digital copyright reform' period, the topic of harmonising the rules of governance of collective rights management organisations had been a concern for the European Commission since 2004, when it published a communication on that subject matter.[47] Following, in 2005, the Commission adopted a Recommendation on collective cross-border management of copyright and related rights for legitimate online music services.[48] In that recommendation, the commission advocates for promoting a regulatory environment effectively suited to a Community level "management of copyright and related rights for the provision of legitimate online music services".[49] The proposal for such a regulatory environment did not arrive until 2012 and became the adopted CRM Directive in 2014. It was not until 2017 that the EU adopted a regulation dealing with copyright matters, the 'Online Content Portability Regulation'[50] It aims to ensure subscribers to an online content service in their own EU country can access it while temporarily staying in other EU countries.

---

[44]Directive 2012/28/EU of the European Parliament and of the Council of 25 October 2012 on certain permitted uses of orphan works, OJ L 299, 27.10.2012, p. 5–12.

[45]European Commission, Communication from the Commission to the European Parliament, the Council, the European Economic and Social Committee and the Committee of the Regions - A Digital Single Market Strategy for Europe, COM(2015) 100 final, 6 May 2015.

[46]See European Commission's Digital Strategy website https://digital-strategy.ec.europa.eu/en

[47]European Commission Communication from the Commission to the Council, the European Parliament and the European Economic and Social - Committee The Management of Copyright and Related Rights in the Internal Market, 16 April 2004, COM/2004/0261 final.

[48]European Commission, Recommendation 2005/737/EC of 18 May on collective cross-border management of copyright and related rights for legitimate online music services, OJ L 276, 21.10.2005, p. 54–57.

[49]*Ibid*, para. 1(a).

[50]Regulation (EU) 2017/1128 of the European Parliament and of the Council of 14 June 2017 on cross-border portability of online content services in the internal market, OJ L 168, 30.6.2017, p. 1–11.

On 30 September 2017, the EU adopted two instruments: the 'Marrakesh Directive'[51] and the 'Marrakesh Regulation'.[52] Both instruments implement the requirements derived from the signature on behalf of the EU of the 'Marrakesh Treaty'.[53] The EU fulfilled such the requirements of such compromise by establishing a mandatory and harmonised exception to copyright and related rights for the making and dissemination of copies, in accessible formats, of certain works and for the cross-border exchange of those copies for the benefit of persons who are blind, visually impaired or otherwise print-disabled. The Directive establishes a mandatory exception to copyright and related rights, and the Regulation provides for a copyright exception that permits the cross-border exchange of copies made under the exception between the EU and third countries that are parties to the Treaty.

The biggest project of the copyright reform since the Digital Single Market strategy was proposed by the Commission on 14 September 2016. The European Commission published two documents: the Proposal for a Directive of the European Parliament and of the Council on copyright in the Digital Single Market[54] and the Proposal for a Regulation of the European Parliament and of the Council laying down rules on the exercise of copyright and related rights applicable to certain online transmissions of broadcasting organisations and retransmissions of television and radio programmes.[55] After nearly 3 years of tough negotiations, polemic discussions, and a bunch of amendments, the Council and the European Parliament adopted the two proposals that introduce and update rules on copyright and related rights in the Digital Single Market. The adopted text is the NetCab Directive

[51] Directive (EU) 2017/1564 of the European Parliament and of the Council of 13 September 2017 on certain permitted uses of certain works and other subject matter protected by copyright and related rights for the benefit of persons who are blind, visually impaired or otherwise print-disabled and amending Directive 2001/29/EC on the harmonisation of certain aspects of copyright and related rights in the information society. OJ L 242, 20.9.2017, p. 6–13.

[52] Regulation (EU) 2017/1563 of the European Parliament and of the Council of 13 September 2017 on the cross-border exchange between the Union and third countries of accessible format copies of certain works and other subject matter protected by copyright and related rights for the benefit of persons who are blind, visually impaired or otherwise print-disabled (...) OJ L 242, 20.9.2017, p. 1–5.

[53] WIPO (2013) Marrakesh Treaty to Facilitate Access to Published Works for Persons Who Are Blind, Visually Impaired or Otherwise Print Disabled. Signed on behalf of the EU on 30 April 2014.

[54] European Commission (2016) Proposal for a Directive of the European Parliament and of the Council on copyright in the Digital Single Market. COM/2016/0593 final - 2016/0280 (COD).

[55] European Commission, Proposal for a Regulation of the European Parliament and of the Council Laying down Rules on the Exercise of Copyright and Related Rights Applicable to Certain Online Transmissions of Broadcasting Organisations and Retransmissions of Television and Radio, COM/2016/0594 final - 2016/0284 (COD).

(or Satellite and Cable II) Directive 2019/789,[56] whose initial text was proposed to become a Regulation, and the Directive 2019/790,[57] namely the DSM Directive.

The NetCab Directive amends and completes the SatCab 1993 Directive, which is still in force, by updating rules applicable to simultaneous retransmission services to the new technologies used. This directive, which was supposed to be a Regulation, as it was the Commission proposal, aims to improve the cross-border availability of television and radio programmes in the EU's single market and facilitates the management of copyright and related rights for online services of broadcasters and the retransmission of television and radio programmes by means other than cable, namely Internet.

As happened with the SatCab Directive, the quickly developed digital society required updated rules in other to regulate the new business models and new users or consumption habits, like content streaming services, content sharing service providers, social media or other platforms. The CDSM Directive was intended to fill the legislation gap as a core of copyright reform. The Directive has three main purposes: (i) to adapt the exceptions regime to copyright to the digital and the cross-border environment; (ii) to improve licensing practices and ensure access to content; (iii) to achieve a well-functioning marketplace for copyright. The DSM Directive amends and completes the InfoSoc Directive, as well as the enforcement (Directive 2004/48/EC), orphan works (Directive 2012/28/EU) and CRM (Directive 2014/26/EU) directives.

2.3.2 Principles of Subsidiarity and Proportionality in the EU Copyright Legislation

So far, when the EU has legislated on copyright matters, it has used its competence in harmonising legislation to properly establish and function the internal market. Since internal market policy refers to a shared competence, EU actions must comply with the subsidiarity and proportionality principles. Article 5 TEU sets the principles of subsidiarity and proportionality, which frame the exercise of competence by the EU. Thus, when EU Institutions exercise their shared competencies, they have to meet the requirements in Article 5 TFUE and follow the indications laid down in Protocol (no. 2) on applying the principles of subsidiarity and proportionality.

The principle of subsidiarity requires that regarding EU competence other than exclusive, the EU can act only if the objectives of the proposed measure are better

[56] Directive (EU) 2019/789 of the European Parliament and of the Council of 17 April 2019 laying down rules on the exercise of copyright and related rights applicable to certain online transmissions of broadcasting organisations and retransmissions of television and radio programmes, and amending Council Directive 93/83/EEC, OJ L 130, 17.5.2019, p. 82–91.

[57] (2019) Directive (EU) 2019/790 of the European Parliament and of the Council of 17 April 2019 on copyright and related rights in the Digital Single Market and amending Directives 96/9/EC and 2001/29/EC, OJ L 130, 17.5.2019, p. 92–125. European Parliament and Council of the EU.

achieved at the Union level rather than by the Member States. That is, goals cannot be sufficiently achieved at a lower level than at the EU level. As it has been mentioned earlier, the existence of 27 different national copyright legislations has become an issue of internal market fragmentation since the 1980s'. It seems evident that the EU is in a better position to successfully remove the obstacles to the internal market than individual Member States. Thus, the EU is in the best position to achieve the harmonisation of copyright rules. However, due to the territoriality principle in copyright law, certain aspects of copyright, like culture or property ownership systems, remain closely related to national legislation. Since the treaties introduced the requirement of compliance with the subsidiarity principle, the EU has generally used the same formula to justify the EU legislation by referring to the harmonisation of rules for internal market cohesion; *"Since the objective of this Directive, [namely…], cannot be sufficiently achieved by the Member States and can therefore, because of its scale and effects, be better achieved at Union level, the Union may adopt measures in accordance with the principle of subsidiarity as set out in Article 5 of the Treaty on European Union"*. This formula is present in 9 of the 15 legal instruments of the current copyright acquis.[58] While there was no requirement for a subsidiarity statement in the earliest ones,[59] the other used indirect formulas,[60] justifying the no intervention of the EU by exposing the leeway given to the MS in certain aspects and consequently reaffirming the idea of territoriality of copyright laws. This is the case of Directive 2001/29/EC (InfoSoc), which in its recital (34) clarifies that Member States keep the option of providing for certain exceptions or limitations; therefore, it justifies the subsidiarity by reserving MS the leeway to determine the system of voluntary exemptions and limitations, stated in Article 5(2) and (3).[61] Indeed, the "harmonisation of the internal market" clause and the other formulas used so far have been generally accepted by national parliaments when exercising control on the subsidiarity principle compliance of the EU legislative proposals.

However, some negative outcomes from national parliaments on subsidiarity tests occurred. One example is the Dutch parliament's outcome on the proposal for the Enforcement Directive, where the Dutch chamber proposed that Member States should give criminal prosecution of piracy of intellectual property priority and suggests that the EU should impose minimum sanctions instead.[62]

---

[58] Directive 2004/48 in recital (31), Directive 2011/77 recital (21), Directive 2012/28/EU in recital (25), Directive (EU) 2017/1564 in recital (23), Regulation (EU) 2017/1563 in recital (12), Regulation (EU) 2017/1128 in recital (36), Directive 2014/26/EU in recital (55), Directive 2019/789/EU in recital (26) and Directive 2019/790/EU in recital (83).

[59] Directive 93/83/EEC, Directive 96/9/EC and Directive 2009/24/EC as a codified version of the Council Directive 91/250/EEC.

[60] See Directive 2001/29/EC recital (34), Directive 2001/84/EC recitals (16)(22) and (27) and Directive 2006/115/EC recital (15).

[61] This Article is the one in Directive 2001/29/EC that has resulted in most cases of an interpretation request to the CJUE through preliminary rulings.

[62] Hugenholtz et al. (2009), p. 29.

A more recent example is the negative outcome of the Polish Parliament (Sejm) in 2012, referring to the proposal of the Directive 2014/26/EU on collective management of copyright and related rights and multi-territorial licensing of rights in musical works for online use in the internal market. The Polish Parliament almost unanimously declared that the proposal was incompatible with the principle of subsidiarity. The Polish resolution only stated that the Commission had not proven why the proposed directives objectives could be more efficiently achieved on the EU level. The resolution argues in particular that ensuring transparency of collective societies can be achieved by EU Member States, and regarding multi-territorial licensing, the resolution only states that the Commission has not proven why European actions will be more efficient.[63] The final text of the Directive 2014/26/EU justifies the efficiency of the EU action in recital (5) when remarking that the remaining substantial disparities in national rules governing the operation of collective management organisations, especially in terms of transparency and accountability to rightsholders, led to inefficiencies in the cross-border exploitation of copyright and related rights within the internal market.[64]

No further relevant feature in copyright literature regarding the subsidiarity principle can be found, as it has not become an issue. As said, the plea to harmonise legislation for the internal market has been largely recognised as a fair motivation for the EU's actions on copyright law.

According to Article 5 TFEU, the principle of proportionality entails that when the EU measures take action, they have to be limited to what is necessary to achieve the objectives of the Treaties. Article 5 TFEU language refers to EU actions, which includes all EU actions when legislating, interpreting, and applying. The following lines focus on proportionality in the EU legislative action in the copyright field. Protocol (no. 2) requires the Commission to make wide consultations, taking into account the regional and local dimensions of the action, before drafting a legislative proposal. Once the legislative proposal becomes a draft, such a document must include a detailed statement considering the proportionality compliance by making an assessment of the proposal's financial impact and implications for the rules to be put in place by Member States, in the case of directives. Furthermore, EU Institutions must take account of minimising any burden that may be on the EU, Member States at any level, economic operators, and citizens. If a burden may arise, it must be balanced to be achieved by the EU, and then the Institutions must act commensurately.

It was not until 2009, when the Lisbon Treaty entered into force that the language in Protocol (n.2) added an explicit reference to the obligation that any legislative proposal has to contain a detailed statement considering the compliance with the

[63] Targosz T (2012) Polish Parliament: proposed directive on collective rights management does not comply with principle of subsidiarity - Kluwer Copyright Blog. In: Kluwer Copyr. Blog. http://copyrightblog.kluweriplaw.com/2012/10/16/the-polish-parliament-thinks-the-proposed-directive-on-collective-rights-management-does-not-comply-with-the-principle-of-subsidiarity/

[64] Directive 2014/26/EU, recital (5).

principles of subsidiarity and proportionality and an assessment of the proposal's impact. Hence, since 2009, the Commission must carry out Impact assessments for each legislative proposal to be adopted. Indeed, impact assessments become a significant part of the Commission's task under the 'Better Regulation' agenda since 2015. The 'Better Regulation' agenda seeks to design and evaluate EU policies and laws to achieve their objectives most efficiently and effectively to ensure the proportionality principle. Impact assessments are required if the EU action's expected economic, environmental, or social repercussions are likely significant. In the impact assessment process, problems and their causes are spotted while evaluating whether EU action is required and examining the benefits and drawbacks of the different options.[65] Such impact assessments promote more informed decision-making, contributing to the correct application of the principles of subsidiarity and proportionality. However, impact assessments are not required when the Commission has no discretion over the policy content. According to the criteria set by the Commission in the *Better Regulation Guidance Toolbox,*[66] there is no need for Impact assessment when: (i) there is little or no choice available for the Commission.; (ii) impacts cannot be clearly identified ex-ante; or (iii) impacts are minor, like in the not relevant or minimum amendments of the act or codified versions.

The green papers are another mechanism that may provide evidence of the need for legislation in one policy area. Green papers are documents published by the Commission to stimulate discussion on specific EU-level topics, inviting stakeholders to participate in a consultation process and debate on those matters. Green papers can potentially also bring about, or at least inspire, the proposal of legislative acts based on their discussions. In the early directives, before impact assessments became mandatory to evidence the accomplishment of the proportionality and subsidiarity principles, the core of the motivation for legislative acts sometimes referred to those papers. As early as 1988, the European Commission affirmed in the Green Paper on Copyright and the Challenge of Technology that in developing European measures on copyright, "due regard must be paid not only to the interests of the right holder but also to the interests of third parties and the public at large". That sentence refers to the importance of considering the stakeholders' position. Figure 2.1 summarises the relation of EU legislative acts on copyright and their 'impact assessment' and includes the green papers that motivated the EU action for each act. The figure shows how impact assessments have become more relevant since 2015. It has to be noticed that since proportionality compliance became a requirement in 1999, no legislative acts adopted by the EU have had an impact assessment since 2008, one year before the Lisbon Treaty came into force and one year after its signature.

---

[65] Commission Staff Working Document 'Better Regulation Guidelines', SWD(2015) 111 final.

[66] European Commission, *Better Regulation Toolbox, Tool #7, 2021 edition*l, available at https://ec.europa.eu/info/law/law-making-process/planning-and-proposing-law/better-regulation-why-and-how/better-regulation-guidelines-and-toolbox/better-regulation-toolbox-0_en

Green papers that boosted legislative acts			GP Date
Act's Year	**Legislative Act's Short Name**	**Impact assesment**	**IA Date**
Television Without Frontiers: Green Paper on the Establishment of the Common Market, Especially by Satellite and Cable' - 1984			1984
1993	Satellite and Cable Directive	not applicable	
GREEN PAPER ON COPYRIGHT AND THE CHALLENGE OF TECHNOLOGY - COPYRIGHT ISSUES REQUIRING IMMEDIATE ACTION - 1988			1988
1991	Software Directive	not applicable	
1993	Rental and Lending Directive	not applicable	
1993	'Term Directive'	not applicable	
1996	Database Directive	not applicable	
2001	Resale Right Directive	not applicable	
GREEN PAPER - COPYRIGHT AND RELATED RIGHTS IN THE INFORMATION SOCIETY - 1995			1995
2001	InfoSoc Directive	not applicable	
2006	Rental and Lending Directive (codified)	**not applicable**	
2006	Term Directive' (codified)	**not applicable**	**2008**
Green Paper - Combating counterfeiting and piracy in the single market - 1998			1998
2004	**IPRED - Enforcement**	**not applicable**	
Green Paper - Copyright in the Knowledge Economy - 2008			2008
2009	**Software Directive (codified)**	**not applicable**	
2011	**Term II Directive' (amendment on 2006 Term Directive)**	Commission staff working document accompanying the proposal for a Council directive amending Council Directive 2006/116/EC as regards the term of protection of copyright and related rights - impact assessment on the legal and economic situation of performers and record producers in the European Union 2008	2008
Green Paper - Unlocking the potential of cultural and creative industries - 2010			2010
2012	**Orphan Works Directive**	COMMISSION STAFF WORKING PAPER IMPACT ASSESSMENT ON THE CROSS-BORDER ONLINE ACCESS TO ORPHAN WORKS Accompanying the document Proposal for a DIRECTIVE OF THE EUROPEAN PARLIAMENT AND OF THE COUNCIL on certain permitted uses of orphan works - 2011	2011
2017	**Marrakech Regulation**	**not required**	
2017	**Marrakech Directive**	**not required**	
2014	**'CRM Directive**	Commission staff working document - Impact assessment reforming cross-border collective management of copyright and related rights for legitimate online music services - 2005	2005
		COMMISSION DOCUMENT IMPACT ASSESSMENT Accompanying the document Proposal for a Directive of the European Parliament and of the Council on collective management of copyright and related rights and multi-territorial licensing of rights in musical works for online uses in the internal market - 2012	2012
2019	**DSM Directive**	COMMISSION STAFF WORKING DOCUMENT IMPACT ASSESSMENT on the modernisation of EU copyright rules Accompanying the document Proposal for a Directive of the European Parliament and of the Council on copyright in the Digital Single Market and Proposal for a Regulation of the European Parliament and of the Council laying down rules on the exercise of copyright and related rights applicable to certain online transmissions of broadcasting organisations and retransmissions of television and radio programmes - 2016	2016
2019	**Satellite and Cable II / NETSCAB**		
GREEN PAPER on the online distribution of audiovisual works in the European Union: opportunities and challenges towards a digital single market - 2011			2011
2017	**Portability Regulation**	COMMISSION STAFF WORKING DOCUMENT IMPACT ASSESSMENT Accompanying the document Proposal for a Regulation of the European Parliament and of the Council to ensure the cross-border portability of online content services in the internal market - 2015	2015

Fig. 2.1 Green papers and Impact assessment corresponding to each EU legislative act in the copyright field. Source Author's elaboration

The figure also reveals that although those impact assessments were already mandatory, not all the legislative acts approved since 2009 have a corresponding document of impact assessment. It corresponds to cases in which impact assessments were not required, like in the Directive and the Regulation implementing the Marrakesh Treaty. In that case, the Commission had minimum discretion, transposing an international agreement with no significant margin for variations.

However, the term "proportionality" in EU law not only refers to the described meaning as an EU general principle in Article 5 TEU, but it also refers to the concept of proportionality arising from constitutional law and the balancing of fundamental rights, as deduced from Article 52(1) of the CFEU. Regarding the exercise of the rights and freedoms, the CFEU accepts that limitations may be made on the fundamental rights and freedoms contained in the Charter, but 'only if they are necessary and genuinely meet objectives of general interest recognised by the Union or the need to protect the rights and freedoms of others, accordingly with the principle of proportionality. This exercise of balancing rights must be carried out not only ex-ante, by the EU Institutions taking part in the legislative process, but also by a judiciary ex-post control before the CJEU.

In conclusion, no issues relating to proportionality in the EU exercising its competence when adopting copyright measures have arisen before the CJEU. However, on many occasions, the CJEU assessed the proportionality in copyright rules when balancing them with other rights recognised by the EU legislation, including fundamental rights.

2.4 Overview: Adequacy of the Legal Basis and Legal Instruments to Advocate for a Unitary Copyright System

The choice of Article 114 does not refrain the EU legislator from using another legal instrument than the Directive. The European Commission, in the Impact Assessment accompanying the CDSMD proposal, when referring to the fulfilment of the subsidiarity principle, highlights the need for an EU intervention to face problems related to online access to content, including cross-border and to avoid further fragmentation in the Digital Single Market. The Impact Assessment also identifies EU intervention as indispensable "to guarantee legal certainty in cross-border situations".[67]

When justifying the choice of instruments for copyright reform, the same Impact assessment first chose a Regulation[68] as the best instrument to implement the rules for online transmissions and retransmissions of TV and radio programmes. The

[67] European Commission, *Impact Assessment on the modernisation of EU copyright rules*.

[68] Although the proposed instrument was Regulation, the act was finally adopted as Directive 789/2019, due to the amendments introduced by the legislative institutions.

European Commission justifies its choice by arguing that a Regulation would uniform application of the rules in the EU, "which is particularly important to guarantee legal certainty to service providers operating in different territories", and the regulation's direct applicability would also "prevent legal fragmentation and provide a harmonised set of rules to facilitate online access" to TV and radio programmes.

However, the European Commission chose a directive as a more suitable instrument for legislating on copyright and related rights in the Digital Single Market. The motivation for that choice was based on the argument that "it would allow MS to determine the technical or practical aspects complementing the EU harmonised rules and to consider the existing national legislative frameworks".

The Commission seems to favour the action and legislative framework of the Member States rather than granting a uniform level of legal certainty to the online cross-border situations and avoiding further fragmentation in the Digital Single Market, as announced when justifying its interventions regarding the subsidiarity principle.

The current system of voluntary exceptions and limitations in Article 5 of the InfoSoc Directive creates uncertainty for users and service providers. This is because actions allowed in some Member States may be prohibited in others. The system also results in a higher level of legislative fragmentation and lack of harmonisation, which the EU aimed to tackle.

Therefore, a Regulation would have been a better instrument to readdress those concerns. The choice of a Regulation would indeed have challenged the territoriality of copyright, but that is the goal behind the idea of 'avoiding further fragmentation of the Digital Single Market'. However, the territoriality of copyright is being challenged by the global nature of the Internet and the concept of the Digital Single Market itself. Using copyrighted works over the internet blurs the idea of the territoriality of copyright. Thus, the acts of communication become ubiquitous rather than territorial and gain global scope. CtoP and copyright, in general, play now in an online field, and their territoriality should be challenged by the EU legislation to face the reality of the digital economy.

Despite the choice of article 114 TFEU appeared as suitable for the last copyright reform, the next step to be taken by the EU copyright legislation should be to achieve a unitary EU copyright title, as in trademark and design matters. In this case, the adequate legal base is set in Article 118. The legal basis in Article 118 aims to provide uniform protection of intellectual property rights within the EU and establish an EU-wide centralised body or authority.

It would have been ideal for the EU to take the chance of copyright reform by introducing in its last legislative act (the DSM Directive) an EU-wide copyright protection, at least for those works to be distributed online. This would facilitate authors and other rightsholders in the registration of works for getting the corresponding royalties. Also, it would simplify the obtention of blanket licences, allowing users, including OCSSP, to use all the EU repertoire in any Member State. Such a situation would prevent CMOs of the 27 Member States from having to conclude reciprocity or representation agreements[69] to collect the royalties on behalf of their partner organisations and their subsequent clearance. A unitary EU-wide copyright title and a centralised management body would provide a more efficient one-stop solution system for creators and users and a higher level of transparency in licensing, collecting, and sharing royalties. This solution would reduce the role and power of the CMOs and the music industry, providing authors, small publishers and record labels a more balanced position in the internal market. However, this proposed system would change the paradigm, taking copyright management out of the private hands of CMOs and the music industry and introducing the control of a public body or agency, like the EUIPO.[70]

The development of such a possibility leaves room for a further research in depth.

References

Craufurd-Smith R (2004) Introduction. In: Culture and European Union law. Oxford University Press, p 414

Dessemontet F (1998) Copyright and Human Rights. In: Kabel JJC, Mom GJHM (eds) Intellectual Property and Information Law: Essays in Honour of Herman Cohen Jehoram. Kluwer Law International

Geiger C, Izyumenko E (2014) Copyright on the Human Rights' trial: redefining the boundaries of exclusivity through freedom of expression. IIC – Int Rev Intellect Prop Compet Law 45:316–342. https://doi.org/10.1007/s40319-014-0181-3

Hugenholtz PB (2009) Is harmonization a good thing? The case of the copyright acquis. In: Hugenholtz PB et al (eds) Harmonising European Copyright Law. The challenges of better law making. Kluwer Law International, pp 57–74

Hugenholtz PB, van Eechoud M, van Gompel S et al (2009) Harmonizing European Copyright Law. Kluwer Law International

Mahalwar V (2017) Copyright and Human Rights: the quest for a fair balance. In: Copyright law in the digital world. Springer Singapore, Singapore, pp 151–174

Ramalho A (2014) Conceptualising the European Union's competence in copyright—what can the EU do? IIC – Int Rev Intellect Prop Compet Law 45:178–200. https://doi.org/10.1007/s40319-014-0161-7

Ramalho A (2017) Beyond the cover story—an enquiry into the EU competence to introduce a right for publishers. IIC Int Rev Intellect Prop Compet Law 48:71–91. https://doi.org/10.1007/s40319-016-0540-3

Ramalho A (2021) The competence and rationale of EU copyright harmonization. In: The Routledge handbook of EU Copyright Law. Routledge, pp 3–17. https://doi.org/10.4324/9781003156277-2

[69]Currently, the most relevant CMO in Spain, SGAE, has signed more than 300 representation or reciprocity agreements with 173 collective management organisations that cover more than 220 countries and territories around the world, including the other 26 EU Member States. https://www.sgae.es/wp-content/uploads/2023/02/Entidades-con-acuerdos-representacion-SGAE-2.2.2023.pdf

[70]EUIPO stands for European Union Intellectual Property Office. https://www.euipo.europa.eu/

Romainville C (2015) The right to participate in cultural life under EU law. J Eur des droits l'homme 2:145–172

Synodinou TE (2021) The desirability of unification of European copyright law. In: The Routledge handbook of EU Copyright Law, pp 39–60. https://doi.org/10.4324/9781003156277-4

Torremans PLC (2007) Is copyright a human right. Mich State Law Rev 2007:271

Chapter 3
The Right of Communication to the Public of Musical Works Online in the EU Copyright Law

After the overview of the general copyright framework in the EU, this chapter aims to clarify the meaning and scope of the communication to the public right in musical works communicated online. It analyses the EU relevant rules on the subject matter, mainly on Directive 2001/29/EC (InfoSoc), as well as the most relevant case law of the CJEU that contributed to the configuration of the CtoP right.

Although the right of communication to the public is referred to in the first copyright directives, none of those legal instruments offered a general definition of CtoP right. The Satellite and Cable Directive[1] offers a specific deception of what shall be understood for such Directive as 'communication to the public by satellite', meaning "the act of introducing, under the control and responsibility of the broadcasting organisation, the programme-carrying signals intended for reception by the public into an uninterrupted chain of communication leading to the satellite and down towards the earth".[2] Article 4 of the Satellite and Cable Directive mentions the related rights of performers, phonogram producers and broadcasting organisations. It refers, for communication to the public by satellite, to the provisions in Articles 6, 7, 8 and 10 of Directive 92/100/EEC[3] for their protection. However, in both cases, the scope of protection and the definition does not go beyond the scope of the directive itself.

Furthermore, the first 1992 Rental and Lending Directive contained the provision in Article 8 on broadcasting and communication to the public regarding the related rights of performers, phonogram producers and broadcasting organisations. The

[1] Directive 93/83/EEC of the Council of the European Communities of 27 September 1993 on the coordination of certain rules concerning copyright and rights related to copyright applicable to satellite broadcasting and cable retransmission, OJ L 248, 6.10.1993, p. 15–21.

[2] Article 1(2)(a), Directive 93/83/EEC.

[3] Council Directive 92/100/EEC of the Council of the European Communities of 19 November 1992 on rental right and lending right and on certain rights related to copyright in the field of intellectual property, OJ L 346, 27.11.1992, p. 61–66.

L. Ballesta Martí, *The Communication to the Public of Musical Works Online in the European Union's Legislation*, Law, Governance and Technology Series 75,
https://doi.org/10.1007/978-3-031-94132-0_3

exact text and same Article numbering can be found in the codified version of the Rental and Lending Directive adopted in 2006.[4]However, neither offers a clear explanation of what constitutes the CtoP right.

The first version, the Rental and Lending Directive implemented Articles 12 and 13(d) of the Rome Convention while allowing Member States to grant broader protection.[5] This Directive regulates the rights derived from the rental and lending of works but also regulates fundamental exclusive and economical-related rights for performers, producers and broadcasters, including the CtoP. Such a combination of rights and matters is because many Member States, by the time of the approval of the Rental and Lending Directive's first version, did not recognise any basic economic and exclusive right related to copyright to those right holders. The need to provide performers and producers with rental rights on the works they invested in or took part in making the European legislator recognise their basic related rights for consistency reasons and a comprehensive approach, including in the Rental and Lending Directive in Chapter II on Rights Related to Copyright.[6]

It was not until 2001 that the InfoSoc Directive introduced a timid definition of the 'communication to the public' term, based on the definition stated in the WCT, including the 'making available' right as part of the CtoP. Since the concept of making available to the public was not granted in the international treaties until 1996, in the WCT, the European legislator, when approved the InfoSoc Directive, could take the chance to amend the 1992 Rental and Lending Directive or repeal its Article 8 and including it to the InfoSoc Directive. Instead of compiling CtoP rights with other copyright and the related rights in one text, as it was done with the *reproduction right* (formerly regulated in Article 7) that was abrogated by Article 11 of the InfoSoc Directive,[7] the EU legislator maintained the CtoP regulated in two different text. Furthermore, in 2006, the EU approved a codified version of the Rental and Lending Directive and maintained the same language as its predecessor 1992 text; thus, the only grant of the making available right regarding the related rights owners was already introduced in 2001 by the InfoSoc Directive. The CtoP right continues having a regulation split into two texts instead.

The conceptualisation of CtoP right given in the EU legislation since 2001 has brought about many cases before the CJEU, which has been reshaping the notion of communication to the public for nearly 20 years since then. The harmonisation of the concept of CtoP run by the CJEU case law has been done in an analogical context as well as to adjust the term to the digital changes and challenges.[8] Under the expected *Copyright Reform* that updated the rules to the digital era, the CDSM Directive in

[4]*Directive 2006/115/EC of 12 December 2006 on rental right and lending right and on certain rights related to copyright in the field of intellectual property (codified version), OJ L 376, 27.12.2006, p. 28–35.*

[5]Recital 16 of the Rental and Lending Directive.

[6]Nérisson (2014), p. 150.

[7]Ibid, p. 182.

[8]Xalabarder Plantada (2016), p. 635.

2019 did not redefine the concept of CtoP, not even clarifying the term by embodying the jurisprudential nuances in the EU legislation. Far from giving a close revised concept of the CtoP, the CDSM Directive updates the liability regime on such right by a regulation that fits in the new acts of communication to the public run by new subjects in the field: the OCSSPs.

The following paragraphs in this section aim to find an appropriate definition of the term CtoP suitable for the current musical industry environment. It is done firstly by assessing its regulation in the InfoSoc Directive and secondly by examining the legislation in the light of the relevant case law of the CJEU.

3.1 The (Non)Conceptualisation of Right of Communication to the Public in the EU Legislation: Article 3 of the InfoSoc Directive Shortcomings

As it has been mentioned in Chap. 1, the right of communication to the public is laid down in the international legislation in Article 8 of the WCT and 10 and 14 of the WPPT.[9] The implementation of such right into the European legislation was done by the means of Article 3 of the Directive 2001/29/EC[10] (InfoSoc Directive). The recital (15) of the InfoSoc Directive states that such Directive serves to implement several of the international obligations derived from the signature and ratification of the WIPO Internet Treaties by the EU. Apart from this objective imposed by the international obligation, the InfoSoc Directive objectives can be divided in general objectives, specific objectives and operational objectives. Recital (2) of the InfoSoc Directive states the aim to "*create a general and flexible legal framework at Community level in order to foster the development of the information society in Europe*" as general objective of the Directive. To achieve that general goal, the Directive responds to two specific objectives: (i) to improve the functioning of the Internal Market for copyrighted works[11] and (ii) to provide adequate incentives to boost the competitiveness of the EU creative content industry.[12] The first was to be achieved through the harmonisation of national copyright laws to prevent differences in national responses to technological developments affecting copyright.[13] Such objectives are underlined in Article 1 when adjusting the scope of the Directive of protecting copyright and related rights, specifically in 'the framework of the internal market'.[14] The harmonisation of copyright and related rights within the internal

[9] See Chap. 1, Sect. 1.2.

[10] Directive 2001/29/EC of 22 May 2001 on the harmonisation of certain aspects of copyright and related rights in the information society, OJ L 167, 22.6.2001, p. 10–19.

[11] Recital 2 of the InfoSoc Directive.

[12] Recital 4 of the InfoSoc Directive.

[13] Recitals 6 and 31 of the InfoSoc Directive.

[14] Article 1 of the InfoSoc Directive.

market is supposed to lay on a high level of protection of exclusive rights "since such rights are crucial to intellectual creation".[15] This is related to the second objective of boosting the creative industry within the EU and its competitiveness. In order to achieve that goal, an adequate legal protection of artistic work of authors and performers, as well as producers' investment, is necessary to guarantee an appropriate reward to creators for the use of their works and provide the opportunity for satisfactory returns on producers' investments.[16] Through to a meticulous and efficient protection of copyright and related rights, the EU should be capable to ensure that 'cultural creativity and production could receive the necessary resources, with a subsequent guarantee of intellectual autonomy for artistic creators and performers and the preservation of their dignity'.[17] Thus, the specific objective of protecting and boosting cultural creative industry in the EU is achieved via those operational objectives of increasing copyright legal protection and expanding the scope of the exclusive rights.[18]

The right of communication to the public is one of those exclusive rights that is granted in the InfoSoc Directive. In particular, Article 3 addresses the communication to the public right, inspired by the Article 8 WCT layout of the CtoP term, and introduces the concept of 'making available' as part of the CtoP right. However, none of these two provisions offer a clear definition of the concept of CtoP; neither explains the content[19] and scope of the right nor what exactly constitutes an act of CtoP. Under the title 'Right of communication to the public of works and right of making available to the public another subject-matter, Article 3 of the InfoSoc Directive states as follows:

> 1. Member States shall provide authors with the exclusive right to authorise or prohibit any communication to the public of their works, by wire or wireless means, including the making available to the public of their works in such a way that members of the public may access them from a place and at a time individually chosen by them.
>
> 2. Member States shall provide for the exclusive right to authorise or prohibit the making available to the public, by wire or wireless means, in such a way that members of the public may access them from a place and at a time individually chosen by them:
>
> (a) for performers, of fixations of their performances;
> (b) for phonogram producers, of their phonograms;
> (c) for the producers of the first fixations of films, of the original and copies of their films;
> (d) for broadcasting organisations, of fixations of their broadcasts, whether these broadcasts are transmitted by wire or over the air, including by cable or satellite.
>
> 3. The rights referred to in paragraphs 1 and 2 shall not be exhausted by any act of communication to the public or making available to the public as set out in this Article.

[15] Recital 9 of the InfoSoc Directive.

[16] Recital 10 of the InfoSoc Directive.

[17] Recital 11 of the InfoSoc Directive, and Recital 5 of the Rental and Lending Directive.

[18] Renda (2015), p. 9.

[19] Rosati (2020), p. 3.

In Article 3, on the surface, one of the clear things that arise is that such provision regulates the communication to the public right separately from the making available right. However, it is stated that the latest is included in the concept of communication to the public, which is not plainly defined.

The first paragraph recognises the exclusive right of authors to authorise the communication to the public of their works. It includes within the concept of communication to the public the notion of making it available to the public. However, the second paragraph of Article 3, corresponding to related rights, refers to the exclusive right to authorise or prohibit the 'making available to the public', but not other means of communication to the public. In the field of musical works, Article 3 (2) recognises the 'making available to the public' for performers, of fixations of their performances, for phonogram producers, of their phonograms and broadcasting organisations, of fixations of their broadcasts.

From the language of the provisions in Article 3, it can be deducted that making available to the public is a form of communication to the public, as when Article 3(1) refers to the latest, it uses the formula "*including the making available to the public*". However, the fact that Article 3(2) does not mention the term *'communication to the public'*, but only the notion of *'making available to the public'*, implies that communication to the public includes other acts different from the 'making available'. The non-recognition of other acts of communication to the public rather than the making available, for performers, phonogram producers and broadcasting organisations in Article 3(2) does not mean that those subjects have no rights regarding communication to the public acts of their object. This is because the communication to the public right in related rights is regulated in Article 8 of the Rental and Lending Directive.[20] Therefore, Article 8 of the Rental and Lending Directive recognises the exclusive right of performers to authorise or prohibit the 'broadcasting by wireless means and the communication to the public of their performances, except where the performance is itself already a broadcast

[20] Article 8 in both Rental and Lending Directives; Directive 92/100/EEC and the codified version of the Directive 2006/155/EC states as follows:

1. Member States shall provide for performers the exclusive right to authorize or prohibit the broadcasting by wireless means and the communication to the public of their performances, except where the performance is itself already a broadcast performance or is made from a fixation.
2. Member States shall provide a right in order to ensure that a single equitable remuneration is paid by the user, if a phonogram published for commercial purposes, or a reproduction of such phonogram, is used for broadcasting by wireless means or for any communication to the public, and to ensure that this remuneration is shared between the relevant performers and phonogram producers. Member States may, in the absence of agreement between the performers and phonogram producers, lay down the conditions as to the sharing of this remuneration between them.
3. Member States shall provide for broadcasting organizations the exclusive right to authorize or prohibit the rebroadcasting of their broadcasts by wireless means, as well as the communication to the public of their broadcasts if such communication is made in places accessible to the public against payment of an entrance fee.

Table 3.1 Regulation of the Communication to the Public and Making Available Rights in the EU Legislation in relation to each rightsholder

Rightsholders (Subjects)	The exclusive right to authorise or prohibit		Economic right	Subject-matters (Objects)
	Communication to the Public	Making Available	Equitable remuneration for broadcasting or CtoP	
Authors	Article 3(1) Infosoc	Article 3(1) Infosoc	–	Musical works
Performers	Article 8(1) rental and lending	Article 3(2) Infosoc	Article 8(2) rental and lending	Performances
Phonogram producers	–	Article 3(2) Infosoc	Article 8(2) rental and lending	Phonograms
Broadcasting organisations	Article 8(3) rental and lending (if entrance fee payment is required)	Article 3(2) Infosoc	—	Broadcasts

Source: Author's elaboration

performance or is made from a fixation'. In the case of phonograms published for commercial purposes, broadcasting or any communication to the public requires a single equitable remuneration, shared between the relevant performers and phonogram producers, to be paid by the user. Article 8(3) recognises broadcasting organisations the exclusive right to authorise or prohibit rebroadcasting or communication to the public of their broadcasts if the communication is made to the public against payment of an entrance fee. Recital 20[21] of the InfoSoc Directive informs that the provisions of the directive should be without prejudice to the provisions of other directives in force, including the Rental and Lending. Hence, the CtoP right has a regulation split into two texts. Consequently, although the making available right is part of the communication to the public right, both rights are regulated separately regarding the related rights. That separated regulation makes finding a definition more difficult. To find a single definition of the CtoP, it is important to clarify the scope of the right. Therefore, before going further in the conceptualisation, it needs to be assessed that the combination of the two provisions of the aforementioned directives gives a different scope of the rights depending on the rightsholders. As shown in Table 3.1, under Article 3 of the InfoSoc Directive, all categories of rightsholders[22] (authors, performers, phonogram producers and broadcasting organisations) have the exclusive right to authorise or prohibit the making available of their corresponding works or related subjects matters (performances, phonograms or broadcasts). However, only authors have such rightfully granted acts

[21] Recital 20 of the InfoSoc Directive.

[22] Article 3 (2) of the InfoSoc Directive includes new rightholders than the recognized by the WPPT since it introduces right on the making available for broadcasting organizations (and for producers of the first fixations of film). It also extends the recognition of the right to audiovisual sector, and not only to music sector as it is in the WPPT.

of communication to the public in Article 3 (1) of the InfoSoc Directive. In contrast, the same right is granted to performers in Article 8(1) of the Rental and Lending Directive. Besides, Under Article 8(3) of the Rental and Lending Directive, broadcasting organisations enjoy the exclusive right to authorise or prohibit the rebroadcasting or communication to the public of their broadcast, but just partly. The exercise of such an exclusive right by broadcasting organisations is conditioned to the fact that the Communication Act must be made in places accessible to the public against payment of an entrance fee. Moreover, phonogram producers only have the economic right of equitable remuneration for CtoP, shared with performers, as stated in Article 8(2) of the Rental and Lending Directive, despite having a full grant of the making available exclusive right.

The different scope of those two provisions was pointed out by the CJEU in the judgement C-135/10, which explained that under Article 3(1) of Directive 2001/29

> "authors have a right which is preventive in nature and allows them to intervene, between possible users of their work and the communication to the public which such users might contemplate making, in order to prohibit such use. On the other hand, under Article 8(2) of Directive 92/100, performers and producers of phonograms have a right which is compensatory in nature which is not liable to be exercised before a phonogram is published for commercial purposes or a reproduction of such a phonogram, has been used for communication to the public by a user. It follows that Article 8(2) of Directive 92/100, on the one hand, requires an individual interpretation of the concept of communication to the public. (...) The right under Article 8(2) of Directive 92/100 is exercised in the event of the use of a work; that right is clearly a right which is essentially financial in nature".[23]

Once clarified the scope of both making available and communication to the public rights according to each rightsholders, either more expansive as an exclusive right or just as a *financial* right, it takes turns to determine the scope of meaning of the terms 'communication to the public' and 'making available', being the last a part of the first.

3.1.1 Communication to the Public and Making Available

Article 3(1) of the InfoSoc Directive refers to the CtoP right as 'the exclusive right to authorise or prohibit any communication to the public of [authors] works, by wire or wireless means, including the making available to the public of their works in such a way that members of the public may access them from a place and at a time individually chosen by them. Thus, from the reading of Article 3(1), it can be concluded that (i)communication to the public can be done by wire or wireless means, (ii) the making available is a form of communication to the public, (iii) and making available implies that the public is able to choose the time and place of the communication. The information provided by this Article opens a gap that leads to a

[23] CJEU Judgment of 15 Mar 2012, *SCF v Del Corso, C-135/10, ECLI:EU:C:2012:140*. paras. 75–77.

bunch of questions rather than offering a conceptualisation of the CtoP right. An act of communication to the public can be accomplished by wire or wireless means, which includes a large range of possible situations, but what shall be considered an act of communication? Which is the scope of the 'making available', right? 'Making available' is a form of communication to the public, but which are the others? Is public performance a way of communication to the public? To consider whether the communication is done to a "public" or not, which criteria shall be applied? If making available implies that the public can choose the time and place of the communication, does it mean that it includes "interactive transmissions" as well as hyperlinking? The Recitals 23 to 27 in the preamble of the InfoSoc Directive clarify some aspects as well as inspired the CJEU decisions[24] that shaped the CtoP right in the EU law.

Recital (23) of the Directive, in relation to the objective of harmonising the right of communication to the public, clarifies that '[this] right should be understood in a broad sense covering all communication to the public not present at the place where the communication originates'. This excludes then any life performance and consequently separates public performance right from CtoP right. In its judgement, C-283/10 (*Circul Globus*),[25] the CJEU focuses on the history and recalls the legislative procedure of the Directive 2001/29 to clarify the core interpretation of its recital 23. The court refers to the Common Position of the Council to adopting Directive 2001/29 to remind that recital 23 to InfoSoc Directive "follows from the proposal of the European Parliament, which wished to specify, in that recital, that communication to the public for the purposes of that Directive does not cover 'direct representation or performance', a concept referring to that of 'public performance' which appears in Article 11(1) of the Berne Convention and encompasses interpretation of the works before the public that is in direct physical contact with the actor or performer of those works". Accordingly, CtoP right "does not cover any activity which does not involve a 'transmission' or a 'retransmission' of a work, such as live presentations or performances of a work",[26] being these two last activities part of the right of public performance.

Apart from differencing CtoP from public performance, recital (23) explicitly includes broadcasting as part of the CtoP since it refines the right by stating that it 'should cover any such transmission or retransmission of a work to the public by wire or wireless means'. The final part of the recital seems to limit the scope of CtoP when states that '[this] right should not cover any other acts. Following Recital (24) sets up the right to make available to the public in related rights, declaring that it has to be understood as covering 'all acts of making available [such subject-matter] to members of the public not present at the place where the act of making available originates, and as not covering any other acts. This Recital does not clarify any

[24] See, Judgements on cases, C-403/08 (Premier League), of 4 Oct 2011, *ECLI:EU:C:2011:631*, and C-283/10 (Circul Globus), of 24 Nov 2011, *ECLI:EU:C:2011:772.*

[25] CJEU Judgment of 24 Nov 2011, *Circul Globus, C-283/10, ECLI:EU:C:2011:772.* para. 35.

[26] *Ibid.* para. 40.

further aspect of the making available than the provided by Article 3(2). However, Recital (25) specifies that the that all rightsholders recognised by the Directive have an exclusive right to make available to the public, which covers, in particular, the interactive on-demand transmission of copyright works over digital networks. Furthermore, the Recital provides a definition of interactive on-demand transmissions, which are characterised 'by the fact that members of the public may access them from a place and at a time individually chosen by them'. However, nothing is said about on-demand transmissions which cannot be considered interactive, either because user can only choose a channel, playlist, music genre, artist, etc., but cannot choose or skip the songs or even hybrid interactive systems in which users can only skip a certain number of songs (i.e. Spotify payment-free subscription accounts). Recital (26) promotes the conclusion of collective licensing arrangements to facilitate the clearance of the rights concerned in the 'making available in on-demand services by broadcasters of their radio or television productions incorporating music from commercial phonograms'. From the reading of this recital, it is implicit that broadcasting and making available are different rights, one from each other. Thus, it states that when a broadcaster offers an on-demand services to users to see or listen to their own productions that have already been broadcasted, the broadcaster has to clear the corresponding rights for 'making available' although the rights for broadcasting had already been cleared. Table 3.2 summarises the difference between 'public performance', CtoP and MA rights according to the aspects found in the text of Article 3 and recitals the InfoSoc Directive.

Finally, Recital (27) asserts that the presumption of an act of communication to the public cannot be derived from the 'mere provision of physical facilities for enabling or making a communication'. That presumption refers to secondary acts of communication, meaning someone that communicates to a public sound recordings or broadcasts that have been transmitted by using sound systems, loudspeakers, audiovisual systems or other means. The fact of having one of those facilities installed in a place open to the public does not necessarily imply that such communication to the public would occur. The same case is when hiring a car equipped with radio receivers or apps installed to connect to the streaming services does not constitute a communication to the public within the meaning of the provisions in InfoSoc, as the CJEU recognised in its judgement in case C-753/18.[27] Agreeing Liliia Oprysk,[28] the current EU legal framework on copyright does not explicitly makes a difference between primary (or initial) and secondary (or subsequent) acts of communication.

---

[27] CJEU Judgment of 2 April 2020, *C-753/18 Stim and SAMI*, ECLI:EU:C:2020:268.

[28] Oprysk (2020), p. 205.

Table 3.2 Difference between 'public performance', CtoP and MA rights in InfoSoc Directive

Right	Action	Place where the public is	Means	Role of the public	Choice of time & place of the action	Acts
Public performance	Recitation, live performance or presentation	At the same place, the performance	Live + loudspeaker	Present + interactive or not	Performer / displayer	Live performances, concerts.
Communication to the public	Transmission / retransmission	Different place from where the transmission originates	Wire or wireless	Not present + non-interactive	Broadcaster, service provider or operator	Broadcasting, streaming, online radio, background music, etc.
Making available	Host, offer and transmit content on demand		On-demand wire or wireless	Not present + interactive (on-demand)	User individually	Podcast, interactive streaming, P2P, content sharing

Source: Author's elaboration

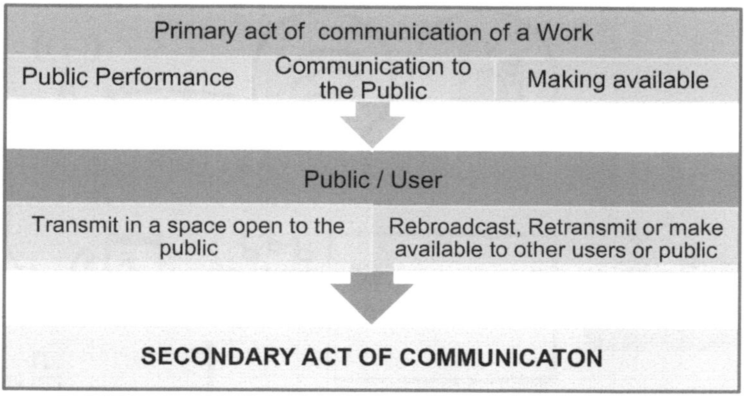

Fig. 3.1 Primary and secondary acts of communication. Source: Author's elaboration

3.1.2 Secondary Acts of Communication and the Non-Exhaustion Principle

Secondary acts of communications do not always refer exclusively to CtoP but to MA or rebroadcasting as well, as shown in Fig. 3.1.

Hence, every act of communication of a work is supposed to be authorised by the rightsholders. This is that every act of communication subsequent or derived from the first or initial act of communication, whether authorised or not by the corresponding rightsholders, generates a new exclusive right each time it is communicated or made available to the public. Consequently, each subsequent act of communication represents a potential liability situation in case of infringement of the exclusive right of rightsholders. The Fig. 3.2 shows an example to clarify the concepts of primary and secondary acts of communication.[29] When bartenders in a bar turn on the radio (analogical or online) or play their favourite playlist from their Spotify account on their devices (computers, phones or tablets), the radiobroadcast or streaming of copyright-protected works represents an initial or primary act of communication to the public. However, when the bartenders want to put some background music and connect their devices to the sound system and loudspeakers in the bar, they share the initial communication (the radiobroadcast or stream) with the customers in the bar place. As long as the customers are able to enjoy the transmitted works from the initial transmission (from the radio station or Spotify to the bartenders' private device) a separate act of communication to the public happens, from the bartenders to the random customers that are in the bar place. This subsequent act of communication represent a 'secondary act of communication' since the sound system and loudspeakers intervene in the initial transmission in order

[29] Example based on the case in CJEU Judgement of 14 Jul 2015 Sociedade Portugesa de Autores, C-151/15, ECLI:EU:C:2015:468.

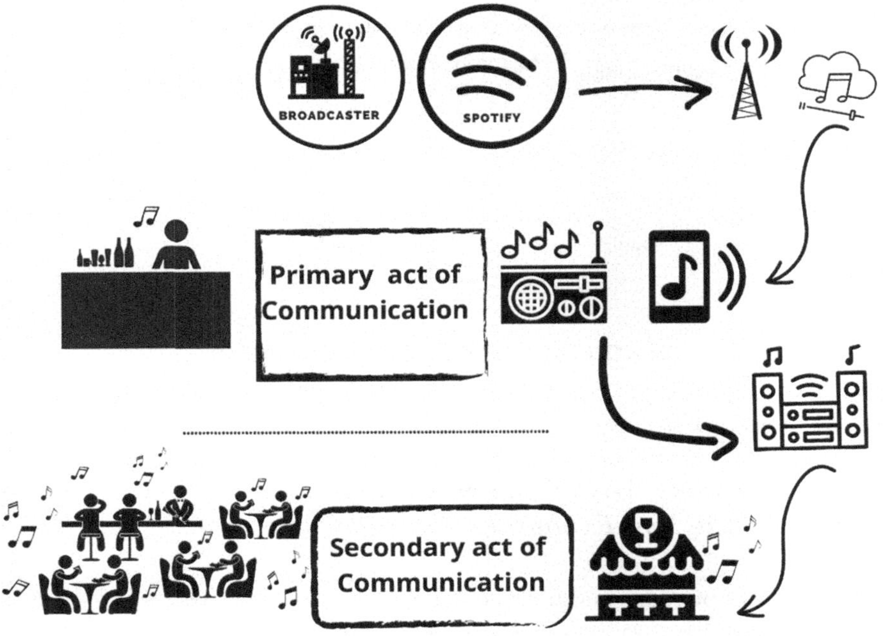

Fig. 3.2 Example of primary and secondary acts of communication to the público. Source: Author's elaboration

to allow customers to enjoy the music in any place or area of the bar, different from the place next to the radio or device.

It has to be noted that any subsequent transmission would potentially be considered as a new act of communication since the CtoP right cannot be exhausted by further acts of communication. That means neither the right of communication nor the making available right are subject to digital exhaustion.[30] Article 3(3) of the InfoSoc Directive explicitly establishes that 'the rights referred to in paragraphs 1 and 2 shall not be exhausted by any act of communication to the public or making available to the public'. Therefore, the exhaustion principle applies to exclusive rights other than CtoP, like right of distribution. This case also applied the principle of exhaustion for the distribution right. The exhaustion principle, which is referred to in Recital 28 of the preamble to the InfoSoc Directive, establishes that the first sale in the EU "of the original of a work or copies thereof by the right holder or with his consent exhausts the right to control resale of that object in the EU [Community]". Moreover, Article 4(2) of the Directive provides that the "distribution right shall not be exhausted within the Community in respect of the original or copies of the work, except where the first sale or other transfer of ownership in the Community of that object is made by the right holder or with his consent". It involves that rightsholders

[30] Quintais (2018), p. 388.

don't have any control on the secondary and subsequent acts of dissemination of a work. In the case of right of distribution, that is, the rightsholders are not allowed to authorise the secondary acts of distribution, like the resale of copies, provided that the initial distribution had already been authorised. Therefore, it is essential to make a distinction between primary and secondary acts. Hence, distribution right refers mainly to the authorisation for disseminating tangible copies; once the primary distribution is authorised, the secondary acts do not need the authorisation of the right holders. Although the explicit prohibition of exhaustion regarding the right of CtoP in Article 3(3), the difference between distribution and communication to the public, referring to both primary and secondary acts, is sometimes unclear concerning digital content online in the music field. For instance, when a music work is made available online on a streaming platform, every time you play that song, it is a primary act of communication to the public. If you connect it to loudspeakers to ambient, your store is a secondary act. But when the music work is made available to be downloaded in a music file, does it concern the making available right or distribution right? Once downloaded in your device, if you reproduce the song to the public (in your store), is it a primary or a secondary act of communication? Following Liliia Oprysk's research, the 'question that arises is whether digital copies could and should be considered equivalent to tangible copies for the purpose of applying the exhaustion principle',[31] which was developed in the analogue era with the aim of enabling the free movement of goods within the internal market[32] and to provide a boundary of exclusive control online.[33] Oprysk suggests that the exhaustion principle in digital works should not be too rigid, as from a yes-or-not approach, when balancing the interests of rightsholders, users, and services. Even though the clear language of Article 3(3) of the InfoSoc Directive, the CJEU, on a few occasions, exempted secondary acts from authorisation based on economic considerations.[34] After assessing the language in Article 3 and the recitals of the InfoSoc Directive, communication to the public right could be described as:

> The right of the rightsholders to prohibit, authorise, or obtain an equitable remuneration for the communication of their works or subject-matters, transmitted by wire or wireless means, to a public not present at the place where the performance of the work takes origin. Such transmission to the public can be initiated either by the transmitting organisation or by the public on their own demand, which is, then, considered a communication to the public by the act of making available the works to be transmitted. Any act of communication can also involve subsequent or secondary acts of communications, which shall require new authorisation of the rightsholders.

Despite the attempt to extract a suitable definition from the text in the legislation, there are still many issues that are not clear enough, and many questions may arise.

---

[31] Oprysk (2020), p. 212.

[32] CJEU Judgment of 8 June 1971.

[33] Oprysk (2020), p. 216.

[34] A further assessment on CEJU judgements on CtoP is done in Section 2 of this Chap. 3.

The lack of precision in the legal texts when defining the concepts and the acts that shall be considered as acts of communication to the public afterward triggered the CJEU to interpret the legislation and delimitate the term 'communication to the public' and the related concepts and elaborating criteria to determine when an act shall be included in the legal concepts and consequently become an infringement.

The following subsection covers the configuration and evolution of the CtoP right through the CJEU case law.

3.2 The CJEU Configuration of the Communication to the Public Right in Musical Works Online: An Approach Through Dynamic Criteria

As assessed in the previous sections, EU legislation does not clearly define what CtoP refers to. As regards the concept of 'communication to the public' appears not only in Article 8(2) of Directive 2006/115, but also in Article 3(1) of Directive 2001/29. On the other hand, as assessed in Chap. 1, the concept of 'communication to the public' is also present in international law, specifically in Article 11bis of the Berne Convention, Article 12 of the Rome Convention, Article 8 of the WCT, Article 15 of the WPPT and Article 14(1) of the TRIPS agreement. However, not all those international rules are part of the EU legal order, as the EU in not part of all those conventions. Decision 94/800 approved TRIPS Agreement signed by the European Union, the Decision 2000/278 authorised the adoption of the WCT and the WPPT treaties by the EU, which means that both instruments bind not only the institutions of the EU but also its Member States. In contrast, neither the Rome Convention nor the Berne Convention have been adopted by the EU, although the Berne Convention rules on Articles 1 to 21 are introduced by the acceptance of Article 1(4) of the WTC.[35]

As the CJEU expressed in recital 51 on its judgment in Del Corso case, the EU "legislation must, so far as possible, be interpreted in a manner that is consistent with international law, in particular where its provisions are intended specifically to give effect to an international agreement concluded by the European Union".[36] Here, the CJEU reproduces its own jurisprudential line regarding the interpretation of EU legislation consistently with the international rules concluded by the EU.[37] However, the statement indicates that interpretation must be consistent with international law in general, not only with EU-concluded agreements. Thus, the statement introduces the specific example of EU-concluded agreements by using the language use "in

[35] See Chap. 1 of this book.

[36] CJEU Judgment of 15 Mar 2012, *SCF v Del Corso, C-135/10, ECLI:EU:C:2012:140.* para. 51.

[37] See CJEU judgement of 14 de july 1998, *Betatti v. Safety Hi Tech*, C-341/95, ECLI:EU:C:1998:353, para. 20, and CJEU judgement of 9 Jan 2003, *Petrotub SA and Republica SA v Council of the European Union*, C-76/00, ECLI:EU:C:2003:4 para. 57.

particular"; therefore, it does not limit the consistent interpretation just to those treaties to with the EU is a party. But in the case of the copyright and related rights international treaties, not all of them have been concluded by the EU, as said before. However, some of the mentioned international treaties are not part of the EU legal system, so in principle shouldn't be binding for the EU. In *Del Corso's* case, referring to the CtoP, the CJEU on its the judgment extends the idea that international law shall be a guide to interpret the provisions in the EU legal order despite not being concluded by the EU. Recital 55[38] refers to the fact that the concepts appearing in Directives 92/100 and 2001/29, such as 'communication to the public', must be interpreted in the light of the equivalent concepts contained in those international agreements and to become compatible with those agreements. It points out that the context in which those concepts are found and the purpose of the relevant provisions of the agreements must be taken into account when making such interpretation. Furthermore, recital 71[39] openly mentions that the concept of CtoP must be interpreted in the light of the equivalent concepts contained in the Rome Convention, a convention not concluded by the EU. The recital also refers to the TRIPS agreement and the WPPT and clauses contained in Articles 2.2 and 1.2, correspondingly confirming the respect and not prejudice of any rights or obligations in the existing conventions, including the Rome convention. Although nothing is said about the compatible interpretation of the former treaties, the mandate of respect and non-prejudice indirectly entails making a consistent interpretation of all those treaties and consequently leads their parties to do so. Furthermore, in 2017, the CJEU clarified that although the Rome Convention:

> does not form part of the legal order of the European Union, concepts appearing in Directive 2006/15 must be interpreted in particular in the light of that convention, in such a way that they are compatible with the equivalent concepts contained in that convention, taking account also of the context in which those concepts are found and the purpose of the relevant provisions of the convention.[40]

After all, neither the EU legislation nor the international legislation offer a clear definition of the term 'CtoP'; consequently, the concept has been shaped through the interpretation made by the courts, particularly the CJEU. Since 2006, up to the date of writing this book, the CJEU has adopted 30 judgements on preliminary ruling cases regarding the concept of CtoP in reference to Article 3 in InfoSoc Directive and Article 8 of the Rental and Lending Directive. Figure 3.3 shows all the CJEU judgements regarding those two provisions being requested for interpretation. The systematisation of the figure is presented by the date of the decision and displays the different rights involved, the criteria used by the Court to determine the existence of an act of CtoP, if the case refers to a primary or a secondary act of communication, a

[38] CJEU Judgment of 15 Mar 2012, para. 55.

[39] Ibid. para. 70–71.

[40] CJEU Judgment of 16 Feb 2017, *Verwertungsgesellschaft Rundfunk*, C-641/15, *ECLI:EU:C:2017:131*.para. 21.

Date	Preliminary rulings	EU Law provision	Rigth	Interpretation Criteria	Primary / Secondary communic.	Main proceding facts	CJEU Judgement	Copyright field
7.12.06	Judgment of 7 Dec 2006, C-306/05 (SGAE v Rafael Hotels)	Art. 3(1) Infosoc Directive	CtoP + MA	CtoP/ Public / profit / knowledge /	Secondary	TV sets on hotels rooms constitute CtoP	Transmission of signal on TV sets on hotels rooms is CtoP	AV
18.3.10	Order of 18 Mar 2010, C-136/09 (Sillogikis)	Art. 3(1) Infosoc Directive	CtoP	CtoP	Secondary	TV sets on hotels rooms constitute CtoP	Confirms C-306/05 judgement	AV
4.10.11	Judgment of 4 Oct 2011, C-403/08 (Premier League)	Art. 3(1) Infosoc Directive	Cto P	CtoP/ Public / profit / knowledge /	Secondary	Transmission of sports broadcast on a TV in a space open to the public	Transmission of broadcast works to cutomers in a bar is CtoP	BROADCAST
24.11.11	Judgment of 24 Nov 2011, C-283/10 (Circul Globus)	Art. 3(1) Infosoc Directive	CtoP	CtoP / Public	Primary	Performance of musical works in a live Public Performance	If the Public is present it can't be considered CtoP	MUSIC
7.3.13	Judgment of 07 Mar 2013, C-607/11 (TVCatchup V ITV BROADCASTING)	Art. 3(1) Infosoc Directive	CtoP	CtoP / Technical means	Secondary	Online Live streaming of commercial television free-to-air broadcasts	An organisation and technical means different from the original broadcaster's primary communication, is a new act of CtoP	BROADCAST
15.3.12	Judgment of 15 Mar 2012, C-135/10 (SCF v. Del Corso)	Art. 3(1) Infosoc Directive + Art. 8(2) R&L Directive	CtoP	CtoP/ Public / profit / knowledge /	Secondary	display of phonograms in a dental practice by radio as background music	No CtoP because ther is no large public, neither benefit for the primary user nor any active choice from the patient.	MUSIC
15.3.12	Judgment of 15 Mar 2012, C-162/10 (Phonographic Performance)	Art. 8 (2) R&L Directive	CtoP	CtoP/ Public / profit / knowledge /	Secondary	Nacional law sets an exeption for devices to play phonograms installed in hotel rooms	National legislation cannot set exceptions to exclude the CtoP; An hotel operator is a 'user' making a CtoP of a phonogram	MUSIC
13.2.14	Judgment of 13 Feb 2014, C-466/12 (Svensson)	Art. 3(1) Infosoc Directive	CtoP	CtoP / Public	Secondary	Internet links giving access to protected work	Website links to works freely available on another website does not constitute an act of CtoP, as there is no new public	PRESS
27.2.14	Judgment of 27 Feb 2014, C-351/12 (OSA)	Art. 3(1) Infosoc Directive	CtoP	CtoP / Public	Secondary	Transmission of works in a spa establishment by radio and TV sets in patients rooms	National legislation cannot set exceptions to exclude the CtoP acts by a spa establishment which is a business	MUSIC / AV
21.10.14	Order of 21 Oct 2014, C-348/13 (BestWater International)	Art. 3(1) Infosoc Directive	CtoP	Technical means / New Public	Secondary	Internet links giving access to free available protected works using the 'framing'	A work is not transmitted to a new public nor using a different technical means from the ones used of the original communication.	AV
26.3.15	Judgment of 26 Mar 2015, C-279/13 (C More)	Art. 3(2) Infosoc Directive + Art. 8(3) R&L Directive	MA	CtoP / Public	Secondary	Online links to sports broadcast free of payment	Is a CtoP as Member states may offer further protection for bradcastes as it does not undermine the protection of copyright.	BROADCAST
14.6.15	Order of 14 Jul 2015, C-151/15 (Sociedade Portuguesa de Autores)	Art. 3(1) Infosoc Directive	CtoP	CtoP / Public	Secondary	Play radio in a cafè via loudspeakers	Constitutes a CtoP as works are communicated to a new public	MUSIC
19.11.15	Judgment of 19 Nov 2015, C-325/14 (SABAM v SBS Belgium)	Art. 3(1) Infosoc Directive	CtoP	CtoP / Public	Primary	TV programmes transmitted via direct injection (point to point)	Not communication to public from broadcaster to individual distributors without potential viewers .	AV
31.5.16	Judgment of 31 May 2016, C-117/15 (Reha Training)	Art. 3(1) Infosoc Directive + Art. 8(2) R&L Directive	CtoP	CtoP/ Public / new public / profit / knowledge /	Secondary	making available of TV broadcasts by means of TV sets in a rehabilitation centre	Constitutes a CtoP, since the number of persons is not insignificant it constitutes a 'new public'	AV
8.9.16	Judgment of 8 Sep 2016, C-160/15 (GS Media)	Art. 3(1) Infosoc Directive	CtoP / MA	CtoP/ Public / new public / profit / knowledge / Technical means	Secondary	posting, on a website, hyperlinks to protected works, freely available on another website, without consent,	Constitutes a CtoP if there is financial gain, so the knowledge of the illegal nature of the publication of those works by the user must be presumed.	PHOTO
16.2.17	Judgment of 16 Feb 2017, C-641/15 (Verwertungsgesellschaft Rundfunk)	Art. 8(3) R&L Directive	CtoP	CtoP	Secondary	Communication of broadcasts by means of TV sets in hotel rooms.	the communication to the public of TV and radio broadcasts by means of TV and radio sets installed in hotel rooms does not fall within the scope of the exclusive right of broadcasting organisations, as tue price of the hotel room can't be considered as an entrance fee	BROADCAST
26.4.17	Judgment of 26 Apr 2017, C-527/15 (Stichting Brein)	Art. 3(1) Infosoc Directive	CtoP / MA	CtoP/ Public / new public / profit / knowledge / Technical means	Secondary	multimedia player with hyperlinks to websites on which copyright-protected works arel available without the consent of the copyright holders.	The concept CtoP includes the sale of the ultimedia player with pre-installed add-ons containing hyperlinks to freely accessible websites copyright-protected works have been made available to the public without the consent of the right holders.	AV
16.3.17	Judgment of 16 Mar 2017, C-138/16 (AKM)	Art. 3(1) Infosoc Directive	CtoP	CtoP / Technical means / Public	Secondary	Simultaneos rebroadcasting of national broadcaster by comunal antena tv	simultaneous and unaltered transmission of national broadcasting doesn't need authorisation from the author, provided that it is merely a diferent technical means of communication, but not a new CtoP	AV
14.6.17	Judgment of 14 Jun 2017, C-610/15 (Ziggo / 'The Pirate Bay')	Art. 3(1) Infosoc Directive	CtoP / MA	CtoP/ Public / new public / knowledge / Technical means	Secondary	peer-to-peer platform costitutes an act of CtoP or as intermediary	A sharing platform which, allows users of that platform to locate protected works and to share them in a P2P context constitutes CtoP	AV/MUSIC
29.11.17	Judgment of 29 Nov 2017, C-265/16 (VCAST)	Art. 3(1) Infosoc Directive	CtoP	Technical means / new public	Primary / Secondary	computer system actively provides remote recording and cloud service for private copies of works protected	Constitutes a CtoP as original transmission and that made by the service provider are made under different and specific technical means and are intended for 'new public'	AV
7.8.18	Judgment of 7 Aug 2018, C-161/17 (Renckhoff)	Art. 3(1) Infosoc Directive	CtoP	CtoP /New public	Primary / Secondary	Post content taken from a website	Is CtoP when there is new comunication, as it is communicated to a new public	PHOTO
14.11.19	Judgment of 14 Nov 2019, C-484/18 (Spedidam)	Art. 3(2)(a)Infosoc Directive	MA	MA	Secondary	National scheme exempting a public institution for promotion of the national audiovisual heritage from obtaining the performer's written consent rights	There is no MA or CtoP, since the presumption that the performer has authorised the fixation and exploitation of his performances, so that it may be broadcast.	MUSIC + AV
19.12.19	Judgment of 19 Dec 2019, C-263/18 (Tom Kabinet)	Art. 3(1) Infosoc Directive	CtoP / MA / Distrib.	CtoP/ Public / new public / knowledge /	Secondary	virtual market of second hand ebooks, by downloading them for permanent use	is covered by 'making available' to the public works in such a way that the public may access the ebooks from a place and at a time individually chosen by them'	eBOOKS
2.4.20	Judgment of 2 Apr 2020, C-753/18 (Stim and SAMI)	Art. 3(1) Infosoc Directive + Art. 8(2) R&L Directive	CtoP	CtoP/ Public / new public	Secondary	Service hiring out cars with radio reciever sytems installed	the hiring out of motor vehicles equipped with radio receivers does not constitute a CtoP	MUSIC
28.10.20	Judgment of 28 Oct 2020, C-637/19 (BY)	Art. 3(1) Infosoc Directive	CtoP	Public	Secondary	Transmission as court evidence	Court is not considered "Public"	PHOTO
18.11.20	Judgment of 18 Nov 2020, C-147/19 (Atresmedia Corporación de Medios de Comunicación)	Art. 8 (2) R&L Directive	CtoP	CtoP	Secondary	Broadcasting AV recording containing the fixation of an AV work in which a phonogram has been incorporated.	phonograms incorporated to AV are not an independent works anymore, so there is no new CtoP and no single equitable remuneration	MUSIC + AV
9.3.21	Judgment of 9 Mar 2021, C-392/19 (VG Bild-Kunst)	Art. 3(1) Infosoc Directive	CtoP	CtoP/ Public / new public / Technical means	Secondary	Embedding, by the process of framing, in a third party's website, of a freely available copyright-protected work	embedding by framing in a website is an act of CtoP if that embedding circumvents measures imposed by the copyright holder to provide protection from framing	BOOKS
17.6.21	Judgment of 17 Jun 2021, C-597/19 (M.I.C.M. Mircom International Content Management & Consulting)	Art. 3(1) and (2) Infosoc Directive	MA	CtoP/ Public / new public / knowledge /	Primary / Secondary	Share, on a P2P network by BitTorrent protocol, pieces of files containing protected films	even though those pieces are unsable in themselves this action constitutes an act of making available to the public	AV
22.6.21	Judgment of 22 Jun 2021, C-682/18 (YouTube / Cyando)	Art. 3(1) Infosoc Directive	CtoP	CtoP	Primary / Secondary	Liability of the operator for infringements of intellectual property rights by users of its platform	video-sharing platform or a file-hosting and -sharing platform, on which users can illegally make protected content available to the public, does not make a CtoP, if is a 'mere conduit'	MUSIC / BOOKS
20.4.23	Judgment of 20 April 2023, Joined Cases C-775/21 and C-826/21 (Blue Air Aviation/ADA)	Art. 3(1) Infosoc Directive	CtoP / MA	CtoP/ Public / profit / knowledge /	Primary / Secondary	Broadcasting of background music in public transport	broadcasting, in a means of passenger transport, of a musical work as background music constitutes a CtoP, but not the mere presensce or installation of equipment or software.	MUSIC
Date	Preliminary rulings	EU Law provision	Rigth	Interpretation Criteria	Primary / Secondary communic.	Main proceding facts	CJEU Judgement	Copyright field

Fig. 3.3 CJEU judgements regarding communication to the public right. Source: Author's elaboration

brief description of main proceeding facts and the CJEU judgement, as well as the copyright related-matter.

The first judgement of the CJEU on the interpretation of the concept of CtoP in the meaning of Article 3(1) of the InfoSoc Directive was on 2006, and since the date of the end of writing this book, the Court has pronounced 30 judgements. Twelve of these cases are related to internet or digital issues, being the Svenson case[41] in 2014 the first judgement dealing with digital acts of communication to the public, particularly by providing access to protected works using the technique of linking from a website to another. Justin Koo[42] divides the case law in two phases: the *pre-Svensson* cases, with a reasoning based on traditional analogical ways of transmissions and broadcasting, and *post-Svensson* or Internet cases, with a difference approach of the criteria used by the CJEU to interpret the legal provisions.

It can be noticed that a number of cases related to the 'making available' right increased with the digital transmissions, mainly for the rise of interactive on-demand transmissions, which are more specifically acts of making available to the public rather than direct communication to the public. Finally, it highlights that most of the cases referred to the Court were asking for an interpretation of secondary acts of communication rather than primary acts, which indicates two things: on one hand, the difficulty to determine a secondary act of communication, and on the other hand that a larger number of infringements take place in secondary acts of communication, either because those secondary acts of communication are more common or because users ignore the liability or their action and even that they are making an act of communication.

For the delimitation of the CtoP concept, there is a starting point in Case *SGAE v Rafael Hotels* (C-306/05) in which the Court pointed out two important issues: the lack of definition of a concept of CtoP in the EU legislation[43] and the need for uniform application of Community law without any express reference to the law of the Member States to determine the meaning and scope of the European legislation, which must be given an autonomous and uniform interpretation.[44] Such lack of legal definition and need for uniformity led the CJEU to develop certain criteria to determine whether an act constitutes "CtoP" within the meaning of the EU legislation or not.

The criteria set up in *Rafael Hotels* in 2006 have evolved in different manners since such attempts to define the "CtoP" term by the European judiciary. The evolution of the criteria became necessary as per the evolution of the new ways to transmit and communicate content online. This is to say, the new digital businesses have brought not only innovative forms of communicating musical works but also

---

41 CJEU Judgment of 13 Feb 2014, Svensson, C-466/12, ECLI:EU:C:2014:76.

42 Koo (2020), p. 106.

43 CJEU Judgment of 7 Dec 2006, *SGAE v Rafael Hotels, C-306/05, ECLI:EU:C:2006:764.*, para. 33.

44 Ibid. para. 31.

reshaped the established criteria in 2006, being the *Svensson* case,[45] the first judgement of the court on CtoP on the Internet. The following paragraphs review the evolution of the different jurisprudential criteria to identify acts of CtoP under the EU law.

Professor Justin Koo[46] divides the CJEU criteria to determine the CtoP into three core ones: (i) Communication, which is made to (ii) a public and the (iii) a new public that will constitute CtoP in retransmissions or rebroadcasting. However, these three core criteria are redundant, as the need for a "new public" is a part of the conceptualisation of the term "public". The criteria developed by the CJEU are based into the two[47] main ideas offered by the language of the term "Communication to the Public" itself: (i) what represents an act of communication and (ii) what shall be considered as "the public". From such basis, the Court has been providing with additional criteria to determine an act of communication to the public; in *Del Corso's* judgement, the Court indicated that to assess whether a user is making a communication to the public 'account must be taken of several complementary criteria, which are not autonomous and are interdependent'.[48] Those complementary criteria are (i) *the role of the user* and the deliberate nature of its intervention, in full knowledge of the consequences of its action by giving access to the public to a protected work; (ii) the *profit-making nature* of the act of communication to the public, maybe a relevant but not a necessary criterion; (iii) the existence of a *´new public´*, different from the public that the primary communication was directed to (iv) and in absence of new public the '*technical means'* used to communicate the work to the public need to be taken into account. The court declared that those criteria ´must be applied individually and in their interaction with one another, given that they may, in different situations, be present to widely varying degrees.[49] However, the last two criteria, mainly the 'new public' criterion, have been undermined and strongly criticised by some relevant authors, like professors Ficsor, Hugenholtz or Rosati.[50] Figure 3.4 shows how each of those complementary criteria are independent but closely linked to one of the two main criteria, either to help to identify what is an ´act of communication´ or to facilitate a definition of ´the public´.

As announced before, all those criteria have not remained immutable but became dynamic, especially since the digital communication and the online services came in, presenting new forms of communication and, therefore, new acts that may result in an infringement. Such dynamism generated the CJEU jurisprudence on CtoP, which

---

[45] CJEU Judgment of 13 Feb 2014.

[46] Koo (2021).

[47] CJEU Judgment of 26 Apr 2017, *Filmspeler, C-527/15, ECLI:EU:C:2017:300.* para. 19. See also CJEU Judgment of 31 May 2016, *Reha Training, C-117/15, ECLI:EU:C:2016:379.* para. 37.

[48] CJEU Judgment of 15 Mar 2012, paras. 79–81.

[49] CJEU judgment of 15 March 2012, *Phonographic Performance (Ireland), C-162/10, EU:C:2012:141*ECJ. para. 30; See also CJEU Judgment of 31 May 2016, *Reha Training, C-117/15, ECLI:EU:C:2016:379.* para. 35.

[50] See Ficsor (2020), p. 81.

See also Hugenholtz and van Velze (2016), p. 797, Rosati (2020).

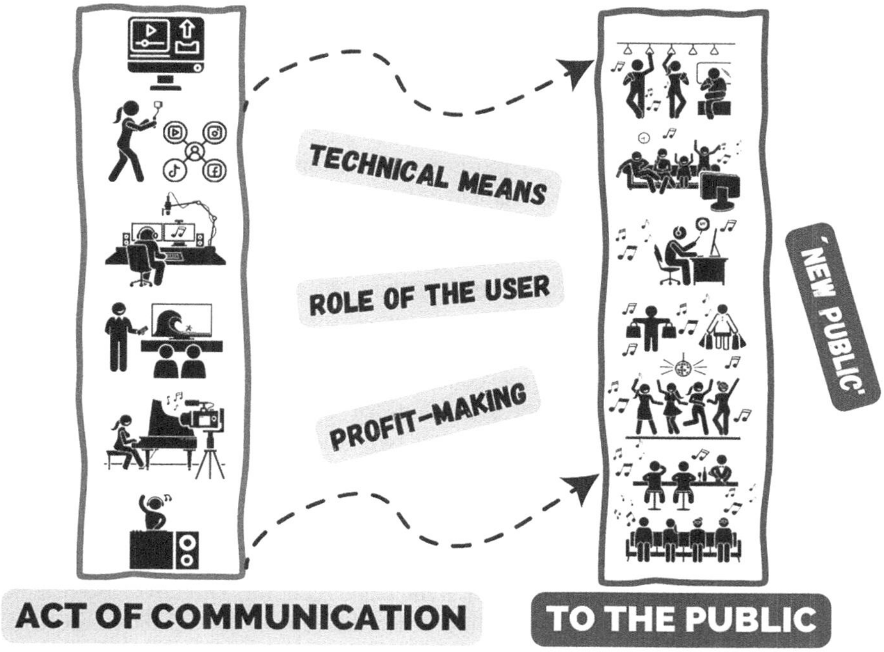

Fig. 3.4 CJEU criteria to determine when an act constitutes a 'communication to the public' in terms of EU legislation. Source: Author's elaboration

led to a certain inconsistency between the different judgements somehow. With the aim to define the concept of CtoP, in the following lines, each one of those criteria, main and complementary, are assessed throughout an analysis of the CJEU caselaw and based on those relevant cases that define each criteria in a clear way to be compatible to acts of communication of online music.

3.2.1 Which Acts Constitute a 'Communication'?

A description of what constitutes an act of communication has been present in most of the cases of the CJEU copyright caselaw in that matter. Although the term ´ communication to the public´ should be commonly understood, courts have not been clear in determining the existence of an infringement when someone exploits a work by disseminating it to many different individuals. The CJEU has not developed a consistent,[51] unique and immutable criteria. As shown in the previous section, the definition of 'communication' in Article 3 of the InfoSoc Directive refers to those

[51] Angelopoulos (2021), p. 195.

communication acts that involve wire and wireless means as well as the making available to the public. As it was said, Article 8(2) of the R&L Directive also rules on the concept of CtoP. The CJEU has declared that Article 3(1) of Directive 2001/29 must be applied without prejudice to the application of Article 8(2) of Directive 2006/115. Furthermore, the Court understands that the concept of 'communication to the public' for the purposes of those two provisions must be given a uniform interpretation because of the requirements of unity and coherence of the European Union legal order, unless the EU legislature has, in a specific legislative context, expressed a different intention.[52] However, as assessed before, the CJEU recognised that the concept of 'communication to the public' appearing in those provisions is used in contexts which are not the same and pursue objectives which, while similar, are, however, in part divergent. Even though the CJEU sees no evidence that the EU legislature wished to confer on the concept of 'communication to the public' a different meaning in the respective contexts of Directives 2001/29 and 2006/115.[53] Hence, the applicability of one of such two provisions depends on the context since the meaning of the concept of CtoP is uniform in both. This equivalence is shown in the judgement *C-135/10 Del Corso,*[54] where the CJEU reformulated the question presented by the national referring court in the preliminary ruling process, which was asking on the interpretation of Article 3(1) of the InfoSoc Directive, and the CJEU led it to the Article 8(2) of Rental and Lending Directive. Both legal provisions must be interpreted according to Recital (23) of the InfoSoc Directive, assessed in the previous section.

Some authors, like Justin Koo, consider two different interpretation approaches of the term communication: the access approach and the transmission approach. The access approach refers to the interpretation given in SGAE case when referring to an act of communication, the fact to facilitate or provide access to a protected work. On the other hand, the transmission approach focuses on the active action of transmitting a work, not just the mere fact of making the work available to a public. More than a different approach of the same communication act, I personally consider that such difference responds to the dual nature of the communication to the public. As assessed in previous sections, the communication to the public includes the making available as part of such communication. Thus, both access and transmission approaches only respond to the same right of CtoP, either run by giving access to works as an act of making available or by an active transmission of such, as an act of communication itself. In its judgement of 4 October 2011 on *Football Association Premier League* case, the CJEU first defined the concept of communication as "any

[52] CJEU Judgment of 4 Oct 2011, *Premier League, C-403/08, ECLI:EU:C:2011:631*, para. 28 and 188.

[53] CJEU Judgment of 31 May 2016, *Reha Training, C-117/15, ECLI:EU:C:2016:379*. para. 29–31.

[54] CJEU Judgment of 15 Mar 2012, *SCF v Del Corso, C-135/10, ECLI:EU:C:2012:140,* para. 18. The applicable R&L Directive by the date of *Del Corso* case, was Directive 92/100. After the codification in the Directive 2006/115/EC the text and numbering in Article 8 remains the same in both directives. See Annex II in Directive 2006/115/EC.

transmission of the protected works, irrespective of the technical means or process used".[55]

One month later, the court, on *Circul Globus case,* set the difference between the concepts of 'communication to the public' and 'public performance'. The CJEU re*defined* an ´act of communication´ as:

> any transmission or retransmission of a work to a public not present at the place where the communication originates, excluding any act communication of a work which is carried out directly in a place open to the public using any means of public performance or direct presentation of the work.[56]

Both definitions refer to analogical situations, as satellite, cable, or other analogical transmissions. It is not until 2014, with the Svensson case, that the CJEU pronounced the first judgements on digital transmissions, or acts of communications on the Internet, specifically a website containing internet links giving access to protected work in another website. Although the way of communicating the different works on the Internet is rather different than the analogical method, the CJEU remains using the same criteria. The criteria for acts of 'communication' or 'making available' have not evolved very differently from the classical judgements.

The single criteria of determining a 'communication' remains referring to any transmission of works by wire o wireless means, but regarding digital acts of communication, the CJEU has been dealing with two main issues: (i) shaping whether the transmission of digital works embodies an act of making available or an act of reproduction or distribution of copies and (ii) determining the cases when using linking techniques to have access to a protected works represents an act of communication.

The CJEU took a holistic approach to solve the matter of distinction between 'communication to the public' and 'reproduction' rights when a work is transmitted digitally. The CJEU approach focuses on the final and most significant use to determine whether an act corresponds to one right or to another or both. The court 'merges' the acts instead of analysing formalistically each separate act of the user formally and emphasises the highly relevant right instead of the accumulation of several rights.[57] A digital copy of the work needs to be done to make it available thereof to communicate it to the public, so the transmission of the work is the relevant act for the CJEU, while the act of reproduction is just an instrument to communicate. This approach is clear in *Renckhoff* judgment, but it is in Tom Cabinet case where the CJEU refers to the explanatory memorandum in the proposal for the InfoSoc Directive to justify its approach. The CJEU quotes the European Commission text of the explanatory memorandum in the proposal, which aims 'to provide for a coherent level playing field for the electronic and tangible distribution of protected material and to draw a clear line between them'.[58] The CJEU recalls that the

---

[55] CJEU Judgment of 4 Oct 2011. para. 193.

[56] CJEU Judgment of 24 Nov 2011. para. 40–41.

[57] Synodinou (2018).

[58] CJEU Judgment of 19 Dec 2019, *Tom Kabinet, C-263/18, ECLI:EU:C:2019:1111.* Para. 43.

Commission pointed out that the Internet offered new forms of exploitation of works, like interactive on-demand transmissions, and reminds that those on-demand transmissions should be covered by the communication to the public right instead of by the distribution right, which applies exclusively to the distribution of physical copies, but does not cover digital transmission. The CJEU, following the Commission memorandum, clarifies that the term 'communication to the public' also applies when "members of the public may have individual access, from different places and at different times, to a work which is on a publicly accessible website, while making clear that that right covers any communication 'other than the distribution of physical copies', since physical copies which can be put into circulation as tangible objects are covered by the distribution right".[59] Although the CJEU refers to the CtoP right on its definition given of 'on-demand transmissions, it should indicate the 'making available right'; more specifically, granting it is included as part of the generic concept of CtoP. No difference is made between if such transmission of works needs to be temporary, such as streaming services, or if it also includes permanent transmissions or transmissions for permanent use, like is the downloading services, as the Tom Kabinet referred case.[60] The CJEU concludes that any communication to the public of a work, other than the distribution of physical copies of the work, should be covered by the term of 'communication to the public' within the meaning of Article 3(1) of the Directive but not by the concept of 'distribution to the public', referred to in Article 4(1) of Directive 2001/29.[61] Accordingly, the concept of 'communication' also includes any digital transmission or making available of works, including streaming or downloading digital files. However, the relevance of this CJEU delimitation entitles the prohibition of the principle of exhaustion in digital transmissions, according to the Article 3.3. of the InfoSoc Directive. Therefore, the CtoP concept carries the fact that the right of communicating and making available to the public of those shall not be exhausted by any digital transmission since are considered acts of communication to the public or making available to the public.

In contrast, the issue of linking or hyperlinks has been treated in a separated manner by the CJEU case law. As Professor Tatiana Synodinou[62] explains, the CJEU's methodology has been based on the interpretative principle of individual assessment. That is, to determine the existence of an act of communication when

[59] Ibid, para. 44.

[60] Mr. Tom Kabinet operated a website offering a virtual market for 'second-hand' e-books, some of them were donated free of charge by members who provided the download link of the book and had to declare that they have not kept a copy of the book. Then the e-book was uploaded from the retailer's website and placed Tom Kabinets' own digital watermark on it, as confirmation that it was a legally acquired copy. See paragraphs 20–29 of the Judgement *C-263/18*.

[61] CJEU Judgment of 19 Dec 2019.

[62] Synodinou. Tatiana (2021) "Framing" the right of communication to the public: the CJEU's decision on the VG Kunst case – Kluwer Copyright Blog. In: Kluwer Copyr. Blog. http://copyrightblog.kluweriplaw.com/2021/03/15/framing-the-right-of-communication-to-the-public-the-cjeus-decision-on-the-vg-kunst-case/.

using the different techniques of digital linking, the concept 'of communication to the public must be tailored to the individual case regarding.

Up to this point the concept 'communication', within the meaning of EU legislation and CJEU caselaw, can be defined as Any transmission or retransmission of works, by wire or wireless means, to a public not present at the place where the communication originates, including the transmission or making available of digital works or their copies. Nevertheless, this definition is incomplete to determine when an act constitutes a CtoP, as it has been assessed, for instance, in the hyperlinking cases in which the CJEU advised that such cases need an individual approach. Only with the previously set conception of 'communication' many acts or situations keep being uncertain regarding if its nature falls under the scope of the definition in the EU legislation. For that reason, it was necessary for the Court to develop complementary criteria to specify when an action should be considered as act of 'communication the public'.

Before describing the conception of 'public,' as the other main criteria to determine the scope of "communication to the public" right, the following lines assess the two additional criteria linked to the conception of an 'act of communication'. These are the 'role of the user', who runs the communication, and the 'profit-making' nature of the acts of communication.

The Role of the User

The importance of the role of the user who makes a communication to a public possible has been pointed out since the first CJEU decisions on the right of communication to the public. Although the level of interaction or degree of the role of the user has not been configurated equally in all the judgements, what remains immutable is the importance of the intervention of the user itself, either active or passive. In *SGAE* case, the CJEU ruled that hotel proprietor carries out an act of communication "when he gives his customers access to the broadcast works via television sets, by distributing in the hotel rooms, with full knowledge of the position, the signal received carrying the protected works".[63] In *Premier League* case the Court made clear the importance of the role of the user, who intentionally gives the access to a broadcast containing protected works and without whose intervention the public would not have been able to the works.[64] So, here, the role of the user is an active role; his intervention is essential to facilitate the transmission and consequently run a communication to the public act. In Reha training case, the Court reviews the indispensable role of the user. It summarises that 'in order for there to be a communication to the public, that user must, in full knowledge of the consequences of its actions, give access to the protected work to an additional public and that it appears thereby that, in the absence of that intervention those 'new' viewers are unable to enjoy the works, although physically within the broadcast's catchment area [...] Thus, the Court has already held that the operators of a

[63] CJEU Judgment of 7 Dec 2006. para. 42.

[64] CJEU Judgment of 4 Oct 2011. para. 195.

café-restaurant, a hotel or a spa establishment are such users and make a communication to the public if they intentionally broadcast protected works to their clientele, by intentionally distributing a signal by means of television or radio sets that they have installed in their establishment".[65] According to that, we could describe the additional criterion of role of the user as there is a communication to the public when the intervention of the user in crucial to communicate the content, either by running the transmission himself or just by giving the public access to the protected works, in the sense that without the user intervention, such communication would not have taken place. This approach works for most of the analogical cases. Still, it is incomplete regarding digital communications, concerning in sharing links that lead to other sites where the protected works are accessible, especially in links or files shared in peer-to-peer platforms. The Court announced that the provision of clickable links to protected works must be considered to be 'making available' and, therefore, an 'act of communication' in *Svensson's*[66] case. However, in this judgement, the Court finally rejected the nature of an act of communication to the public within the meaning of Article 3 (1) of the InfoSoc Directive as the works were already freely available on the Internet, and due to the lack of a 'new public' (criterion that will be analysed hereafter). Following the approach of 'the role of the user' made in *Svensson*, all the linking acts would be potential acts of communication but wouldn't fulfil the requirement communicating to a public as the works have already been made available on the Internet. Thus, all the linking cases would escape from the right of CtoP. Fifteen years after the *Svensson* judgement, the CJEU in *VG Bild-Kunst* case[67] amended its approach on do not consider linking as an act of communication to the public since the works are already available and there is no communication to a new public. In 2021, the technology and linking practices have evolved in many different techniques. However, the Court has rejected to make a distinction between the different linking methods when assessing the communication to the public cases, even though the AG Szpunar, in his opinion on the VG Bild-Kunst case,[68] clearly explained and made a systematisation of the different linking techniques, being critique with the Court approach of linking cases and suggesting to evaluate the linking cases taking into account each linking technique used for acts of communication.[69]

However, previously, in 2016, in the *GS Media* case, the CJEU reshaped the criterion of the 'role of the user' by introducing the non-presumption of knowledge. The Court stated that when making a work available to the public by providing

[65] CJEU Judgment of 31 May 2016. para. 46–47. See also, to that effect, judgment of 7 December 2006 in *SGAE*, C-306/05, *ECLI:EU:C:2006:764*, para. 42 and 47; judgment of 4 October 2011, para. 196; and judgment 27 February 2014, *OSA*, C-351/12, *ECLI:EU:C:2014:110*, para. 26).

[66] CJEU Judgment of 13 Feb 2014. para. 18–23.

[67] CJEU Judgment of 10 September 2021, Case C-392/19, VG Bild-Kunst v Stiftung Preußischer Kulturbesitz, ECLI:EU:C:2020:696.

[68] Opinion of Advocate General Szpunar delivered on 10 September 2020.VG Bild-Kunst v Stiftung Preußischer Kulturbesitz. Case C-392/19, ECLI:EU:C:2020:696.

[69] For further discussion see Padrós Reig (2022).

internet users with direct links to access to the work freely available on another website, it is needed to take account of whether the user who provides such links does or does not know and cannot reasonably know, that the work had been published on the internet with or without the consent of the copyright holder. So the user that provides the hyperlinks "does not, as a general rule, intervene in full knowledge of the consequences of his conduct in order to give customers access to a work illegally posted on the internet. In addition, where the work in question was already available with unrestricted access on the website to which the hyperlink provides access, all internet users could, in principle, already have access to it even in the absence of that intervention. Consequently, if the user providing the link 'knew or ought to have known that the hyperlink he posted provides access to a work illegally placed on the internet, then the provision of that link constitutes a 'communication to the public' within the meaning of Article 3(1) of Directive 2001/29.[70]" Accordingly, the criterion of 'role of the user' has a double dimension: the existence of an essential intervention of the user in providing the public access to a work, as well as the consideration of whether the user has or should reasonably have full knowledge of the consequences of his action, regarding the legality of the content linked to.

'Profit Making'

The CJEU set in SGAE case that even the "pursuit of profit is not a necessary condition for the existence of a communication to the public",[71] the profit-making nature of a communication is not irrelevant. Such a profit-making nature does not only mean the existence of a fee or price for having access to the communication but an indirect financial gain. This point of indirect profit-making nature was described by the Court in Premier League as the "transmission in question has an effect upon the number of people going to [an] establishment and, ultimately, on its financial results".[72] That is, the act of communication has an attractive effect on the people, that is an added value. In *Reha Training* case, the Court explained that if the act of communication constitutes the supply of additional services, different from the main activity of the communicating user, it has an impact on the establishment's standing and attractiveness, thereby giving it a competitive advantage,[73] thus the communication carries a profit-making nature.

The 'profit making' criterion has been used in a different sense in digital cases by the CJEU. In analogical cases, it is pictured as an additional evidence of the existence of an act of communication. Contrary in digital cases, the profit-making criterion is closely connected to the knowledge criterion. In GS Media case, the Court stated that the lucrative aspect of the communication creates a presumption of

[70] CJEU Judgment of 8 Sep 2016, GS Media, C-160/15, ECLI:EU:C:2016:644. para. 46–49.

[71] CJEU Judgment of 7 Dec 2006. para. 44.

[72] CJEU Judgment of 4 Oct 2011. para. 205–206.

[73] CJEU Judgment of 31 May 2016. para. 49–52 and 63.

full knowledge of the possible illegal nature of the communication.[74] Where the posting of a link is carried out for profit, it creates the presumption that the person who posted the link knew or ought to have known that the link provides access to a work published on the internet illegally. In which case, the person who posted the link should ensure that the work to which that hyperlink leads is not published illegally. This approach of the 'profit making' criterion has been used in other digital cases following GS Media in cases like *Stichting Brein(Filmspeler)*[75] or Zigo (Pirate Bay). However, the CJEU in Youtube/Cyando case declared that the presumption created in GS Media is not comparable to that of the operator of a video-sharing platform or of a file-hosting and -sharing platform, as the platforms act as intermediaries and do not post the link by themselves thus such interpretation cannot be transposed. The Court states that the mere fact that the operator of a content -hosting/-sharing platform has the aim of making a profit "neither establishes that its intervention in the illegal communication of protected content by some of the users of that platform was deliberate nor gives rise to an presumption that that is the case. The fact that it provides information society services for profit does not mean in any way that the provider of such services consents to their being used by third parties to infringe copyright."[76] Although at the date of the judgement, the liability of intermediaries had changed after the new CDSM Directive got into force, the variation in the aforementioned approach of the 'profit-making' criterion was still done under the InfoSoc Directive scope. Under the new directive, it seems that there is no room for such interpretation of the profit-making criterion regarding the content sharing platforms.

3.2.2 *Who Is the 'Public'?*

When the EU copyright legislation refers to the 'communication to the public,' neither describes the term "public". Who constitutes the 'public, how many people need to b recipient of the communication to consider that an act is being communicated to the public are unanswered questions by the legislator that had been clarified by the CJEU case law. In the early judgement SGAE, the court considered as "public" the hotel guests, and potential guests, that have access to works through the TV and radio devices installed in the hotel rooms to determine the existence of an act of 'communication to the public'. In such case, the term 'public' was defined as "an indeterminate number of potential listeners" and "a fairly large number of persons". But both concepts 'indeterminate' and 'fairly large' are vague terms themselves, and consequently, they had to be clarified by the court later. In In

74 CJEU Judgment of 8 Sep 2016. para. 51–54.

75 CJEU Judgment of 26 Apr 2017. para. 49.

76 CJEU Judgment of 22 Jun 2021, YouTube/Cyando, C-682/18, ECLI:EU:C:2021:503. Para. 85–89.

contrast to SGAE case, in the judgement *del Corso*, the CJEU determined that broadcasting of music in a dental practice for the benefit of the patients present and not interactive on-demand transmission cannot be considered as an act of communication to the public, due to the potential listeners are a very consistent group of persons that constitute a determinate circle of potential recipients,[77] so cannot be considered as public.

To reach its decision, the Court defines the terms used in SGAE judgement; 'indeterminate' and 'a fairly large number of people'. To clarify the concept 'indeterminate' nature of the public, the Court recalls the definition of the concept of 'communication to the public' given by the WIPO glossary. Accordingly, CtoP means 'making a work … perceptible in any appropriate manner to persons in general, that is, not restricted to specific individuals belonging to a private group'.[78] Thus, the term 'public' refers to a generality of people not part of a private or restricted group. In Recital 86, the CJEU defines the criterion of 'a fairly large number of people as "a certain *de minimis* threshold, which excludes from the concept groups of persons which are too small, or insignificant". The CJEU continues its judgement, explaining how to determine the number of people to be considered as public. The Court took account of "the cumulative effect of making works available to potential audience" being relevant to know how many persons have access to the same work at the same time but also to know how many of them have access to it in succession.[79]

The CJEU uses an additional element, or a precondition, to shape the concept the 'public' as a targeted group of people: the 'accidental' access'. The Court defines the public, which is the subject of the communication in these establishments, is not merely 'caught' by chance but is targeted by their operators.[80] This means that if there is no active choice on the public's part and their access or listening to the works is 'accidental', therefore cannot be considered as 'public'. Following the CJEU line, it could be stated that the communication of protected phonograms made either by professionals in their private practice or by small businesses where a limited group of clients become "accidental" listeners does not constitute a communication to the public.

Regarding Internet cases, the concept 'public' as an indeterminate and fairly large number of recipients becomes even more ethereal. In those cases, almost anyone with Internet connection can have access to protected works shared online. Thus, the public turns out to be all Internet users.

However, the CJEU, already in SGAE case, elaborated a sub-criterion to determine when an act of communication infringes the copyright protected in the legal provisions: the 'new public' criterion. Such criterion has been present in CJEU judgements since then, despite the strong criticism received from the literature.

[77] CJEU Judgment of 15 Mar 2012, SCF v Del Corso, C-135/10, ECLI:EU:C:2012:140. para. 95.
[78] Ibid. para. 85.
[79] CJEU Judgment of 15 Mar 2012, para. 87.
[80] Ibid. para. 48.

Likewise, the CJEU has also used the criterion of new 'technical means', especially in those cases where the 'new public' criterion was not met. The following lines explain those two additional the criteria and asses the different theories that challenge both of them.

New Public and Technical Means

As mentioned above, the Court in SGAE set the 'new public' criterion to shape the existence of an act of communication to the public when a transmission "is made to a public different from the public at which the original act of communication of the work is directed, that is, to a new public". The CJEU, in its section [41] of the same judgement, referred to the Guide to the Berne Convention as an interpretative document drawn up by the WIPO to build up the 'new public criterion'. The Court reasoning is based on the interpretation made in such a guide of the Article 11bis of the convention, that sets whether a reception is for a larger audience other than the direct receivers and their close private circle is a secondary act of communication. The Guide states that there is a secondary communication when "a communication is made by an organisation other than the original one" as well as the "public communication of a broadcast by loudspeaker or on a television screen".[81]

From that, the Court deducts that such an independent act "through which the broadcast work is communicated to a new public."

However, in 2003, 2 years before the judgement, a new Guide to copyright and related rights[82] was launched by the WIPOs and authored by Mihály Ficsor, former WIPO Director. This new guide, which also included the Berne Convention Interpretation, focuses on the point that "the communication is made by an organization other than the original one",[83] that is, that the author or other rightsholders has a right to authorise any secondary act of communication. The Guide mentions the concept of 'new communication' but not the 'new public' term. Following Eleonora Rosati's arguments, in the SGAE case, the concept of 'new public' was not necessary to determine the existence of an act of communication to the public, then was rather a consequence of the secondary act of communication, that is, the activity of the user. As it was said, the 'new public' criterion has been challenged by and wide number of academics, who have considered the 'new public' criterion as unsuitable, incoherent, and overall contrary to international law.[84] Rosati reinforces such idea[85] by referring to AG Szpunar's words, who described the 'new public' criteria as a *'legal fiction'*.[86] In her Article, Rosati[87] makes a systematic distribution of the CJEU cases according the role the criterion 'new public' takes in the final decision. The author points out

[81] WIPO (1978). Article 11bis paragraph (1) sections 4 and 5, p. 67.

[82] Ficsor (2003).

[83] Ibid. at BC-11*bis*.14.

[84] Rosati (2020), p. 15.

[85] Ibid, p. 16.

[86] AG. Szpunar, Opinion of Advocate General Szpunar in *VG Bild-Kunst v Stiftung Preußischer Kulturbesitz, C-392/19, ECLI:EU:C:2020:696,* para. 56.

[87] Rosati (2020), p. 20.

that, even in some cases, the concept of 'new public' has not been relevant in the CJEU analysis; the rejection of the 'new public' criterion, although being desirable, is difficult as a re-calibration of the role of other criteria. Rosati suggests the CJEU should end up considering the 'new public' as a requirement in situations in which the there is a new act communication to the public, that is a secondary act of communication. If those cases, Article3(1) of the InfoSoc Directive clearly applies, and it is irrelevant whether the public targeted by the secondary act is new and whether the technical means in such secondary act are the same or different.[88] The use of 'the new public' criterion has carried some undesirable solutions. Rosati points out that, like in Svensson's[89] case, and other linking cases, the 'new public' should be considered only in cases of linking to freely accessible, licensed content. In internet linking cases, there is no 'new public', as the content is already on the Internet, so everyone with internet access is 'the public'. In cases concerning linking to unlicensed content, as there is no 'new public,' the result of the application of the criteria could bring up an adverse result, as there is liability for making available illegal content, the lack of new public could exclude the secondary liability of the one who makes available the link to illegal content in other websites. For instance, in GS Media case, the 'new public' is irrelevant almost detrimental; the criteria of knowledge and profit-making intention are sufficient to determine the liability.[90]

Furthermore, P. B. Hugenholtz, and S. C. van Velze remind us that the exclusive rights protected under copyright are absolute rights that apply to and can be enforced against third parties and, as property rights, should be defined in precise and objective terms, with clear meaning which not depend on subjective elements, like the rightsholders intentions. For these authors, if the 'new public' criterion test links the scope of the (secondary) communication right to the authorisation by the authors for the initial (primary) act of communication, it means that introduces a subjective element in the definition of the exclusive right of communication to the public. They agree that "whether or not a new public is or was 'taken into account' by the right holder should, therefore, not play a role in delineating the right of communication to the public".[91] The authors state that the 'new public' test is not needed and suggest abandoning it to increase legal certainty without materially affecting the scope of the communication right.

Finally, Ficsor, making a historical assessment of the CJEU criterion, totally rejects the 'new public' theory. The former WIPO Director and Assistant Director, author of the 2003 WIPO Guide to Copyright, directly criticises the Court for creating the criterion without having historical respect for the scenario. Ficsor states that the records of the negotiation history of the 2003 Guide to Copyright Treaties do not confirm but rebut the criterion of "new public" as a condition of application of the right of communication to the public because this theory that it was not accepted

[88] Ibid, p. 21.

[89] CJEU Judgment of 13 Feb 2014.

[90] Rosati (2020), p. 29.

[91] Hugenholtz and van Velze (2016), p. 810.

in the negotiations meetings. Also declares, the 1978 Guide to Berne Convention neither confirms the 'new public' criterion.[92] For Ficsor, in the *TvCatchup* judgement,[93] the CJEU introduced the new criterion of 'technical means' as clarification for the 'new public' criterion. In that case, the Court recognised the application of the right of communication to the public also in the absence of a "new public" by introducing a new formula; the communication has to be subject to the condition that different "specific technical means" is to be used. In the lack of a new public, 'new technical means' are required to determine the communication to the public. In Ficsor's point of view, this new criterion was neither in accordance with the Berne Convention, the WCT, nor the InfoSoc Directive, under which rebroadcasting of a broadcast work using exactly the same technical means is clearly covered by the communication to the public right.[94]

This study totally supports Ficsor's clear conclusion that the Court should have stated that when new acts of communication had taken place, the communication to the public right is concerned. There is no need to determine the existence of a new public or new technical means as it is neither relevant nor always applicable. In contrast, if there is a new act of communication, it turns out to be a secondary act of communication which is covered by the right of communication to the public and needs to be authorised by the author and the corresponding rightsholders.

Once both legislation and case law on CtoP have been analysed, up to now, this study explored an approach to determine the existence of primary or secondary acts of communication. Figure 3.5 summarises the conceptualisation of what a CtoP consist of.

The CJEU in the judgement of 20 June 2024 in the case C-135/23, GEMA v GL,[95] makes a clear summary of all the criterion to determine the existence of a communication to the public act by the means of article 3 (1) of the InfoSoc Directive. The judgement in its paragraph 18 reminds the lack of definition of the CtoP in the European legislation and continues by following the checklist of the criterion; existence of a transmission (para. 19), with an active role of the user (para. 23), who obtains or seeks a benefit or profit (para. 24), in communicating the works to a public (para. 38–42), through technical means (para. 43). In this case, the CJEU refers to the national court to determine the existence or not of a public, by taking into account the number of people that receives the communication and possibility of existence of a "new public" (para. 44–46).

In summary, and following all those jurisprudential criterion, a possible definition of what a CtoP act is could be as follows:

> *There is an act of Communication to the public when individuals or entities transmit a work or make it available via wire or wireless means to an indeterminate and fairly large group of people who are not present at the place where the communication originated. Such*

---

[92] Ficsor (2020), pp. 6–8.

[93] CJEU Judgment of 7 Mar 2013, TVCatchup, C-607/11, ECLI:EU:C:2013:147.

[94] Ficsor (2020), p. 9.

[95] CJEU Judgment of 20 June 2024, GEMA, C-135/23, ECLI:EU:C:2024:526.

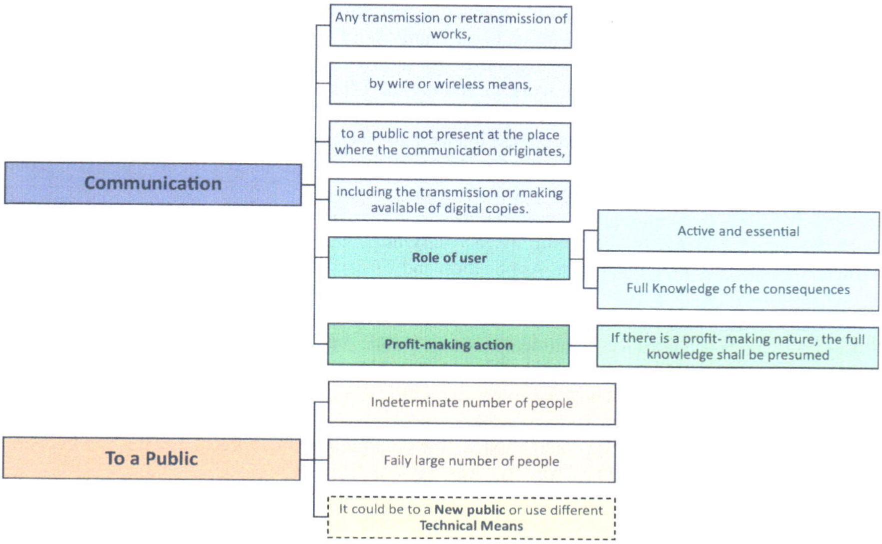

Fig. 3.5 Conceptualisation of acts of communication to the public. Source: Author's elaboration

transmission or availability of works must be performed with the active role of those communicating individuals or entities. To be considered as an act of Communication to the public, communicating individuals or entities should have full knowledge of the consequences of their actions and ensure that their acts are legal, especially if the communications lead to a profit-making nature.

References

Angelopoulos C (2021) Primary and accessory liability in EU copyright law. In: The Routledge handbook of EU Copyright Law. Routledge, pp 193–214. https://doi.org/10.4324/9781003156277-13

Ficsor M (2003) Guide to the copyright and related rights treaties administered by WIPO and glossary of copyright and related rights terms. WIPO, Geneva

Ficsor M (2020) From Madrid to Cordoba—the emergence and the (welcome) decline of the CJEU'S erroneous "new public" theory concerning the right of communication to the public. Cuad Jurídicos del Inst Derecho Autor 1:81–98

Hugenholtz PB, van Velze SC (2016) Communication to a new public? Three reasons why EU copyright law can do without a "new public". IIC Int Rev Intellect Prop Compet Law 47:797–816

Koo J (2020) The right of communication to the public in EU copyright law. Hart Publishing

Koo J (2021) The EU right of communication to the public – still looking for a good link. In: The Routledge handbook of EU Copyright Law. Routledge, pp 173–192. https://doi.org/10.4324/9781003156277-12

Nérisson S (2014) The rental and lending rights directive. In: Stamatoudi I, Torremans P (eds) EU copyright law: a commentary. Edward Elgar Publishing Ltd, Cheltenham, pp 149–202

Oprysk L (2020) Secondary communication under the EU copyright acquis after Tom Kabinet: between exhaustion and securing work's exploitation. J Intellect Prop Inf Technol E-Commerce Law 11:200–214

Padrós Reig C (2022) Internet vs. propiedad intelectual. Nuevos límites a la técnica de transclusión de enlace o framing según la STJUE (Gran Sala) de 9 de marzo de 2021. As. C-392/19. Quad IEE Rev l'Institut d'Estudis Eur 1:120–130

Quintais JP (2018) Untangling the hyperlinking web: in search of the online right of communication to the public. J World Intellect Prop 21:385–420. https://doi.org/10.1111/jwip.12107

Renda, A. *et al.* The Implementation, Application and Effects of the EU Directive on Copyright in the Informat, *CEPS Special Report No. 120*, Centre for European Policy Studies Publications (2015).

Rosati E (2020) When does a communication to the public under EU copyright law need to be to a 'new public'? SSRN Electron J. https://doi.org/10.2139/ssrn.3640493

Synodinou T (2018) The Renckhoff judgment: the CJEU swivels the faces of the copyright Rubik's cube (Part I). Kluwer Copyr Blog

WIPO (1978) Guide to the Berne convention for the protection of literary and artistics works (Paris Act, 1971). World Intellectual Property Organization, Geneva

Xalabarder Plantada R (2016) The role of the CJEU in harmonizing EU copyright law. IIC – Int Rev Intellect Prop Compet Law 47:635–639. https://doi.org/10.1007/s40319-016-0509-2

Part III
Liability and Enforcement of Infringements of Communication to the Public Right in Online Music

Chapter 4
The Directive 2019/790 on Copyright in the Digital Single Market

The previous chapter has tackled the difficulties of finding a clear conceptualisation of the CtoP right. The lack of definition in the legislation plus the CJEU dynamic, and sometimes even inconsistent, criteria system could be more helpful to assert those acts infringing the CtoP right of authors and other rightsholders. Consequently, it also becomes a hassle to establish the liability of those acts. To determine liability for CtoP infringement, several liability limitations and exceptions must also be considered apart from the conceptual troubles. The main problem with the limitations and exceptions regime in the EU copyright legislation is the need for harmonisation. Furthermore, just 6 out of the 29 exceptions set in the different EU copyright directives are mandatory for the Member States to implement in their national legislations. At the same time, most of them, precisely 21, are voluntary.

Figure 4.1 shows, 15 limitations and exceptions may affect the CtoP right of online music works, but just six are mandatory. Those are introduced by three of the 'new directives' approved copyright reform. Regarding the exceptions of quotation for criticism or review and caricature, parody or pastiche were introduced by the InfoSoc Directive as voluntary exceptions, according to the CJEU approach of Article 17(7) of the Digital Single Market Directive, those exceptions must be considered as mandatory. The other optional exceptions and limitations are settled in the InfoSoc Directive, Article 5. This implies a less harmonised system of exceptions and limitations, as many Member States have not adopted some of them, and those implemented into national legislations contain different approaches, depending on the interpretation made by the domestic legislator of the European text, either restrictive or board.[1]

This study does not intend to cover exceptions and limitations since it does not present any assessment of them. Still, it is relevant for the subject of this dissertation

[1] See the website copyrightexceptions.eu for a quick view on the national implementations of the exceptions and limitations to copyright and related rights foreseen in the EU copyright directives.

L. Ballesta Martí, *The Communication to the Public of Musical Works Online in the European Union's Legislation*, Law, Governance and Technology Series 75,
https://doi.org/10.1007/978-3-031-94132-0_4

Exeption	RightS affected	Mandatory /Optional	Article	Directive	Efects on online music
Text and data mining for scientific research	Reproduction	M	3	CDSM	✗
Exception or limitation for text and data mining	Reproduction	M	4	CDSM	✗
Use in digital and cross-border teaching activities	CtoP	M	5	CDSM	✓
Preservation of cultural heritage	Reproduction	M	6	CDSM	✓
Use of out-of-commerce works by cultural heritage institutions	CtoP (MA)	M	8	CDSM	✓
Temporary acts of reproduction	Reproduction	M	5.1	InfoSoc	✓
Photocopying/photo-reproduction	Reproduction	O	5.2 (a)	InfoSoc	✗
Private copying	Reproduction	O	5.2 (b)	InfoSoc	✓
Reproductions by Libraries, Archives & Museums	Reproduction	O	5.2 (c)	InfoSoc	✓
Ephemeral recordings made by broadcasters	Reproduction	O	5.2 (d)	InfoSoc	✓
Reproduction of broadcasts by social institutions	Reproduction	O	5.2 (e)	InfoSoc	✓
Illustration for teaching or scientific research	CtoP (MA) + Repr.	O	5.3(a)	InfoSoc	✓
Use for the benefit of people with a disability	CtoP (MA) + Repr.	O	5.3(b)	InfoSoc	✓
Press review	CtoP (MA) + Repr.	O	5.3(c)	InfoSoc	✗
Reporting by the press on current events	CtoP (MA) + Repr.	O	5.3(c)2	InfoSoc	✓
Quotation for criticism or review	CtoP (MA) + Repr.	O	5.3(d)	InfoSoc	✓
		M	17(7)	CDSM	✓
Use for public security purposes	CtoP (MA) + Repr.	O	5.3(e)	InfoSoc	✓
Use of public speeches and public lectures	CtoP (MA) + Repr.	O	5.3(f)	InfoSoc	✗
Use during religious or official celebrations	CtoP (MA) + Repr.	O	5.3(g)	InfoSoc	✓
Use of works of architecture or sculptures in public spaces	CtoP (MA) + Repr.	O	5.3(h)	InfoSoc	✗
Incidental inclusion	CtoP (MA) + Repr.	O	5.3(i)	InfoSoc	✓
Use for advertising the exhibition or sale of works of art	CtoP (MA) + Repr.	O	5.3(j)	InfoSoc	✗
Use for the purpose of caricature, parody or pastiche	CtoP (MA) + Repr.	O	5.3(k)	InfoSoc	✓
		M	17(7)	CDSM	✓
Use for the demonstration or repair of equipment	CtoP (MA) + Repr.	O	5.3(l)	InfoSoc	✓
Use for the purpose of reconstructing a building	CtoP (MA) + Repr.	O	5.3(l)	InfoSoc	✗
Use for the purpose of research or private study	CtoP (MA) + Repr.	O	5.3(m)	InfoSoc	✓
Pre-existing exceptions of minor importance	CtoP (MA) + Repr.+Dist.	O	5.3(o)	InfoSoc	✓
Make and disseminate accessible format copies of works	CtoP (MA) + Repr.+ Dist	M	4	Marrakech Directive	✓
Permitted uses of orphan works	CtoP (MA) + Repr.	M	6	Orphan Works	✓

Fig. 4.1 Copyright exceptions and limitations in the EU and its affection on CtoP of online music works Source of data: https://copyrightexceptions.eu/. Author's elaboration

to mention the significance of the not-harmonized system of exceptions on the CtoP of online music works and the liability for its infringement. The European Copyright Society (ECS), in their opinion in 2015, criticises that even in harmonising the copyright legislation, the system of exceptions and limitations still needs to be genuinely harmonised. Authors and rightsholders would benefit from a harmonised legal framework for the ECS. An increased lawful international online exploitation of works would be possible. Additionally, users would benefit from laws that are easy to understand and follow, making it clear when a work can be used without infringement. Furthermore, the ECS states that "harmonisation, or even unification, of exceptions and limitations, should, so far as possible, respect the imperative of legal certainty, while allowing a degree of flexibility to permit the adaptation of the copyright system to changing circumstances and social needs".[2]

In terms of CtoP, this lack of harmonisation means that once an action has been spotted as an act of communication to the public, according to the legal text and following the CJEU criteria, all the exceptions and limitations must be considered to

[2]Geiger et al. (2015), p. 93, para. 5–10.

conclude if such an act must be viewed as an illegal act of CtoP or not. Consequently, it complicates determining the corresponding liability. The several and varied voluntary exceptions and limitations have been implemented in various ways, or even not, by a diverse number of Member States. Therefore, when an act of CtoP of musical works is done online, such communication is spread in several countries. The music work will likely be communicated differently and used for various purposes. Acts of online communication are run in all Member States and will be determined as illegal or not, depending on the Member State in which those acts occur. This discrepancy arises from the varying degrees of implementation of voluntary exceptions across Member State. Thus, the same act of CtoP of a music work online will be lawfully allowed in one Member State or determined as lawful and liable in another. For example, if a user makes a musical work available online on a free access website without the rightsholder's consent, such primary communication is illegal in the EU. But if another user plays such music work from the free website during a religious or official celebration, that later secondary act of communication to the public would be illegal in France, Italy, Estonia, or Austria but not in Spain, Ireland, Romania, Bulgaria or Slovakia.[3]

A significant overhaul of the copyright regulatory framework aimed to harmonise it at the EU level began in 2015 with the so-called "Copyright Reform"[4] as part of the Digital Single Market Strategy, presented by President Junker.[5] This reform of EU copyright rules was launched to modernise copyright, reduce differences between national legislations, and allow users wider online access to works across the EU through further harmonisation measures.[6] The Copyright Reform led the Commission to release the "Copyright Package", formed by different legislative proposals. Such a legislative activity concluded in April 2019 by adopting the controversial Directive on Copyright in the Digital Single Market. The Commission or any of the two legislative institutions, the Council and the European Parliament, could have clarified the conception of the CtoP right and unified the exceptions and limitations system. On the contrary, introducing a new liability system for the acts of communication to the public carried by users on online content-sharing platforms became a polemic. This introduction in Article 17, among other reasons, turns the directive into a controversial matter. From the online musical works perspective, the CtoP right in the CDSM Directive is presented and assessed in the following section.

The Directive 2019/790 on Copyright in the Digital Single Market has already been mentioned in Chaps. 2 and 3. Still, the following section studies the reasons for and meaning of this Directive on the CtoP right. It also analyses Article 17, the provision dedicated to that subject matter. On September 14, 2016, the Proposal for a

[3] See the comparison in copyrightexceptions.eu

[4] For a comprehensive analysis of the EU Copyright Reform, see Stalla-Bourdillon et al. (2017).

[5] European Commission, Communication from the Commission to the European Parliament, the Council, the European Economic and Social Committee and the Committee of the Regions - A Digital Single Market Strategy for Europe, COM(2015) 100 final (2015).

[6] Rosati (2021a), p. 10.

Directive on Copyright in the Digital Single Market[7] was released, along with an Explanatory Memorandum and an Impact Assessment.[8] The proposal was sent to the two legislative bodies to start the negotiations and complete the procedure. However, the process took almost 3 years until the final text of the directive was approved. On May 25, 2018, the Council's permanent representatives committee (Coreper) reached an understanding on the content of the Proposal.[9] This agreement would serve the Council as the foundation for negotiations with the Parliament. The proposal's text was discussed and assessed by the Parliament's Parliamentary Committee on Legal Affairs (JURI). In June 2018, after a long and fierce period of hearings, debates, and amendments,[10] the JURI Committee endorsed their Report on the proposed Directive. This first Report was rejected by the Plenary of the Parliament, which, on July 6, 2018, voted against the document. Non-institutional actors entered this legal and political battleground, including digital platforms (headed by Google) and tech trade associations, collecting societies, creative industries and publishers, and other stakeholders representing Internet users.[11] According to Professor Dussolier, 'the level of lobbying and media interest was unprecedented, with large sums of money poured into public campaigns and social media posts in an attempt to influence EU civil society'.[12] Such lobbying activities aimed to influence Members of the European Parliament's vote. On September 12, 2018, the Plenary approved the text of the last JURI Committee Report, which ultimately introduced 86 amendments to the text proposed by the Commission. This text constituted the Parliament's negotiating mandate. The behind-closed-door trialogue negotiations occurred between the last quarter of 2018 and the beginning of 2019. Finally, on April 17, 2019, the text of the Directive was adopted by the Parliament and the Council, and the CDSM Directive entered into force on June 7, 2019, following its publication in the EU Official Journal. The CDSM Directive comprises 86 recitals and 32 Articles. As assessed in Chap. 2, the CDSM Directive has more than one legal basis, but Article 114 TFEU is the main one. Like in the InfoSoc Directive, the

[7] European Commission (2016) Proposal for a Directive of the European Parliament and of the Council on copyright in the Digital Single Market. COM/2016/0593 final - 2016/0280 (COD).

[8] European Commission, Impact Assessment on the Modernisation of EU Copyright Rules, SWD (2016) 301 final (2016), available at https://eur-lex.europa.eu/legal-content/EN/TXT/PDF/?uri=CELEX:52016SC0301&from=EN

[9] Council of the European Union, Proposal for a Directive of the European Parliament and of the Council on copyright in the Digital Single Market—Agreed negotiating mandate (25.05.2018), Interinstitutional File: 2016/ 0280 (COD), 9134/ 18.

[10] See the legislative procedure file in the Legislative Observatoriy of European Parliament 2016/ 0280(COD) https://oeil.secure.europarl.europa.eu/oeil/popups/ficheprocedure.do?lang=en&reference=2016/0280(COD).

See also the Procedure 2016/0280/COD in Eur-lex https://eur-lex.europa.eu/legal-content/en/HIS/?uri=CELEX:32019L0790&qid=1688486435340

[11] Ferri (2020), p. 22.

[12] Dusollier (2020), p. 1005.

chosen legal base is the generic one that allows the adoption of measures or acts to ensure the establishment and functioning of the internal market.[13]

The Directive states its objectives in Recital 2, and as other directives adopted in the area of copyright and related rights, aims to contribute to developing and operating the EU internal market. It is regarded as an incentive-based understanding of copyright as a catalyst for innovation, creativity, investment, and the creation of new content, and to the EU's aim to respect and promote culture and cultural diversity, following Article 167(4) TFEU.[14] That general objective set on the well-functioning of the internal market is reached in the CDSM Directive by providing rightsholders with a high level of protection, enabling the rights-clearing process, and adjusting the playing field for the exploitation of works and other protected works. Recital 3 puts in relevance the need to address the interpretive uncertainties caused by technological development, the emergence of new business models, and actors, as well as sets the goal of ensuring that such technological advancement is not constrained concerning certain uses, including cross-border exploitation of works in the digital environment. Recital 3 also announces that the CDSM Directive provides rules to adapt certain exceptions and limitations to copyright and related rights to that digital and cross-border environment. Moreover, Recital 3 introduces that the CDSM Directive also contains rules on the use of works by online service providers storing and giving access to user-uploaded content, on the transparency of authors' and performers' contracts, on authors' and performers' remuneration, as well as a mechanism for the revocation of rights that authors and performers have transferred on an exclusive basis.[15] Article 2(6) of the CDSMD defines those 'online content-service providers' (OCSSPs) as any "provider of an information society service of which the main or one of the main purposes is to store and give the public access to a large amount of copyright-protected works or other protected subject matter uploaded by its users, which it organises and promotes for profit-making purposes."[16] The second paragraph of Article 2(6) lists different examples of information society service providers which shall not be considered as OCSSP within the meaning of the Directive. Such services excluded from the meaning of 'online content-service providers' are not-for-profit online encyclopaedias (like Wikipedia), not-for-profit educational and scientific repositories, open-source software-developing and sharing platforms, providers of electronic communications services,[17] online

[13] Ferri (2020), p. 22.

[14] See Chap. 2 in this book.

[15] CDSM Directive, Recital 3.

[16] CDSM Directive, Article 2 (6).

[17] As defined in Article 2.4 of Directive (EU) 2018/1972 establishing the European Electronic Communications Code, an 'electronic communications service' means a service normally provided for remuneration which encompasses content transmitted using electronic communications networks and services, like: 'internet access service', interpersonal communications service and services consisting in the conveyance of signals such as transmission services used for the provision of machine-to-machine services and for broadcasting. The provision excludes services providing or exercising editorial control over the files or transmissions.

marketplaces, business-to-business cloud services and cloud services that allow users to upload content for their use. However, Recital 63 of the Directive gives a direction to determine when a service provider shall be considered an OCSSP under the provisions of the CDSMD. The text clarifies that the assessment of whether an OCSSP "stores and gives access to a large amount of copyright-protected content should be made on a case-by-case basis and should take account of a combination of elements, such as the audience of the service and the number of files of copyright-protected content uploaded by the users of the service".[18]

Following the objectives and recitals 2 and 3, the CDSM Directive in Article 17 introduces a new regime of liability of those online content-sharing service providers for the content uploaded by their users. That is the same as a new criterion of liability for illegal acts of communication to the public of copyright-protected works. Indeed, Article 17 was created to protect the financial interests of rightsholders generated by the exploitation of their works online. The same provision also aims to limit the power of big platforms, as just intermediary players, to profit from rightsholders' creative productions and investments.[19] Those were part of why Article 17 was at the core of the mentioned polemic since the beginning of the negotiations on the legislative act. Regarding the legislative discussion on Article 17 of the CDSM Directive, the former Member of the European Parliament Felix Reda stated that the debate "was dominated by rightsholders' statements in favour of Article 17 (then Article 13), while online platform operators and especially civil society organisations were fiercely critical of the proposal".[20] The CDSM Directive has been controversial before, during and after its approval and, as professor Severine Dusollier describes, Article 17 of the CDSM Directive is its 'monster provision, both by its size and its hazardousness'.[21] Furthermore, apart from the polemic, such provision became the object of an annulment procedure that Poland referred to CJEU, as well as requires the development of a document of guidance for its implementation into Member States that redesigned the role of a "stakeholder" for some of the actors affected by the new EU copyright legislation.

The main issues in Article 17 are relevant for this dissertation since such a provision is the only one in the CDSM Directive directly related to the CtoP right. A more detailed account of Article 17 and its meaning for online musical works is given in the following lines of this section.

[18] CDSM Directive, Recital 63.

[19] Ferri (2020), p. 12.

[20] F. Reda, *Article 17: What Is It Really Good for? Rewriting the History of the DSM Directive Part 1*, 2020, Kluwer Copyright Blog, available at https://copyrightblog.kluweriplaw.com/2020/09/28/Article-17-what-is-it-really-good-for-rewriting-the-history-of-the-dsm-directive-part-1/

[21] Dusollier (2020), p. 1023.

4.1 CtoP of Online Music Works Under Article17 CDSM Directive: A New Liability Regime or a redefinition of CtoP?

The first paragraph of the first Article of the CDSM Directive (from now on in this section referred to as CDSMD or "the Directive"), under the title 'Subject matter and scope', runs through the Recitals mentioned above 2 and 3. Under the general objective of harmonisation of copyright and related rights law in the framework of the internal market, Article 1 points out the idea of focusing on 'digital and cross-border uses of protected content', seeking to provide a fair balance between the different actors taking part in the exploitation of works online. This goal is also reflected in Recital 61 when it refers to the legal uncertainty of whether the corresponding OCSSPs need to obtain authorisation from rightsholders for copyrighted content uploaded by their users. According to Recital 61, such uncertainty "affects the ability of rightsholders to determine whether, and under which conditions, their works and other subject matter are used, as well as their ability to obtain appropriate remuneration for such use" and affirming that "Rightholders should receive appropriate remuneration for the use of their works".[22] The copyright reform aims to fit the new uses of digital content into EU copyright legislation, and the CtoP right is one of the most closely linked to the exploitation of works in a digital environment. Therefore, it was expected that the CDSMD would update and reshape the definition of CtoP while clarifying its content, but this was not done. Instead, the liability regime was introduced in Article 17. Additionally, the justification for Article 17 is anchored in the need to address what has come to be known as a "value gap" or "transfer of value". The term "value gap" describes a divergence between the value that some digital user-uploaded content platforms are said to derive from the exploitation of protected works and the revenues paid out to the corresponding rightsholders.[23] The Impact assessment accompanying the proposal of the CDSM Directive[24] highlights the claim of the rightsholders in the music industry regarding OCSSP. It explains that OCSSPs are an important part of the online distribution of protected works and obtain considerable revenue from advertising or paid subscriptions. Still, they do not remunerate rightsholders in proportion, not even fairly.

Regarding musical works, in 2017, the International Federation of Phonographic Industry (IFPI) described the notion of 'value gap' as "the growing mismatch between the value that user upload services, such as YouTube, extract from music and the revenue returned to the music community those who are creating and investing in music. The value gap is the biggest threat to the future sustainability

[22] Recital 61 of the CRDSM Directive.

[23] Rosati (2021a), p. 314.

[24] European Commission, *Impact Assessment on the modernisation of EU copyright rules*. Impact Assessment Part 1/3, pp. 137, 139 and 142, and Part 3/3, Annex 12B.

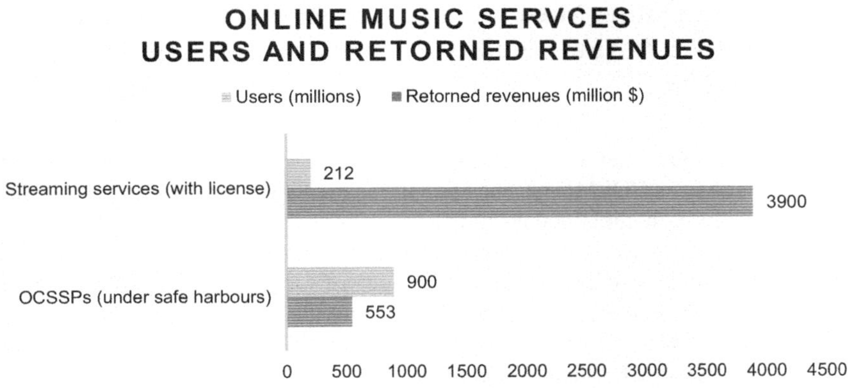

Fig. 4.2 Online Music Services number of users and revenue returned to music rightsholders per user. Source: Author's elaboration. Adapted from 2017 IFPI's Global Music Report (International Federation of the Phonographic Industry (IFPI), "Rewarding creativity: Fixing the value gap" in IFPI Global Music Report 2017, p. 6)

of the music industry".[25] That is because OCSSPs claim they are not legally liable for the music distributed on their websites or platforms, avoiding licencing music on fair conditions as other digital providers do, like streaming platforms, also creating a situation of unfair competition. Since 2000, OCSSPs have sought protection under the "safe harbour" or exception of liability for hosting providers under Article 14 of the Directive on Electronic Commerce 2000/31[26] (E-commerce Directive). This safe harbour is built on the statement that where an information society service consists of the storage of information provided by a user of the service, such service provider is not liable for the data stored at the request of a user of the service, as long as the provider does not have actual knowledge or is not aware of illegal activity or its facts or circumstances.[27] Article 14 adds that in case providers may have knowledge or awareness of the illegality, they must act expeditiously to remove or restrict access to the illegal content to apply the exception of liability. The benefit that OCSSPs obtained from applying the hosting safe harbour regarding copyright infringements is quite relevant.

As Fig. 4.2 illustrates, the above-mentioned IFPI 2017 report[28] estimated that in 2016, OCSSPs benefiting from such "safe harbours" already had more than 900 million users, being the world's largest on-demand music audience. Nevertheless, 2016

[25] International Federation of the Phonographic Industry (IFPI), *"Rewarding creativity: Fixing the value gap" in IFPI Global Music Report 2017*, 2017, pp. 24–27.

[26] Directive 2000/31/EC of the European Parliament and of the Council of 8 June 2000 on certain legal aspects of information society services, in particular electronic commerce, in the Internal Market, OJ L 178, 17.7.2000, pp. 1–16. The European Parliament and of the Council.

[27] Directive 2000/31/EC, Article 14.

[28] International Federation of the Phonographic Industry (IFPI), "Rewarding creativity: Fixing the value gap" in IFPI Global Music Report 2017, p. 5.

revenue returned to rightsholders through these services accounted for $553 million. In contrast, audio subscription services, including paid and ad-supported accounts, estimated 212 million users in the same year and contributed more than US$3.9 billion in licences to compensate rightsholders for CtoP usage. As calculated by the IFPI, in 2015, Spotify paid record labels $20 per user, while YouTube returned less than US$1 for each music user.[29]

The hosting safe harbour in Article 14(1) of the E-commerce Directive sets liability of intermediary services, but it is unclear if this framework also applies to acts that constitute a primary liability. The question about conditions of application of Article 14's safe harbour regarding OCSSP was referred to the CJEU in YouTube/ Cyando join cases C-682/18 and C-683/18.[30] The core question is if OCSSPs can benefit from such hosting safe harbour if they don't perform an act of communication to the public, and consequently, primary liability for copyright infringement is rejected.[31]

Advocate General Saugmandsgaard Øe, in his opinion of the joined cases YouTube/Cyando, considers that Article 14(1) of the E-commerce Directive covers both primary and secondary liability for the information provided and the activities initiated by users.[32] In its judgement, the CJEU clarified that for an internet service provider to fall within the scope of Article 14's safe harbour, "it is essential that it be an 'intermediary' service provider".[33] regardless if the infringement results in a primary liability or secondary liability. Accordingly, an OCSSP, acting as an intermediary, must not play an active role that gives it knowledge or control over the contents of users' communications,[34] as the legal provision requires. The Court concludes that the activity of an OCSSP is covered by the hosting safe harbour as long as such a provider does not play "an active role of such a kind as to give it knowledge of or control over the content uploaded to its platform".[35] Likewise, the exemption from liability in Article 14(1) is not applicable where the OCSSP "has knowledge of or awareness of specific illegal acts committed by its users relating to protected content uploaded to its platform."[36]

The liability questioned in the YouTube/Cyando case was whether platforms like YouTube perform themselves as an act of communication or make it available to the public under Article 3(1) of the InfoSoc Directive. The Court explained in paragraph 102 of the referring judgement that an OCSSP does not make an act of

[29] Ibid, p. 6.

[30] CJEU Judgment of 22 Jun 2021, YouTube/Cyando, C-682/18, ECLI:EU:C:2021:503.

[31] Reda and Selinger (2021), available at https://copyrightblog.kluweriplaw.com/2021/07/01/youtube-cyando-an-important-ruling-for-platform-liability-part-2/

[32] Advocate General Saugmandsgaard Øe Opinion delivered on 16 July 2020 on Joined Cases C-682/18 and C-683/18. ECLI:EU:C:2020:586, para. 138.

[33] CJEU Judgment of 22 Jun 2021, *YouTube/Cyando,* para. 105.

[34] Reda and Selinger, 'YouTube/Cyando an Important Ruling for Platform Liability Part 2'.

[35] CJEU Judgment of 22 Jun 2021, para. 117.

[36] Ibid, para. 118.

communication to the public of the uploaded content, within the meaning of Article 3(1) of the InfoSoc Directive, "unless it contributes, beyond merely making that platform available, to giving access to such content to the public in breach of copyright".[37] Professor Hümmer summarises the CJEU's reasoning in the judgement that considers online content-sharing platforms as not liable despite the fact they know or are supposed to know about the availability of copyright-infringing material on its platform. This happens in three situations when the OCSSP: (1) refrains from putting in place the appropriate technological measures that can be expected from a reasonably diligent operator, (2) or provides tools on its platform specifically intended for the illegal sharing of such content, (3) or knowingly promotes such sharing, which is indicated if the operator has adopted a financial model that encourages users of its platform illegally to communicate protected content to the public.[38] The judgement was released on 22 June 2021, after the CDSM Directive entered into force and 2 weeks after the deadline for the directive's transposition expired. The Court made a special consideration in paragraph 59 of the judgement, reminding that the questions referred to in the cases concern the InfoSoc Directive, the Directive on Electronic Commerce and the Enforcement Directive as were applicable at the material time of the main proceedings. Likewise, the Court clarified that the "interpretations provided by the Court in answer to those questions do not concern the set of rules established by Article 17"[39] of the CDSM Directive, avoiding making any other reference to the new regime introduced by the CDSM Directive. Professor Rosati underlines that the CJEU did not provide a definite answer regarding whether the platforms in the case perform directly copyright-restricted acts,[40] which would also link to the new CDSM provisions.

Article 17 is found in CDSM Directive's Title V, *Measures to Achieve a Well Functioning Marketplace for Copyright*, in its second chapter, labelled as *Certain uses of protected content by online services*. Under the title *Use of protected content by online content-sharing service providers,* Article 17 is the only reference to the CtoP right done in CDSMD; as said, it introduces a new regime of liability for OCSSPs, establishing specific general guidelines while allowing some complex exceptions. This provision determines that the OCSSPs are performing an act of CtoP by giving access to the copyright-protected content uploaded by their users. Furthermore, the second paragraph of the Article requires online content-sharing service providers to get authorisation from the rightsholders of copyrighted works to communicate to the public such works. Article 17, in paragraphs 1 and 2, states as follows:

[37] Ibid, para. 102.

[38] Hummer F (2022) News in YouTube/Cyando: German Federal Court rules following CJEU decision. In: IPKat Blog. https://ipkitten.blogspot.com/2022/06/guest-post-news-in-youtubecyando-german.html

[39] CJEU Judgment of 22 Jun 2021, para. 56

[40] Rosati (2021b), 10/06/2021. Available at https://ipkitten.blogspot.com/2021/06/cjeu-rules-on-platform-liability-under.html

> (1). Member States shall provide that an online content-sharing service provider performs an act of communication to the public or an act of making available to the public for the purposes of this Directive when it gives the public access to copyright-protected works or other protected subject matter uploaded by its users.
>
> An online content-sharing service provider shall, therefore, obtain an authorisation from the rightsholders referred to in Article 3(1) and (2) of Directive 2001/29/EC, for instance by concluding a licensing agreement, in order to communicate to the public or make available to the public works or other subject matter.
>
> (2). Member States shall provide that, where an online content-sharing service provider obtains an authorisation, for instance by concluding a licensing agreement, that authorisation shall also cover acts carried out by users of the services falling within the scope of Article 3 of Directive 2001/29/EC when they are not acting on a commercial basis or where their activity does not generate significant revenues.

Montagnani defines the obligation imposed to OCSSPs in Article 17 as "a two-fold duty upon such providers to conclude licencing agreements with rightsholders for the use of their works or to (make best efforts to) prevent the availability on their services of works identified by rightsholders through the cooperation with the service providers".[41] Besides, the duty of OCSSPs to obtain authorisations is also a double-decker burden. OCSSPs must obtain authorisations to cover their acts of CtoP, but those licenses are taken on behalf of their users for their acts of CtoP. Indeed, users are the ones that upload the copyright-protected content and realise an act of communication to the public, as refereed in Article 3 (1) and (2) of the InfoSoc Directive. On the other hand, OCSSPs are the ones that are making benefit from such actions.

Professors Quintais and Husovec consider that such an obligation on OCSSPs to license their own use of protected content is a special law. In their study, the authors suggest the possibility that Article 17 creates a 'new right' of communication to the public in the EU copyright acquis and they support the idea that such a new right exists in its special regime, either because it is a 'special right' to Article 3 InfoSoc Directive, or because it goes beyond that provision, constituting a 'new sui generis right'".[42] To reach these two possibilities, the authors went through four different theories of the nature of Article 17 conception: (a) As a sub-type of right of communication to the public within international minimum standards, (b) as a sub-type of right of communication to the public outside international minimum standards, (c) as a 'special' right of communication to the public outside international.

minimum standards but within the earlier EU copyright acquis, and (d) a 'new sui generis' right of communication to the public outside international minimum standards and outside the earlier EU acquis.[43] Likewise, the authors state that Article 17 "is not a 'clarification' of existing law". They provide two main reasons for such a statement. The first is that Article 17 sets the scope of the 'new' right while introducing a special liability exemption mechanism, an exemption of OCSSPs

---

[41] Montagnani (2020), p. 301.

[42] Husovec and Quintais (2021), p. 5.

[43] *Ibid.* p. 15.

from direct liability. The second alleged reason is that Article 17 merges exploitation acts of users and OCSSPs in some circumstances. Although conceiving Article 17 is creating a 'new right' of communication to the public, the authors recognise that the practical consequences of such an interpretation are limited. Their argument for that limitation is that the "exploitation acts by OCSSPs under Article 17(1) presuppose an exploitation act by users, covered by Arts. 2 and 3 InfoSoc Directive".[44] Quintais and Husovec's discussion does not come to an end; rather, it leaves two possibilities on the nature of the provision. They conclude that Article 17 is either a 'special right', perceived as a deviation from the existing CJEU case law, or a 'new *sui generis*' right, which departs from the InfoSoc Directive's established framework and goes beyond the current CJEU case law's interpretation. The conclusion is open, so the authors refer to a final solution given by the future CJEU interpretation in the upcoming judgements.

As many scholars do,[45] the present study disagrees with Quintais and Husovec on the qualification of Article 17 as a special or sui generis right. This study supports the theory that Article 17 establishes a new regime rather than just clarifying the CtoP, following Professor Rosati's research.[46] Considering the language in the provision, it appoints OCSSP as subjects of the action, the ones who perform an act of CtoP; "Member States shall provide that an online content-sharing service provider performs an act of communication to the public (…)".[47] But that Article 17 constitutes a new right cannot be directly deducted from the provision's text. Conversely, when making the same language test to Articles 3 (1) and (2) of the InfoSoc Directive, it is clear that those provisions establish the exclusive right of CtoP and make it available as part of the first right. In this case, the provisions require Member States to "provide [authors] *with the exclusive right* to authorise or prohibit any communication to the public of their works (…)".[48] It is evident that Article 3 recognises the exclusive right of CtoP. However, Article 17 does not set any new rights for authors or other rightsholders nor reshapes the concept of CtoP, as the European legislator asserted in Recital 64. Recital 64 in CDSMD is aimed to clarify that online content-sharing service providers perform an act of communication to the public or of making available to the public when they give the public access to copyright-protected works or other protected subject matter uploaded by their users. It also requires OCSSP to obtain authorisation from the corresponding rightsholders. The recital explicitly states that such recognition and requirement is not reconceptualising the CtoP right when it declares that "[t]his does not affect the

[44] Husovec and Quintais (2021), p. 25.

[45] See also Dusollier (2020), p. 1013; Grisse (2019), p. 887; Rosati, *Five Considerations for the Transposition and Application of Article 17 of the DSM Directive - The IPKat*, 16 February 2021, The IPKAT, available at https://ipkitten.blogspot.com/2021/02/five-considerations-for-transposition.html

[46] Rosati (2021a), p. 324.

[47] CDSM Directive, Article 17(1).

[48] InfoSoc Directive, Article 3(1).

concept of communication to the public or of making available to the public elsewhere under Union law, nor does it affect the possible application of Article 3(1) and (2) of Directive 2001/29/EC to other service providers using copyright-protected content."[49] Furthermore, the European Commission's *Guidance on Article 17*,[50] considering the wording of recital 64, clarifies that Article 17 is a *lex specialis* to Article 3 of the InfoSoc Directive 2001/29 and Article 14 of the E-commerce Directive. The Commission's document also confirms that Article 17 does "not introduce a new right in the Union's copyright law. Rather, it fully and specifically regulates the act of 'communication to the public' in the limited circumstances covered by this provision" or affects the application of Article 3 of the InfoSoc Directive to "other service providers using copyright-protected content".[51] Rosati explains that the "relationship between the Directive and the InfoSoc Directive 2001/29 is special only insofar as the treatment of certain liability aspects is concerned."[52] Likewise, Article 17 does not create a new 'sui generis' right nor a special right on the existing CtoP in Article 3(1) of the InfoSoc Directive, nor a new conception of the CtoP. Agreeing with Rosati's position, the concept of CtoP and making available to the public in Article 17 CDSMD is to be interpreted in accordance with the corresponding concept in the InfoSoc Directive and other international legislation. Rosati also reminds us that following the CJEU settled case law, "identical concepts should be attributed the same meaning". Therefore, even though Article 17 CDSMD could be considered a 'sub-right of Article 3 of the InfoSoc Directive 2001/29, it is still the same right and must be interpreted similarly. Summarising, Article 17 does not create a new 'sui generis' right nor a special right on the existing CtoP in Article 3(1) of the InfoSoc Directive, nor a new conception of the CtoP. Article 17 introduces a new regime of liability for OCSSPs, who won't be protected by the hosting safe harbour in Article 14 E-commerce Directive, despite being an intermediary service with no direct intervention and no knowledge of the copyright infringement committed by their users.

4.2 The New Liability System for CtoP: OCSSPs' Liability and Exemptions

The new liability system in Article 17, despite not creating or reshaping any right by itself, recognises a determinate action as an act of CtoP. Since Article 17 declares that when OCSSPs give the public access to copyright-protected works uploaded by

[49] CDSM Directive Recital 64.

[50] European Commission, Communication from the Commission to the European Parliament and the Council 'Guidance on Article 17 of Directive 2019/790 on Copyright in the Digital Single Market', COM(2021) 288 final, 4 June 2021.

[51] *Ibid.* p. 3.

[52] Rosati (2021a), p. 328.

its users, they are performing an act of CtoP, the provision is simply identifying a 'new' type of act of CtoP, which, if completed without the corresponding authorisation implies the liability of the intermediary service. As assessed in the previous chapter, the CtoP implies any communication or transmission works by wire or wireless means, including the making available to a public that may have access to the protected works from a place and at a time individually chosen by them. Therefore, explicitly recognising that when OCSSPs, by means of their websites/ platforms, give access to the public, at any time or place, to protected works is basically to define an act of CtoP. Although the definition in Article 17 of an act of communication may seem redundant, it is not. Article 17(1) needs to specify the liability regime of OCCSPs to avoid them being covered by the liability exemption of intermediary services in Directive 2000/31. The limitation of the "hosting safe harbour" is clearly stated in Article 17(3),[53] which explicitly excludes the application of that exemption in situations under Article 17. This is in OCSSP's acts of communication. However, such intermediaries' liability regime requires making a difference between primary and secondary acts of CtoP. Therefore, the OCSSPs acts are always secondary acts of communication because they could not be done without a primary act of uploading, where the users run the communication act. Hence, those secondary acts may become, at the same time, acts of CtoP in an intermediary stage. This is the case where the user is not really the final user because he communicates the work displayed online to the public. For instance, when playing YouTube videos in a café open to the public as background music, the YouTube user communicates the musical work to the public and represents a new liable act of communication, according to the CJEU criteria exposed in the previous chapter. So, in this case, the final user's acts would not be covered by the authorisation or license that the OCCSP may obtain, according to Article 17.2.

The language used in the second part of Article 17(2),[54] precisely the word "also", indicates that the authorisations that OCSSPs shall get cover two kinds of CtoP acts: (1) the primary act of uploading and consequently communicating to the public or making available copyright-protected works (2) and the secondary act of giving the public access to copyright-protected works or other protected subject matter uploaded by users, run by OCSSPs. However, the final user that accesses the works ('recipient-user') is not covered by the same license or authorisation. The provision refers to acts carried out by users of the services falling within the scope of Article 3 of Directive 2001/29/EC when they are not acting on a commercial basis or where their activity does not generate significant revenues. Recital 69 on the

[53] The CDSM Directive's Article 17(3) states the following:

> When an online content-sharing service provider performs an act of communication to the public or an act of making available to the public under the conditions laid down in this Directive, the limitation of liability established in Article 14(1) of Directive 2000/31/EC shall not apply to the situations covered by this Article.

[54] Article 17.2 states as follow: "(…) that authorisation shall also cover acts carried out by users of the services falling within the scope of Article 3 of Directive 2001/29/EC when they are not acting on a commercial basis or where their activity does not generate significant revenues."

CDSMD clarifies that the double umbrella of the authorisation covers OCSSPs acts, on the one hand, and only the 'uploading-users' acts. Identifies that the authorisations obtained by OCSSPs cover the use on their service of content uploaded by the users of the service and the "copyright relevant acts in respect of uploads by users in cases without any profit-making purpose, or where the revenue generated by their uploads is not significant. When referring to the uploads by users, the recital means the primary act of communication of uploading. That excludes any act of CtoP performed by the recipient-user, which in any case constitutes a new act of CtoP. Additionally, Recital 69 explores the possibility that rightsholders have explicitly authorised users to upload and make available works in an online content-sharing service. In that situation, recital 69 grants that the act of communication to the public run by the OCSSPs is also authorised within the scope of the authorisation granted by the rightsholder to the user. However, it clarifies that this grant does not constitute any presumption in favour of OCSSPs that their users have cleared all relevant rights.[55] Based on Article 17(1), it can be inferred that OCSSPs consistently engage in secondary acts of communication by making available content uploaded by users in a previous primary act of communication. As Fig. 4.3 illustrates, the end-user or *recipient-user* may do eventual subsequent acts of CtoP, online or offline. Those subsequent acts are clearly out of the scope of the authorisation in Article 17(2) CDSMD and require a new authorisation under Article 3(1) of the InfoSoc Directive.

Returning to the requirement of not-profit making acts, according to Article 17(2), when the uploading-user is acting *'on a commercial basis or where their activity generates significant revenues'*, those users 'acts are not covered by the authorisation that OCSSPs shall obtain, and users require a separate license from the rightsholders.[56] This exclusion of commercial uses is intended to keep the obligation of obtaining authorisation for the communication to the public for those users doing profit-making acts like marketing or promotion, either directly or indirectly. The approach towards Article 17(2) appears to align with the CJEU's criteria of considering the user's profit-making situation.[57] It requires a new license as it constitutes a new act of communication to the public. Apart from "commercial uses", the provision excludes other uses that generate 'significant revenues'. That section referring to "significant revenues" is unclear as it does not specify the activities involved or define "significant revenues". Should we consider revenues as any income, or does it only refer to monetary value? When interpreting the term broadly, significant revenues can be considered equivalent to significant benefits. This interpretation includes any benefits besides monetary compensation that users may receive, directly or indirectly, from sharing content on platforms that may become viral. Various benefits can be considered profit-making acts, like products, services, trips, potential sponsorships, and even increased relevance, fans, or followers. An example

[55] CDSM Directive, Recital 69.

[56] Husovec and Quintais (2021), p. 5.

[57] See Chap. 3, section 2 in this book.

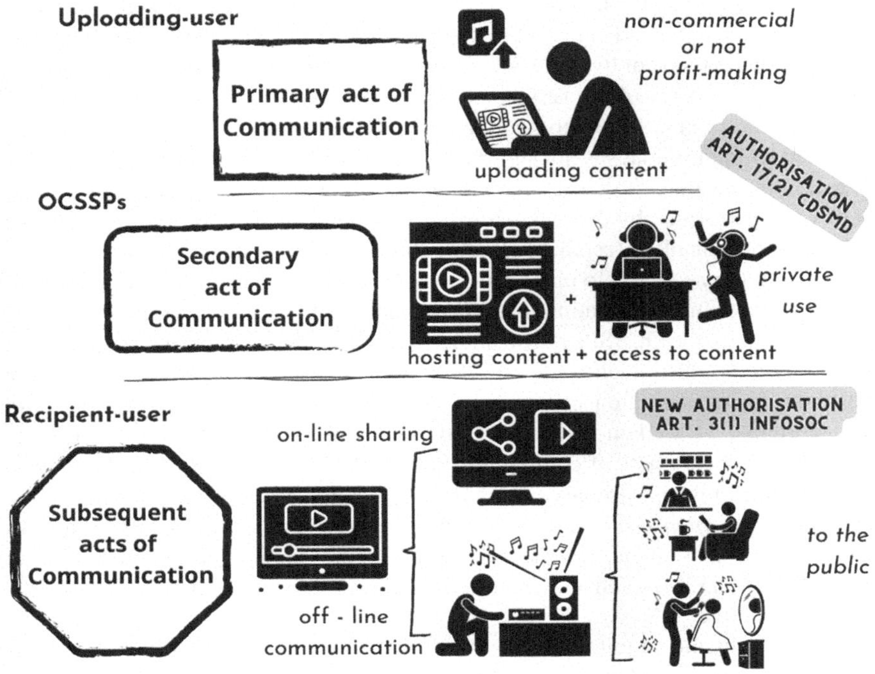

Fig. 4.3 Sequence of communication acts and the corresponding authorisation types under InfoSoc and CDSM directives. Source: Author's elaboration

of this practice is when a more or less relevant user uploads a video or meme containing music that goes viral on YouTube or Social Media (SM). On the one hand, those viral actions can result in further benefits different from economic revenues for the user. On the other hand, sometimes those actions are undercover commercial activities run by companies or other entities with undisclosed commercial intentions. In this scenario, a company reaches out to users. It requests them to upload videos on YouTube or social media platforms like TikTok or Instagram to promote their product, service, or event. The videos should appear authentic and not deliberately promotional. Sometimes, videos can become very popular and spread rapidly, which can be a way to avoid paying for a commercial use license. The person who originally posted the video may argue that it was intended for personal or private use despite it going viral and reaching a wider audience, resulting in some benefit. In this case, it falls under the authorisation obtained by the OCSSP, as stated in Article 17(2). Furthermore, both the company and the user receive benefits. However, there is a lack of authorisation in two aspects: first, for the commercial intention of the company, and second, for the "significant benefit" that the user gains. Article 17(1) intends to address the "value gap," while Article 17(2) connects profit-making activities to the requirement for authorisation. Therefore, users, particularly influencers, who gain any advantage from using a musical work on a content-sharing Social Media platform must obtain special authorisation from the rightsholders. This approach may be seen as an overprotection of rightsholders' rights that may affect the normal traffic of content on the internet and penalise the users for that. This is to say that such an interpretation could refrain users from uploading videos using musical works to avoid paying for a license. Which should be the criteria to consider the existence of "significant revenues" to require the authorisation for a subsequent act of communication to the public? A consistent approach would be to follow an analogue criterion of the existing "profit-making" standards that the CJEU has applied to offline situations[58] and online cases.[59] The consideration of the criterion of "the public" is not equivalent among online and offline. In online situations, the content is accessible to all the users of a certain platform or even the whole internet community.[60] Determining the profit-making nature of SM users and influencers is not easy. The theory in *GS Media's* judgement that the lucrative aspect of the communication creates a presumption of full knowledge of the possible illegal nature of the communication is obvious in those cases where the user makes the communication[61] to get a benefit. The CJEU profit-making criterion has been considered relevant when there is an effect on the financial results or becomes an additional service different from the main activity of the communicating user. Accordingly, since the activity of content-sharing is based on acts of communication, such a criterion is not acceptable to determine which users could be considered acting under the "significant revenues" scope. The problem is determining the standard to measure and the "significant revenues" level. Shall the number of followers, "likes", or "shares" be taken into account to measure the impact of the post and its potential revenues? Such an approach could be inconsistent, massive and unfair for many users. Those users are the ones who share content just for entertainment but unexpectedly start becoming viral and gaining visibility and benefits. Since there is no fixed standard to rely on, and their aim was not commercial, most users ignore their obligation to obtain authorisation from rightsholders and consequently their liability. Such vagueness and the lack of fixed standards require a case-by-case approach. The case-by-case approach, combined with the incorporation of 27 different national rules to implement the directive using varying criteria, undermines the level of consistency and may result in legal ambiguity.

[58] See CJEU Judgment of 31 May 2016, *Reha Training, C-117/15, ECLI:EU:C:2016:379,* para. 49–51, and CJEU Judgment of 4 Oct 2011, *Premier League, C-403/08, ECLI:EU:C:2011:631,* para. 205–206.

[59] See CJEU Judgment of 14 Jun 2017, *Ziggo, C-610/15, ECLI:EU:C:2017:456, para. 46,* CJEU Judgment of 26 Apr 2017, *Filmspeler, C-527/15, ECLI:EU: C:2017:300, para. 49,* CJEU Judgment of 8 Sep 2016, *GS Media, C-160/15, ECLI:EU:C:2016:644,* para. 51–54.

[60] Rejecting the theory of "new public", a definition of "the public" is a targeted indeterminate and large number of people, out of a determinate circle of potential recipients, which is too wide to determine it in online cases. See Chap. 3, section 2 in this book.

[61] CJEU Judgment of 8 Sep 2016, *GS Media, C-160/15, ECLI:EU:C:2016:644.*

Once the new liability regime of the OCSSPs is determined, as in the first three paragraphs of Article 17, the fourth paragraph introduces certain limitations to the OCSSPs liability. The first part of Article 14(4) confirms that the lack of authorisation to run public communication acts, including making available copyright-protected works, makes content-sharing service providers liable for unauthorised acts. That general liability of OCSSP is limited as long as service providers demonstrate that they have:

> (a) made best efforts to obtain an authorisation, and
>
> (b) made, in accordance with high industry standards of professional diligence, best efforts to ensure the unavailability of specific works and other subject matter for which the rightsholders have provided the service providers with the relevant and necessary information; and in any event
>
> (c) acted expeditiously upon receiving a sufficiently substantiated notice from the rightsholders to disable access to, or to remove from their websites, the notified works or other subject matter, and made best efforts to prevent their future uploads in accordance with point (b).[62]

The new liability regime requires OCSSPs to obtain a licence from rightsholders, but rightsholders do not have to grant an authorisation.[63] Recital 61 justifies that "as contractual freedom should not be affected by those provisions, rightsholders should not be obliged to give an authorisation or to conclude licensing agreements".[64] The limitation of liability in Article 17(4) operates in three cumulative stages. The first step is that the OCSSP must have requested a license but could not obtain it. However, the provision requires the OCSSP to make the "best efforts" to obtain authorisation. Using another unclear term adds extra uncertainty to determine whether an OCSSP is liable or can be exempt under Article 17(4). The European Copyright Society (ECS), in their Comment on Selected Aspects of Implementing Article 17 CDSMD into National Law,[65] declares that the fact of making best efforts to obtain an authorisation, plus the other requirements in paragraphs (b) and (c), become an exemption of liability may appear as a contradiction to Article 17(1). However, following Timm Pravemann's[66] theory that Article 17(1) and 17(4)(a) are interpreted as expressions of the same duty of the OCSSP, the *ECS* finds reasonable that 17(1) and 17(4)(a) considered together may be "applied as a cascade of different rules for different scenarios",[67] so Article 17(4)(a) applies only if OCSSP lacks authorisation from rightsholders and the corresponding license agreement. The term "best efforts" is not defined, raising the question of its meaning. Although Recital 66 does not define the requirements to consider "best efforts" have been made, it refers to the standards "in accordance with high industry standards of professional

---

62 Article 17(4) of CDSM Directive.

63 Shapiro and Hansson (2019), p. 408.

64 CDSM Directive, Recital 61.

65 Metzger et al. (2020).

66 See Pravemann (2019).

67 Metzger et al. (2020), p. 3.

diligence".[68] Rosati has understood such Industry standards of professional Diligence as "whether the steps that the service provider has taken are the steps that could be expected from a diligent operator of its kind."[69] The diligent operator concept was used by the CJEU case when discussing the liability of intermediary services in the *L'Oreal v eBay* case,[70] but without giving a definition of it. Matthias Leistner offers another approach of "best efforts", taking into account the systematic context of EU secondary law as well as the contextual relationship of Article 17 (1) and Article 17 (4)(a); Leistner considers the standards of the expression "best efforts" should follow a "similar direction of a rather strict standard",[71] Accordingly, OCSSPs' action in obtaining authorisation should not be minimal; on the contrary, OCSSPs must act proactively to conclude licensing agreements with all or at least, the most relevant collective management organisations (CMOs) in each Member State they operate in or the record labels to get a license for their catalogue. The ECS advices that the OCSSP active search should not require seeking adequate licenses for each and every item of protected content and its rightsholders because it may generate a blocking scenario. Hence, such an interpretation "would entail a general monitoring obligation for all uploaded content, and conflicts with Article 17(8) DSMD, Article 15 E-Commerce Directive and the fundamental freedom of OCSSPs to conduct a business under Article 16 of the Charter of Fundamental Rights".[72] The ECS also rejects the idea of obliging the rightsholders to take a leading role in providing OCSSPs with a license. This interpretation would turn OCSSPs into a passive role, merely reactive, and consequently, a reactive position cannot be considered as making "best efforts". On the other hand, the scope of best efforts should be proportionate and consider that OCSSPs cannot always easily identify the rightsholders, and licenses can not be obtained beforehand.[73] This is the case for orphan works,[74] emerging artists and minor and independent record labels.[75] Mandatory collective licenses are generalised in the music sector. If an OCSSP wants to operate within the EU, it is obliged to conclude general or blanket licenses with all the relevant CMOs, covering all their repertoire, in each Member State.[76] They can also apply for multi-territorial licenses[77] covering the catalogue of

---

68 CDSM Directive, Recital 66.

69 Rosati (2021a), p. 331.

70 CJEU Judgement of 12 July 2011, *L'Oreal v eBay, Case C-324/09, ECLI:EU:C:2011:474*, para. 124.

71 Leistner (2020), p. 23.

72 Metzger, et al. (2020), p. 5.

73 Leistner, (2020), p. 25.

74 This study is not covering the case of Orphan Works and its regulation in *Directive 2012/28/EU on certain permitted uses of orphan works of 25 October 2012, OJ L 299, 27.10.2012*, pp. 5–12.

75 Leistner (2020), pp. 30–37, proposes. in those situations, the application of the Extended Collective Licensing (ECL) system in Article 12 of the CSDM Directive as a solution for getting an ex-ante license. For further information related to this topic see: Quintais (2020), pp. 11–14.

76 For a further details on licensing see Hviid et al. (2017), p. 256.

77 For a further approach on Multiterritorial licenses see: Navas Navarro (2019), p. 81.

different CMOs in part of the EU territory.[78] Another option for OCSSP would be to negotiate blanket licenses directly from the main record labels in the music industry, also known as the "majors" (Universal Music Group, Sony Music Entertainment, and Warner Music)[79] and from other Indie record labels (Associated as IMPALA).[80] Despite the process of obtaining a license, music users, including OCSSPs, should not face difficult or even impossible barriers when fulfilling their obligation of obtaining rightsholders' authorisation. In that way, Article 16 of the CMOs' Directive[81] indicates that CMOs have the legal duty to negotiate, with any interested user, for the licensing of rights in good faith and onbased on the necessary information and see objective and non-discriminatory criteria. Moreover, paragraph (3) states that CMOs, once they have received the end users' required information, "shall, without undue delay, either offer a licence or provide the user with a reasoned statement explaining why it does not intend to license a particular service".[82]

If the OCSSP, after its best efforts, fails to obtain a license, Articles 17(4) (b) and (c) add two more conditions to limit the liability of service providers. Section (b) of the Article requires that OCSSPs ensure the *unavailability of those works* the rightsholders provided the *relevant and necessary information.* When ensuring the unavailability of this work, OCSSPs must make the "best efforts." the provision also specifies that it needs to be made according to the *high industry standards of professional diligence.* Likewise, the following paragraph (c) requires notice-and-take-down actions to OCSSPs. This requires that when rightsholders consider that there is a copyright infringement regarding one of their works, they take an active role and send a sufficiently substantiated notice to OCSSPs, who must "disable

[78] Since the CMOs 'Directive entered into force, allowing multi-territorial licensing many CMOs set up alliances to license their repertoires on a multi-territorial basis. Also, emerging collective rights management organisations, like Unison, (https://www.unisonrights.es/) broke into the market, ending with the traditional monopolies and generating a more diverse offer and fairer playing field for both, creators and users. However, this has disseminated the obtention of licences that usually was a one-stop, as most of CMOs operated as pseudo-monopolies in each Member State.

[79] The European Commission approved on 26 Oct. 2018 the acquisition of EMI Music Publishing by Sony Music America (See https://competition-cases.ec.europa.eu/cases/M.8989). After that the three major labels in today's industry are Universal Music Group, Sony Music Entertainment and Warner Music Group—with each having their own subsidiaries. See also https://www.musicgateway.com/blog/record-label/music-labels-top-record-labels and https://www.billboard.com/music/music-news/record-labels-billboard-explains-1235296400/

[80] The Independent Music Companies Association (IMPALA) is a pan-European industry body representing independent labels and distributors. They lobbied the European Commission and made a frontal opposition against the acquisition of EMI Music Publishing, first in 2012 against the attempt of Universal Music Group and finally in 2018 to stop the full acquisition by Sony Music. See https://www.impalamusic.org/news/

[81] Directive 2014/26/EU of the European Parliament and of the Council of 26 February 2014 on collective management of copyright and related rights and multi-territorial licensing of rights in musical works for online use in the internal market. (2018). OJ L 84, 20.3.2014, p. 72–98 (CMOs' Directive).

[82] CMOs'Directive, Article 16(3).

access to, or to remove the notified works from their websites and made best efforts to prevent their future uploads."[83]

However, the requirements in Article 17 (4) don't apply to all OCSSPs, as per the exception in Article 17(6), which aimed to make things easy for emerging companies and start-ups. Those OCSSPs that have been available to the public in the EU for less than 3 years and have an annual turnover below ten million Euros are only required to comply with the first preventative obligation of Article 17(4) (a). If such OCSSPs receive *sufficiently substantiated notice*, they must act immediately to remove or disable access to the notified works from their websites. Only if their average number of monthly unique visitors exceeds five million in the previous calendar year will they be required to demonstrate that they have done their best to prevent further uploads of the notified works for which the rightsholders have provided the relevant and necessary information.

If an OCSSP does not meet any of the conditions listed in Article 17(4), or none of them, Article 17 (5) determines the approach that needs to be done in light of the proportionality principle and requires considering the relevant case's key aspects. Article 17(5) contains a non-exhaustive list of elements that must be taken into account. When determining the liability of an OCSSP national judiciaries, and eventually the CJEU, when required, must consider "(a) the type, the audience and the size of the service and the type of works or other subject matter uploaded by the users of the service; and (b) the availability of suitable and effective means and their cost for service providers",[84] among others. It has to be understood that OCSSPs have to use the technological tools available, including algorithmic tools based on AI, etc., to detect and block the unauthorised copyright-protected content that can be identified as such. OCSSPs, to avoid liability, are required to review all uploaded content to ensure that it does not infringe copyright, according to Article 17(4). Angelopoulos and Quintais point out that given the massive amounts of content that platforms host, this requires the adoption of automatic content identification systems, also known as "upload filters", in practice. The authors also highlight that critics argue whether performed manually or through automated filtering, requires general monitoring, incompatible with the preexisting EU legislation and even the EU Charter of Fundamental Rights.[85] Although Article 17(8) in the CDSMD declares that the provision "shall not lead to any general monitoring obligation",[86] this provision does not set a prohibition of such general monitoring, but a lack of obligation to monitor for OCSSPs. On the other hand, authors like Shapiro and Hansson believe that the obligation of monitoring does not affect those OCSSPs that fulfilled all the requirements and met all the new duties and conditions in Article

[83] CDSM Directive, Article 17(4)(c).

[84] CDSM Direcive, Article 17(5).

[85] For a comprehensive analysis of the compatibility between automated filtering and fundamental rights, consider the following: Geiger and Justin Jütte (2021), available at https://digitalcommons.wcl.american.edu/research

[86] CDSM Directive Article 17(8).

17 beyond what is relevant to and necessary for compliance with that provision. The authors consider that the "monitoring performed to comply with Article 17 should not be considered general monitoring".[87]

4.3 The compatibility of Article 17 with the EU Charter of Fundamental Rights: An Attempt for Annulment

The compatibility of Article 17(4) with the EU legislation and the EU Charter of Fundamental Rights has been controversial. In May 2019, just a few weeks after the approval of the CDSMD, the Polish government an action for annulment with the CJEU,[88] challenging the validity of the filtering obligation contained in Article 17 on the grounds that it will lead to censorship and will limit the freedom of expression and the freedom to receive and impart information guaranteed in the EU Charter of Fundamental Rights. The Polish request was the annulment of the preventive measures in Article 17(4) (b) and (c) in fine in light of the right to freedom of expression and information in Article 11 of the Charter of Fundamental Rights of the EU (Charter). In the alternative, should these provisions not be detachable from Article 17, the Republic of Poland required the Court to annul Article 17 in its entirety. The Court rejected the petition of partial annulment, considering that point (b) and point (c) are not severable from the remainder of Article 17. The CJEU prompted that the "requirement of severability is not satisfied where the partial annulment of an act would have the effect of altering its substance".[89] Following the Opinion of the Advocate General Øe on that case,[90] the Court points out that Article 17 of the CDSM Directive establishes a new liability regime in respect of online content-sharing service providers and its provisions as a whole, resulting from the interpretation of recitals 61 and 66, seek to strike a balance between the rights and interests of OCSSPs and those of rightsholders. Consequently, the partial annulment of only point (b) and point (c) would alter the substance of Article 17 since it would result "in that liability regime's being replaced by a regime that is both substantially different and significantly more favourable to those providers".[91]

Therefore, the core issue before the Court was determining the compatibility of Article 17 with fundamental rights. In other words, whether Article 17 effectively ensures compliance with fundamental rights through the safeguards in paragraphs 5–9. In paragraphs 27–28, the Court recalls the conception of communication to the

[87] Shapiro and Hansson (2019).

[88] CJEU Judgment of 26 April 2022, Ibid.

[89] *Ibid*, para 17.

[90] Opinion of the Advocate General Øe delivered on 16 July 2020 on Joined Cases C-682/18 and C-683/18. ECLI:EU:C:2020:586.

[91] Judgment of the Court of 26 April 2022, para. 20.

public in its YouTube/Cyando judgement. It later clarifies that the CDSMD provided a new specific liability mechanism with a limited scope for OCSSPs.[92]

The Court clarifies that the specific liability regime, introduced in Article 17(4) of the CDSM Directive, is further specified and supplemented in Article 17(5) to (10). Additionally to the measures mentioned above in Article 17 paragraphs (5) (6) and (8), the provision in Article 17(7) states that online content-sharing service providers and rightsholders must not prevent the availability of user-uploaded works or protected subject matter that do not infringe the copyright or related rights, especially if an exception or limitation covers them. That provision lists those exceptions and limitations that shall be allowed by the Member States to rely on, including exceptions for quotation, criticism, review, caricature, parody or pastiche. Ferri[93] explains that Article 17(7) makes these exceptions mandatory, whereas, in InfoSoc Directive's Article 5(3), subparagraphs (d) and (k), the same exceptions were considered optional. Professor Pedro A. de Miquel defends that those exceptions and limitations on quotation, criticism, review, caricature, parody or pastiche usages become mandatory under the CDSMD but only regarding content generated and uploaded by users on an online content-sharing platform.[94] Additionally, Professor Garrote Fernández-Diez believes that Article 17(7)(b) does not oblige the legislators of the Member States to adopt a new limit of general scope in relation to uses of the works or services for the purposes of caricature, parody or pastiche. He considers that the limit remains optional for Member States in accordance with the InfoSoc Directive. The author concludes that "the limit mentioned in Article 17(7)(b) CDSMD it is compulsory for Member States to incorporate, but only in relation to acts of loading and provision of user-generated content on online content sharing services".[95]

Accordingly, the Court affirms that the EU legislature considered the particular importance of those exceptions and limitations for freedom of expression and freedom of the arts and, therefore, for the abovementioned fair balance, it was necessary to make those exceptions and limitations mandatory, in order to ensure that users receive uniform protection in that regard across the European Union.[96]

Article 17(7) first subparagraph states that the "cooperation between online content-sharing service providers and rightsholders shall not result in the prevention of the availability of works or other subject matter uploaded by users, which do not infringe copyright and related rights, including where such works or other subject matter are covered by an exception or limitation" of those rights. The Court referring to that "unambiguous wording" of Article 17(7) declares that it prescribes a specific result to be achieved, instead the limited requirement to OCSSPs to make their 'best efforts'.[97] The Court acknowledges that Article 17(7) requires Member States to

---

[92] *Ibid*, para. 30–32.

[93] Ferri (2020), p. 25.

[94] De Miguel Asensio (2020), p. 212.

[95] Garrote Fernández-Diez (2023), p. 8.

[96] Judgment of the Court of 26 April 2022, para. 87.

[97] Ibid, para 77–78.

ensure those exceptions are respected despite the preventive measures in paragraph (4). Quintais assumes that the Court sets "a normative hierarchy between the higher-level obligation in paragraph (7) and the lower-level obligation in paragraph (4)".[98] Furthermore, the Court reminds that the third paragraph of Article 17(9) states that the CDSMD "shall in no way affect legitimate uses, such as uses under exceptions or limitations provided for in Union law".[99] It is important to note that Article 17-(8) explicitly excludes any general monitoring obligation from Article 17(4). The CJEU determines the provision of Article 17(8) as an additional safeguard for ensuring that the right to freedom of expression and information of users of OCSSPs is observed. The Court clarifies that this means that the OCSSPs "cannot be required to prevent the uploading and making available to the public of content which, in order to be found unlawful, would require an independent assessment of the content by them in the light of the information provided by the rightsholders and of any exceptions and limitations to copyright".[100] In other words, the case-by-case assessment of the content cannot be ex-ante, as it represents general monitoring, but only after notice from the rightsholders. This allows only ex-post notice-and-take-down mechanisms. Quintais agrees that the judgment clarifies that Member States' laws should prioritise limiting ex-ante filtering measures. In that case, "additional application of ex-post safeguards is an adequate means to address remaining over-blocking issues".[101]

Article 17(9) mandates the creation of efficient and expeditious complaint and redress mechanisms for users in the event of disputes arising from disabled access or the removal of works uploaded by users. This requirement is crucial to ensuring all users' fair and just treatment. The Court recognises that Article 17(9) introduces several procedural safeguards, additional to those provided for in Article 17(7) and (8), to protect the right to freedom of expression and information of users that, despite the safeguards laid down in those other provisions, the OCSSPs have erroneously or unjustifiably block lawful uploaded content.[102]

Apart from those mechanisms offered by the OCSSPs, Member States must also guarantee out-of-court redress mechanisms for the settlement of disputes, supplementing judicial remedies. The Court has determined that in order to protect users' right to freedom of expression and information, enshrined in Article 11 of the Charter. The fair balance between various rights and interests, the EU legislature has laid down provisions of Articles 17(7) and (9) that the implementation of obligations on OCSSPs, in Article 17(4) points (b) and (c) cannot lead to measures affecting

[98] Quintais (2022) 'Between Filters and Fundamental Rights: How the Court of Justice saved Article 17 in C-401/19 - Poland v. Parliament and Council', available at https://pure.uva.nl/ws/files/145379774/verfassungsblog.de-How_the_Court_of_Justice_saved_Article_17_in_C-40119_-_Poland_v_Parliament_and_Council.pdf

[99] Judgment of the Court of 26 April 2022, para. 79.

[100] Ibid. para. 90.

[101] Quintais (2020), p. 4.

[102] Judgment of the Court of 26 April 2022, para. 93.

users' fundamental rights.[103] Thus, the obligations in Articles 17(7) and (9) protect the fundamental rights of OCSSPs 'users who share content which does not infringe copyright and related rights.

The Court concludes its judgement by declaring that the obligation resulting from the specific liability regime established in Article 17(4) of the CDSM Directive, and in particular from the conditions for exemption from liability laid down in point (b) and point (c), has been accompanied by appropriate safeguards by the EU legislature to ensure respect for the right to freedom of expression and information of the users guaranteed by Article 11 of the Charter, and a fair balance between that right, and the right to intellectual property, protected by Article 17(2) of the Charter.[104] Furthermore, the CJEU closes its judgement, recapping that when transposing Article 17 into national law, Member States must grant a fair balance between the different fundamental rights protected by the Charter. When implementing the measures transposing Article 17,[105] the authorities and courts of the Member States must interpret their national law consistently with that provision and ensure that their approach is compliant with the principle of proportionality and respectful of fundamental rights and the other general principles of EU law.

During the pendency of the annulment action before the CJEU, the Commission conducted Stakeholder Dialogues as required under Article 17(10) CDSMD. The CJEU, in its judgement, also refers to Article 17(10) as a supplementing the system of safeguards. That provision requires the European Commission to organise stakeholder dialogues in cooperation with the Member States to discuss best practices for cooperation between OCSSPs and rightsholders. Article 17(10) specifies that, when discussing best practices, special consideration should be given to balancing fundamental rights and the use of exceptions and limitations. That is why the CJEU defines such a provision as a supplement to the system of safeguards. From the results of those dialogues, the Commission is required to issue a document of

---

[103] *Ibid*, para. 80.

[104] *Ibid*, para. 98.

[105] Dr. Christina Angelopoulos made an analysis of the national implementation of the DCDSM in 11 Member States and its compatibility. See the legal report in different formats:

For a visual summary of the project report, visit: C. Angelopoulos, *Copyright Lab.*, 2022, Informationlabs.Org, available at https://informationlabs.org/copyright/*Articles 15 & 17 of the Directive on Copyright in the Digital Single Market.*

For the full report see *Comparative National Implementation Report* (2022), available at https://informationlabs.org/wp-content/uploads/2022/09/Angelopoulos-Report-Full-Report.pdf.

For an Article of the highlights of the report, see: Angelopoulos, 'Comparative Report on the National Implementations of Articles 15 & 17 of the Directive on Copyright in the Digital Single Market – Part 1 and Part 2', *Kluwer Copyright Blog* (2022), available at https://copyrightblog.kluweriplaw.com/2022/12/01/comparative-report-on-the-national-implementations-of-Articles-15-17-of-the-directive-on-copyright-in-the-digital-single-market-part-2/

guidance on the application of Article 17. The *Guidance on Article 17*[106] was published on 4 June 2021, just three days before the deadline for the CDSM Directive's transposition.

4.4 The CDSM Directive and the Role of Stakeholders in the Music Field

The requirement of Article 17(10) refers to stakeholders. Still, it does not indicate who must be identified as such and consequently be entitled to take part in the consultation process and elaboration for the Guidance on Article 17. The following lines analyse the concept of stakeholders, especially in the music field, and assess their importance or role in each stage of the legislative process. This study on the stakeholders aims to determine which of them were considered during the CDSM Directive legislative process and how the approval of the Directive benefits certain stakeholders more than others. This tries to demonstrate if the Directive's main objectives, like closing the value gap and balancing the rights of the different players, were achieved.

The seminal definition of stakeholder analysis comes from strategic management theories. One of the early definitions was given by Freeman in 1984,[107] who referred to Stakeholders as "any who can affect or is affected by the achievement of the organisation's objectives". Modern theories offer a broader definition of stakeholders by describing them as a 'group or individual that can be influenced by, or can itself influence, the activities of the organisation',[108] including anyone that can be involved somehow, either as an active or as a passive subject, in the transformations generated by any action of an organisation. Classical management stakeholder analysis has been adopted in policy or law-making processes. In the policy-making process, the stakeholder's analysis is applied to determine the validity of the current theoretical models, the relation of such theoretical models with the major players' working practices and behaviours, and the need for changes in that policy area. Furthermore, stakeholders' analysis assists in determining whether there should be a policy shift.[109]

Including stakeholders in the policy-making process involves, at first instance, identifying the different institutions, subjects and interest groups concerned in the law-making and the implementation of a particular policy and its further effects.

[106] European Commission, Communication from the Commission to the European Parliament and the Council 'Guidance on Article 17 of Directive 2019/790 on Copyright in the Digital Single Market', COM(2021) 288 final.

[107] Freeman (1984).

[108] Friedman and Miles (2006).

[109] Suthersanen (2007), p 126.

Therefore, stakeholders can be of very different natures[110] depending on the policy to be developed. Although there is a wide range of subjects that can become stakeholders, they can be divided into three main categories: (i) natural persons, concerned by self-interest; (ii) enterprises or legal entities with economic interest; (iii) advocacy or organisations NGO's, interested in defending certain rights or legal interests that may be affected. Accordingly, Suthersanen divides primary stakeholders into creators, producers and users in the copyright field. Copyright law and policy aim to find the balance between creators, who generate artistic or scientific works; producers or publishers, who invest in the distribution and communication of such works; and users, who are interested in having access to cultural and scientific works. Since the last decades of the twentieth century, technology changed the cultural and scientific industries, and new stakeholders in the scene have interfered in those three primary groups, like streaming services providers, online content-sharing service platforms (OCSSPs), social media, intermediary service platforms, etc. Among copyright stakeholders, there is a wide range of subjects because copyright law scope is also varied, including any literary (books, poems, journalistic Articles, etc.), artistic (fine arts, performing arts, audiovisual, musical works, photographs, etc.) and scientific works (scientific research, academic papers or lectures, software, databases, codes, etc.). Furthermore, copyright law does not only deal with authors and publishers strictly; it also covers rights ancillary to copyright to other subjects taking part in the creative process (like performing artists, translators, musicians, broadcasters, etc.), namely related or neighbouring rights. Accordingly, each discipline protected by copyright and related rights has its subjects directly or indirectly affected by copyright law or policy development. To streamline, as this study is focused on copyright in online musical works, we refer to the role of stakeholders in online music.

The different classic stakeholders in the music field are directly related to the general categories of "creators" and "producers". The "creators" group includes not only authors of musical works, who are the copyright owners—namely composers and lyricists-but also all those who take part in the creative process and hold any related rights—like musicians, performers, and music producers when making music arrangements. As "producers" are included, those with an economic interest in a musical work either during the creation process—publishers and phonogram producers at the distribution level—record labels—or when communicating to the public—broadcasting companies regarding their broadcast.

In the music field, the royalties share of the copyright's economical rights system is very complex. As Fig. 4.4 shows, part form different subjects and objects and has different rights and economical share of royalties.

Economical Rights in the music fields are divided into performing rights and mechanical rights. Performing rights are directly linked to the musical work, to the composition, and those rights are the public performance right and the communication to the public right. Authors and publishers are subjects that receive the share of

[110]Vetulani-Cęgiel and Meyer (2020), p. 7.

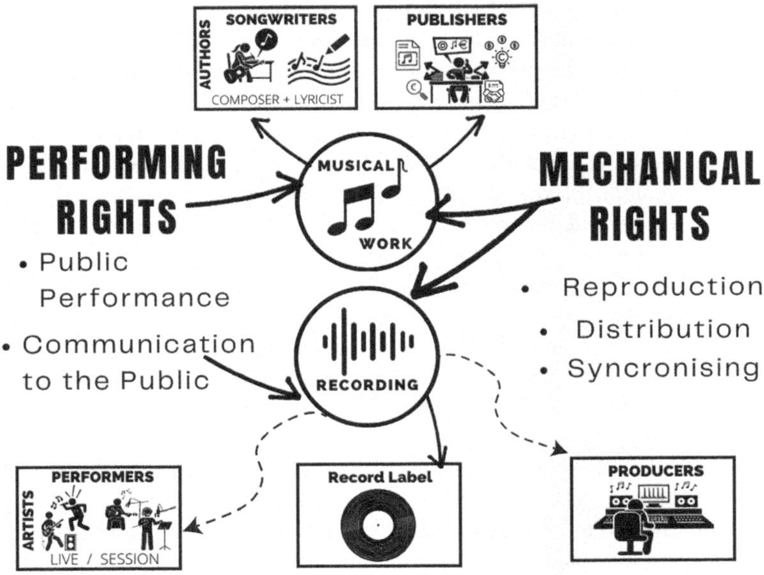

Fig. 4.4 Type of economical rights and their corresponding share. Source: Author's elaboration

copyright royalties generated by the exploitation of the musical work related with those rights. However, when there is a live performance of a musical work artist get their share of related rights, but not on the object of the musical work but on their performances.

Another type of rights is the so called mechanical rights. Mechanical rights are critical for the exploitation of music recordings, whether physical or digital. Those mechanical rights are reproduction, distribution and synchronization rights. Reproduction and distribution royalties refer to those for making copies of the sound recording and distributing it physically or digitally. Royalties for the synchronization right, are generated when copyrighted music is paired or 'synchronised' with visual media, for example a song used as part of the soundtrack of a film. The royalties share of mechanical right is shared among the recording and the musical work owner's, the record label, and publishers and authors. The percentages of the share for each part are set in the agreements signed between record labels and creators. Since

The royalties are due to the licensing agreements of digital platforms, radio, tv or other broadcasters, that sign to use the musical works and their recordings.

For example the stream a song on Spotify in Europe generates is considered a 75% for communication to the public, as a public performance right, and 25% for mechanical rights, including reproduction and a download.

The licensing, collection and distribution of royalties is run by CMO's, on behalf of authors, publishers or artists. Those CMO's administrate a catalogue of works, and the larger the work the more power to negotiate the licensing fees with the platforms. Regarding the mechanical rights, big record labels, also named masters, negotiate their catalogues directly with the platforms.

All those primary stakeholders that create, invest or produce musical works, don't have the same position. It is clear that those ones who has the power are masters that on one hand negotiate with the digital platforms and on the other screw authors and artist by setting unfair shares of the royalties in their agreements.

All those musical works and sound recordings are consumed, used or exploited by the third general group of stakeholders: the users. Users are interested in having access, as much as possible, to cultural and creative content. Thus, such users' interests must be balanced with the creators' interest in their moral recognition and remuneration and the producers' economic interest. As mentioned above, in a digital world, classic stakeholders in the field of musical works converge with new subjects or even categories of stakeholders resulting from the new business models, which gives a prominent role to the information technology and digital services industry. Thus, a new category of stakeholders can be introduced in this schema: the online intermediaries. As online intermediaries, music service providers have previously obtained authorisation and licences by signing agreements with the rightsholders and their representatives, namely collecting societies.

As previously assessed in this chapter, a big part of users' music consumption is based on creating social media content, using copyright-protected music, and sharing such content with other users on the OCSSPs (like Instagram, YouTube, TikTok, etc.). Hence, final users do not have any authorisation or licence from the rightsholders to use, exploit and share their musical works. Still, the intermediary service should be on their behalf instead. The important influence of those intermediaries in nowadays music and copyright industry is obvious, and their role and opinion must be considered in the policy-making and law-making process. This elevates those intermediaries to a new category of stakeholders. Also, the interests or affectation of such intermediaries are far from the primary stakeholders' concerns.

Although Chap. 2 in this book[111] analyses the Copyright acquis and the legislative process of its instruments, the following lines analyse the involvement of those stakeholders in the European Union law-making process of the CDSM Directive. The assessment of ex-ante Stakeholders analysis conducted before the approval of the CDSM Directive is assessed in this chapter to provide consistency to the ex-post Stakeholders analysis under Article 17(10) CDSMD, and the conclusion drawn from both parts, ex-ante and ex-post. In the recent EU Copyright reform, we can identify two types of stakeholders' analysis: ex-ante and ex-post. Before the law-making process, ex-ante stakeholders' analyses control the proportionality in the EU competencies exercise. As seen in Chap. 2, consultation with stakeholders is essential when elaborating impact assessment reports that accompany the legislative proposals and justify the proportionality principle. The CDSM Directive proposal was accompanied by an Impact Assessment containing an ex-ante stakeholders process. Another ex-ante stakeholders' consultation process the CDSMD can be found in the

[111] See Chap. 2 in this book.

Reports on the corresponding Parliamentary Committee's legislative proposals. The *Report on the proposal for a directive of the European Parliament and of the Council on copyright in the Digital Single Market*[112] was adopted on 29 June 2018 before presenting the final text, with the related amendments, to be discussed and voted approved by the European Parliament in the Plenary session. That report contains the opinion of the Parliamentary Committee of Legal Affairs after different hearings held with the stakeholders.

On 14 September 2016, the European Commission published the Commission Impact Assessment on the modernisation of EU copyright rules[113] (from now onwards IA). That IA document accompanied the document of the legislative proposals of the CDSM Directive and the final Directive 2019/789[114] on copyright and related rights applicable to certain online transmissions of broadcasting organisations and retransmissions of television and radio programmes (Broadcasting Directive). This text was conceived as a Regulation instead of a Directive in the Commission proposal. In the IA, three types of mechanisms were taken for the stakeholders' analysis: public consultations, surveys and stakeholder meetings. Figure 4.5, in next page, categorises the main topics, discussions and stakeholders participating in each mechanism. Despite some sectorial consultations, public consultations were open to all stakeholders. Users and consumers were asked mainly via surveys (by telephone and online). Likewise, surveys were only used for those types of stakeholders. However, some meetings also congregate consumers' representatives for sectors like audiovisual or education. But most of the stakeholders' meetings were led to hear the rightsholders, whether they are the industry[115] or creators. Intermediaries were only met in specific conferences to discuss the role of online intermediaries and cross-border access to content.

The overall conclusion of the IA evaluates the impact of the copyright reform on stakeholders and remarks that it would affect all types of stakeholders differently. Still, no disproportionate impact on a specific category of stakeholders was expected. Hence, the draft legislative acts were elaborated considering the results of the stakeholder analysis done in the IA, based on the existing evidence and the different stakeholder consultations. The IA states that a balance was considered between the

---

[112]Committee on Legal Affairs of the European Parliament, Report - A8–0245/2018 on the proposal for a directive of the European Parliament and of the Council on copyright in the Digital Single Market, 2018.

[113]European Commission, Impact Assessment on the modernisation of EU copyright rules, SWD (2016) 301 final, 14 September 2016.

[114]Directive (EU) 2019/789 of the European Parliament and of the Council of 17 April 2019 Laying down Rules on the Exercise of Copyright and Related Rights Applicable to Certain Online Transmissions of Broadcasting Organisations and Retransmissions of Television, OJ L 130, 17.5.2019, p. 82–91.

[115]From now onwards the term 'industry' refers to above mentioned stakeholders primary group of 'producers', meaning any legal entity, corporate, guilt or professional association, that contributes in the creation process (not creative) by contributing to make the literary artistic or scientific works possible, including investors, producers, publishers, masters.

Type of Action	TOPIC	Time	Main points covered	Implied Stakeholders
Public consultations	Public consultation on the review of the EU copyright rules	05/12/13 - 05/03/14	Commission's review of the EU copyright rules, including in the areas of access to cross-border content, exceptions, and remuneration of authors and performers	All
	Public consultation on the review of the EU Satellite and Cable Directive	24/08/15 - 16/11/15	the functioning of the rules related to the clearance of rights for satellite broadcasters regarding cross-border access and the possible need to extend these rules to online transmissions	All
	Public consultation on the role of publishers in the copyright value chain and on the 'panorama exception'	23/03/16 - 15/06/16	the possible introduction in EU law of a new neighbouring right for publishers and the so-called 'panorama exception	PUBLISHING SECTOR AND CONSUMERS
Surveys	Eurobarometer on "Cross-border access to online content"	01/01/15 - 31/01/15	information on consumers' experience and interest with online; as regards cross-border portability of online subscriptions and cross-border access to online content.	CONSUMERS
	Eurobarometer on "Internet users' preferences for accessing content online"	01/01/15 - 31/01/15	Online content consumption patterns for music, films and TV series, news and images. Type of services chosen by Internet users to access content online . Criteria for choosing a service to access and consume content online.	Internet Users aged 18-45
Meetings with stakeholders	Round table discussion : Access to content	30 January 2015	Territoriality and cross-border access to content	AV, MUSIC and PRINT sectors: right holders, broadcasters, VoD/SVoD platforms, cable and telecom companies, and consumer organisations
	Round table discussion in the context of the Berlinale Film Festival	February 2016	Cross-border access to audiovisual works as well as ways to tackle copyright infringements	AUDIOVISUAL SECTOR
	Round table discussion in the context of the Cannes Film Festival	May 2016	Online transmissions and retransmissions of TV/radio programmes. Access to and availability of EU audiovisual works on VoD platforms.	AUDIOVISUAL SECTOR
	Meetings of the ad hoc "IPR and copyright reform" Working Group of the European Parliament	February and June 2015	Ways to improve cross-border accessibility and availability of audiovisual works in the EU. Licensing mechanisms and exceptions, in particular in relation to the print sector. Remuneration of authors and performers	ALL
	Bilateral Meetings: TV and Radio online	between 2014 and 2016	Online transmissions and retransmissions of TV and radio programmes	TV and radios, CMOs, broadcasters, telecommunications operators and right holders.
	Meetings and discussions on Availability of EU audiovisual works on VoD platforms	1s semester 2016	The reasons of the limited availability of European audiovisual works on VoD platforms and possible solutions	VoD platforms, distributors, film producers, aggregators and organisations representing audiovisual authors
	Meetings on digitisation and dissemination of out-of-commerce (OOC) works in the collections of Cultural Heritage Institutions	between 2014 and 2016	Digitisation and dissemination of out-of-commerce (OOC) works in the collections of Cultural Heritage Institutions. Copyright issues and the practicalities of the preservation of works in cultural heritage collections	Cultural Heritage Institutions, practitioners on the field, epresentatives of authors, publishers and producers, CMO's
Meetings with stakeholders	Roundtable on exeptions on access to knowledge and heritage through libraries, education and cultural heritage institutions	19-02-2015	need to adapt the exceptions for preservation and illustration for teaching to digital and cross-border uses	representatives of universities, libraries, cultural heritage institutions, consumers, representatives of authors, scientific and educational publishers, film producers, and CMOs
	Meetings interviews and surveys on uses of protected content in the context of teaching	between 2014 and 2016	Uses of protected content in the context of teaching. Copyright framework on digitally supported education and training practices	representatives of universities and, , educational users, educational and academic and sheet music publishers, CMOs
	Meetings with Licences for Europe group: text and data mining	2015	Explore solutions such as standard licensing models as well as technology platforms to facilitate TDM access	researchers and universities, scientific publishers, news and books publishers, technology and life science companies, consumer representatives
	Well-functioning marketplace for copyright ; the role of online intermediaries	2015-2016	The role of online intermediaries	ALL / Bilateral meetings with online intermediaries assosiations
	Well-functioning marketplace for copyright ; the role of publishers	2016	The role of publishers in the copyright value chain and the rights in publications	journalists, consumers, publishers, media monitoring services, digital media associations, online service providers of access to news and other publications
	Well-functioning marketplace for copyright ; Remuneration of authors and performers	2013-2015	Remuneration of authors and performers	representatives of authors, performers and producers, publishers, broadcasters, record labels

Fig. 4.5 Stakeholders, and topics in the Impacts Assessment. Source: Author's elaboration

interests of consumers/users and rightsholders. Therefore, the derived legislative proposals aimed to provide substantial benefits to consumers/users and rightsholders by introducing measures related to broader access to content, exceptions and the better functioning of the online copyright marketplace. Evaluating the IA conclusions regarding the impacts on the different types of stakeholders, rightsholders, and users would benefit more than negative impacts from the proposed actions to be taken in the IA. On the one hand, rightsholders would get advantages like improved licensing mechanisms, a higher level of control on their content uploaded by users or more accessible and more transparent clearance of rights, but to face the burden of the exceptions on educational, preservation and text and data mining. On the other hand, users and consumers would benefit from broader access and availability to content. However, online service providers—also refered as online intermediaries—would be affected differently depending on their business models and the nature of the content they host. These impacts are rarely beneficial. Nevertheless, certain burdens or obligations, such as those faced by Online Content-Sharing Service Providers (OCSSPs) that handle large volumes of uploaded content, require the implementation of appropriate measures to identify protected material, increase transparency, and comply with the prohibition on general monitoring.

The main conclusion taken from the ex-ante stakeholders' analysis before the text of the proposal of the CDSM Directive is that all the stakeholders taking part in the consultations affected by the law-making process can be categorised into three main types. The categories of stakeholders taken into account before the approval of the CDSM Directive were: (i) rightsholders, including the two principal categories of creators and industry; (ii) intermediaries, namely internet services providers and platforms; and (iii) users, also referring to consumers and institutional users. After the consultations and once the IA was published together with the draft legislation, the significance of each stakeholder varied. Thus, some become clear beneficiaries of the legal actions after the ex-ante stakeholders' analysis, namely rightsholders. While others, the intermediaries, would be burdened by the legislative act rather than a benefit. Besides, users got stuck in the middle of the other two stakeholders. Despite being beneficiaries of wider content availability, users would also have to indirectly bear the interference of the intermediaries' obligation when sharing content online, as their fundamental right to freedom of expression could be engaged.

Once the CDSM Directive was approved, the OCSSPs' obligation of obtaining authorisation was materialised in Article 17 of the CDSM Directive, as assessed in the previous section of this chapter. Article 17(10) additionally requests the Commission to organise stakeholder dialogues to discuss best practices for cooperation between OCSSPs and rightsholders, and taking into account the results of the stakeholder dialogues, the Commission issued guidance on the application of Article 17. This, in essence, means a requirement for taking an ex-post stakeholders' analysis.

The guidance was elaborated considering the results of stakeholders' dialogues organised to discuss best practices for collaboration between OCSSPs and rightsholders. Following an open call for interest, the Commission invited up to

80 individual representatives of stakeholder organisations to the dialogue meetings. The number of seats per organisation varied depending on their composition and representativeness. The Commission targeted and selected which representative organisations had a seat at the meeting. The organisation's eligibility was based on the criteria stated by the Commission. To participate in the discussions, the representative organisations must operate at the European level and represent the interests of rightsholders, online content-sharing service providers or users. Users' organisations also included consumer and fundamental rights organisations concerned with the application of Article 17. Organisations with a legitimate interest in and directly impacted the discussion on the best practices for cooperation between OCSSPs and rightsholders were also invited. Finally, the meetings were also open to other organisations, referring to any practical experience related to the matters regulated by Article 17. The Commission organised six stakeholder dialogue meetings between October 2019 and February 2020. A targeted written consultation was carried out from 27 July to 10 September 2020 to finalise the stakeholder dialogue.

Those meetings aimed to elaborate a guidance document[116] to support the Member States in making an adequate transposition of Article 17. The guidance was also led to those market players obliged to comply with the obligations derived from implementing Article 17 into national legislation. The topics covered in the stakeholders meeting that were finally laid down in the guidance mainly referred to the relation between rightsholders and OCSSPs and the liability of service providers under Article 17. Likewise, it also addressed how to facilitate the obtention of authorisations and the need for a specific liability mechanism in the absence of a license, for instance, ensuring the unavailability of specific protected content. A minor part also referred to users' role, basically the establishment of 'notice and take down' and 'notice and stay down' mechanisms when users share unauthorised content. Those mechanisms must grant users fundamental rights; therefore, safeguards for legitimate uses of content and complaint and redress mechanisms for users were assessed. As Article 17(10) provides, the guidance has to mainly deal with the cooperation between online content-sharing service providers and rightsholders to fulfil the obligations imposed by Article 17 to OCSSPs. That is why the two main stakeholders for that purpose, content-sharing service providers and rightsholders, were at the core of such ex-post stakeholders analysis.

Regarding disputes that may arise in the application of Article 17, the CJEU shall not be bound by the text of the Commission's guidance when interpreting such provision since the guidance is "soft law." Following Rosati's research,[117] national authorities and courts must consider the Commission's recommendations when deciding issues due to the indirect impact of non-binding law. Nevertheless, the

[116] European Commission, Communication from the Commission to the European Parliament and the Council 'Guidance on Article 17 of Directive 2019/790 on Copyright in the Digital Single Market', COM(2021) 288 final, 4 June 2021.

[117] Rosati et al. (2021), p. 1139, available at https://link-springer-com.are.uab.cat/Article/10.1007/s40319-021-01082-6

Commission's document will not grant persons any rights they may rely on before such courts and other authorities, which means it is not enforceable in front of national courts, according to established case law. However, the "soft-law" status of the Commission's guidance does not preclude requests for preliminary rulings on itself since the CJEU, in its judgement C-322/18, has consistently insisted that "Article 267 TFEU confers on the Court jurisdiction to give a preliminary ruling on both the validity and the interpretation of all acts of the Union institutions "without exception".[118]

This research suggests that the classical categorisation of stakeholders in copyright law of 'creators-producers-users' is not valid anymore. Nowadays, other players appear in the copyright scene, where musical works are exploited digitally. The irruption of these new stakeholders, namely online intermediaries, changes the classical categorisation schema of copyright stakeholders to an updated version as follows: 'Primary stakeholders' including rightsholders (meaning creators plus industry) and users, and 'secondary stockholders' with non-primary interest, namely online intermediaries. As it has been assessed, the different stakeholders have different degrees of implication whether an ex-ante or an ex-post stakeholders analysis is taken. When making an ex-ante stakeholders analysis, the division into primary and secondary stakeholders can be considered valid before the copyright legislation has been adopted. Hence, the reason for regulating copyright is the balance between users and creators, while the concern of online intermediaries is secondary. Thus, the intermediaries act as such; they interfere in the user-creator biome to achieve the economic interest of their businesses, which are based on the user's usage of the rightsholders' works on their platforms, being mere intermediaries. Even before the CDSM Directive was approved, at the IA and proposal stage, it can be observed that the legislation is aimed to improve or benefit just one group of stakeholders, the rightsholders while imposing burdens on intermediaries and maintaining users in between the benefits, derived from wider access to content, and the possible negative impact on their rights, derived from the burdens imposed to intermediaries. At this point, can rightsholders be considered stakeholders, or are they not stakeholders but a beneficiary of copyright law? When EU copyright law protects the rightsholders' interest to grant the public's interest of having access to culture and having cultural works created, then the industry should not be considered a stakeholder anymore but a beneficiary of the copyright law. Therefore, after the law-making decision, a stakeholders' analysis made ex-post reveals that rightsholders are set at the primary position of benefit-stakeholders. At the same time, intermediaries become *duty stakeholders*. Finally, users remain as mere stakeholders whose interests, duties and benefits depend on how good the cooperation between intermediaries and rightsholders turns out to be and how well the Member States transpose the Directive into their national laws.

---

[118] CJEU Judgement of 13 December 1989, C-322/88, Salvatore Grimaldi v Fonds des maladies professionnelles, ECLI:EU:C:1989:646. para. 19.

4.5 Overview: Rightsholders as Beneficiaries of the Copyright Legislation, CDSM Directive and Fundamental Rights Balancing

The CDSM Directive, apart from the general objective of contributing to the development and operation of the EU internal market, also aims to adjust the playing field for the exploitation of works by addressing the "value gap" and providing rightsholders with a high level of protection. The European Commission put rightsholders' interests at the centre of the legislative process of the CDSMD, and also after the approval of the Directive when discussing a set of guidelines for its implementation.

Article 17 of the CDSM Directive, with its goal of reducing the "value gap", positively changes the playing field for the unauthorised use of such works. However, this playing field does not seem equal for all the players. The new liability regime requires OCSSPs to obtain rightsholders' authorisation for the communication to the public of copyright-protected musical works. Those authorisations also cover users' non-commercial CtoP act when uploading the content to those platforms. Although the value gap has been reduced, the balance between stakeholders' interests has not been completely met. The CDSM Directive regime in Article 17 benefits only one part of the stakeholders: the rightsholders, specifically the music industry. The music industry has a privileged position among other rightsholders. Therefore, only those authors, artists and musicians under the umbrella of a relevant record label or a significant CMO can obtain fair remuneration and guarantee their rights.

Under the CDSMD, rightsholders, in practice, this is the music industry, decide whether to provide platforms with licences for the CtoP of their works. They also hold the power to require the OCSSPs to block and remove user-generated content. OCSSPs, after receiving notice from the rightsholders, must remove the content uploaded by their users. Otherwise, they are at risk of infringement. OCSSPs must implement notice-and-take-down without general monitoring actions and preserve users' fundamental rights, mainly their freedom of expression.

The CDSMD provides a high level of protection for the interests of rightsholders. Still, it is not well balanced with the responsibility required of OCSSPs when handling possible copyright infringements of their users and addressing their fundamental rights. The users' interest in accessing a wide range of content is also not balanced with the gains of rightsholders. Therefore, platform users must bear the risks of potential infringement of their fundamental rights to ensure fair remuneration for the music industry.

Thus, the imposition of art. 17 new liability regime for the OCSSPs when hosting and now also communicating the public copyright-protected works jeopardises users' fundamental rights when sets the obligation of OCSSPs to take-down supposed unauthorised content. As the CJEU pointed out, the Directive transfers responsibility for guaranteeing the protection of users' rights to the different Member States when implementing the measure in their national laws. Such a scenario can create two problematic situations. On one hand, it can lead to a lower level of harmonisation among Member States. On the other hand, it can put the safeguards of users' fundamental rights at risk if not all Member States achieve adequate protection.

The EU left users' fundamental rights in the hands of private organisations like OCSSPs, but also the music industry and the CMOs. This is a risk that Member States are in charge to control and address. The success of users' rights protection will result from how good are Member States' laws implementing the CDSM Directive. Although the European Commission has published a set of Guidelines for the implementation of Article 17, it does not avoid the differences arising from the 27 different laws implementing the CDSM Directive.

References

De Miguel Asensio PA (2020) Conflict of Laws and the Internet, 1st edn. Edward Elgar Publishing

Dusollier S (2020) The 2019 directive on copyright in the digital single market: Some progress, a few bad choices, and an overall failed ambition. Common Mark Law Rev 57:979–1030

Ferri F (2020) The dark side(s) of the EU Directive on copyright and related rights in the Digital Single Market. China-EU Law J 71(7):21–38. https://doi.org/10.1007/S12689-020-00089-5

Freeman RE (1984) Strategic management: a stakeholder approach. Pitman, Boston

Friedman AL, Miles S (2006) Stakeholders: theory and practice. Oxford University Press, Oxford

Garrote Fernández-Diez IJ (2023) La transposición al ordenamiento español de la Directiva 2019/790, de derechos de autor y derechos afines en el Mercado Único Digital. LA LEY Unión Eur 60:2

Geiger C, Justin Jütte B (2021) Platform liability under Article 17 of the copyright in the digital single market directive, automated filtering and fundamental rights: an impossible match. GRUR Int 70(6):517–543

Geiger C, Griffiths J, Senftleben M et al (2015) Limitations and exceptions as key elements of the legal framework for copyright in the European Union Opinion of the European Copyright Society on the Judgment of the CJEU in Case C-201/13 Deckmyn. IIC Int Rev Intellect Prop Compet Law 46:93–101. https://doi.org/10.1007/s40319-015-0297-0

Grisse K (2019) After the storm—Examining the final version of Article 17 of the new Directive (EU) 2019/790′. JIPLP 14:887–890

Husovec M, Quintais JP (2021) How to license Article 17? Exploring the implementation options for the new EU rules on content-sharing platforms under the copyright in the digital single market directive. GRUR Int 70:325–348. https://doi.org/10.1093/grurint/ikaa200

Hviid M, Schroff S, Street J (2017) Regulating collective management organisations by competition: an incomplete answer to the licensing problem? J Intellect Prop Inf Technol Electron Commer Law 7:256

Leistner M (2020) European copyright licensing and infringement liability under Art. 17 DSM-directive. Zeitschrift für Geist Eig 12:123. https://doi.org/10.1628/zge-2020-0008

Metzger A, Senftleben M, Derclaye E et al (2020) Selected aspects of implementing Article 17 of the directive on copyright in the digital single market into National Law comment of the European Copyright Society. SSRN Electron J. https://doi.org/10.2139/ssrn.3589323

Montagnani ML (2020) A new liability regime for illegal content in the digital single market strategy. In: Frosio G (ed) Oxford handbook of online intermediary liability. Oxford Academic, pp 295–311

Navas Navarro S (2019) Plataformas de servicios de música online y licencias multiterritoriales (estado de la cuestión). In: Serrano Gómez E (ed) Medios de comunicación, contenidos digitales y derecho de autor. Reus, pp 81–98

Pravemann T (2019) Art. 17 der Richtlinie zum Urheberrecht im digitalen Binnenmarkt - Eine Analyse der neuen europäischen Haftungsregelung für Diensteanbieter für das Teilen von Online-Inhalten. Gewerbl Rechtsschutz und Urheberr 8:783

Quintais JP (2020) The new copyright in the digital single market directive: a critical look. Eur Intellect Prop Rev 42. https://doi.org/10.2139/SSRN.3424770

Reda F, Selinger J (2021) YouTube/Cyando an Important Ruling for Platform Liability Part 2. Kluwer Copyr Blog 1/07/2021

Rosati E (2021a) Copyright in the digital single market: article-by-article commentary to the provisions of directive 2019/790. Oxford University Press

Rosati E (2021b) CJEU rules on platform liability under copyright law, safe harbours, and injunctions. IPKat Blog

Rosati E, Rosati E, of Intellectual Property Law P (2021) The DSM directive two years on: do things ever get easier? IIC Int Rev Intellect Prop Compet Law 529(52):1139–1142. https://doi.org/10.1007/S40319-021-01082-6

Shapiro T, Hansson S (2019) The DSM copyright directive: EU copyright will indeed never be the same. Eur Intellect Prop Rev 141:404–414

Stalla-Bourdillon S, Rosati E, Turk K et al (2017) An academic perspective on the copyright reform. Comput Law Secur Rev 33:3–13. https://doi.org/10.1016/j.clsr.2016.12.003

Suthersanen U (2007) Copyright law: A stakeholders' palimpsest. In: Macmillan F (ed) New directions in copyright law. Edward Elgar, pp 119–134

Vetulani-Cęgiel A, Meyer T (2020) Power to the people? Evaluating the European Commission's engagement efforts in EU copyright policy. J Eur Integr 43:1–19. https://doi.org/10.1080/07036337.2020.1823382

Chapter 5
Enforcement of Communication to the Public Right

To ensure that the rights of creators and other rightsholders are fully protected, not only is it necessary to establish liability for unauthorised actions by CtoP, but also to provide for its enforcement. In order to determine the liability, Justin Koo proposes to make simpler the determination of an act of CtoP by only focusing on three requirements: (1) the existence of an act of communication, (2) the presence of a public (3) and the case of involving a new act of communication run by an organisation other than the original one it shall need a new authorisation.[1] However, this theory does not take into account the liability regime in Article 17 of the CDSM Directive, nor does it consider the role of the OCSSP and their users. It is essential to consider all the possible liable acts of CtoP to determine the appropriate enforcement instruments. Apart from determining those acts, it is required to identify the potentially liable subjects and all the possibly affected rightsholders. It is also essential to determine where those liable acts of communication take place.

Based on the communication and public concepts discussed in Chap. 3 and the liability regime outlined in Chap. 4, and drawing on Justin Koo's approach, this study proposes a method for determining liability by categorising acts of communication as primary, secondary, or subsequent. See Fig. 5.1 for a visual representation. Dividing acts of CtoP into three levels simplifies determining liability and enforcement. Any act of CtoP is performed by a subject who is potentially liable if acting without the corresponding rightsholders' authorisation.

Every stage or level of acts requires a new assessment to determine the liability of the related subject, considering the existence of a communication act and a "public". To properly assess the potential liability of an act and the relevant subject, it is important to identify the level or stage at which a new CtoP act takes place. Doing so lets us determine whether previous related acts or subjects authorise the act. If it is

[1] Koo (2020), p. 107.

L. Ballesta Martí, *The Communication to the Public of Musical Works Online in the European Union's Legislation*, Law, Governance and Technology Series 75,
https://doi.org/10.1007/978-3-031-94132-0_5

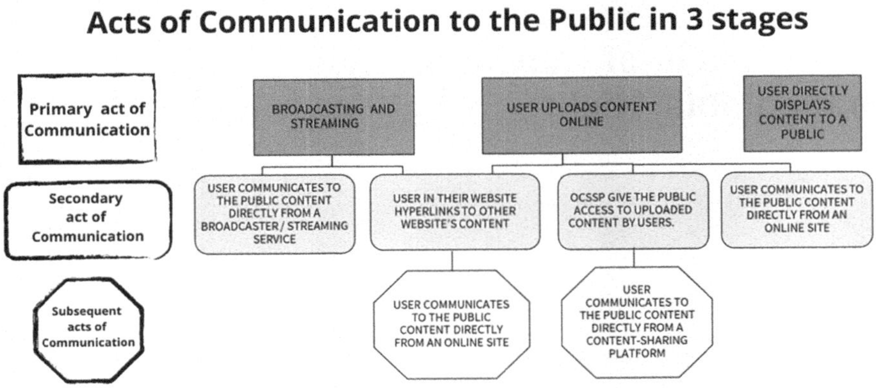

Fig. 5.1 Acts of Communication to the Public in 3 Stages. Source: Author's elaboration

not authorised, we can determine the liability and take appropriate enforcement action.

Primary acts of communication refer to the direct transmission or making available of works to the public. This category encompasses actions such as directly displaying phonograms (using CDs, MP3s, etc.), broadcasting or streaming musical content (transmited by broadcasters or streaming service providers), and uploading files containing copyrighted content online (by uploading the original music file or derivative works that use the musical content). The secondary communication stage also involves displaying music to the public. In this case, the person who communicates the phonogram to the public does so by playing the music from a radio, streaming service, or internet site. This type of secondary communication includes hyperlinks to broadcasting or streaming services and sites with previously uploaded content (especially by embedding). As per Article 17(1) of the CDSMD, the act run by OCSSPs of giving the public access to copyrighted works uploaded by users is also a secondary act of communication. Subsequent acts of communication are all those acts of displaying a musical work to the public directly a from previous secondary act of communication, this is through an OCSSP or a linked website. When a musical work is displayed or directly communicated to the public, it can be categorised as a primary, secondary, or subsequent act of communication, depending on the source of the phonogram. An example of this is illustrated in Table 5.1 by the very common case of a subject playing background music in a store.

Each of the stages in the example needs an authorisation. However, the uploader user in level III(1) is covered by the authorisation obtained by the OCSSP if not acting for commercial or monetary purposes. The store owner always needs to obtain an authorisation, despite having a paying subscription account on Spotify (as they pay for the services of private use, not for the CtoP right compensation). Although OCSSPs perform secondary acts of CtoP, they are directly liable for not obtaining the authorisation required in Article 17 of the DSM Directive. There may be situations where a user uploads protected content to a content-sharing platform,

Table 5.1 Example of the stages of an act of communication to the public. Source: Author's elaboration

Stage	Act of communication	Potential liable subject	Authorisation Needed
I—Primary act of communication	The subject (owner) directly displays music in the store using a CD or MP3 files connected to an audio system.	Owner	Yes
II—Secondary act of communication:	The owner connects the audio system to a cell phone o or a computer and displays the music from a playlist in their Spotify account.	Owner	Yes
1. Previous Primary act of communication:	The streaming from Spotify to the user (owner).	Spotify	Yes
III—Subsequent act of communication:	The owner connects the audio system to an internet-connected device and plays music from a YouTube playlist, uploaded by a user	Owner	Yes
1. Previous Secondary act of Communication:	The hosting of YouTube, as a OCSSP, that makes available the works to the public	Youtube	Yes
2. Former Primary act of communication:	The user's music files are uploaded on YouTube.	User	No; Covered by the OCSSP authorisation
		User with commercial porpouses	Yes

but the corresponding OCCSP has authorisation that does not cover the uploaded content. In such cases, if the notice-and-take-down mechanisms have not been activated and the content has not been removed or blocked, it creates doubt about the existence of direct or indirect liability of the OCSSP. Following the division proposed, each stage of CtoP acts generates a new liability. Accordingly, in this later situation, the OCSSP would also be directly liable for direct infringement of Article 17 when not fulfilling the requirements of removing or blocking the copyrighted content unless it can prove that it has made the best efforts according to 17(4) the exception. The uploader of the content is also responsible for it and can defend themselves by arguing that they believed the OCSSP had authorisation, and the absence of notice or locking of the content gave them the impression of acting legally. The division into three stages of liability aims to prevent indirect liability by making each subject responsible for their acts at each stage.

Determining jurisdiction and applicable law should be simplified once the responsible parties and actions have been identified. However, the Internet's borderless nature makes any online communication of works multi-territorial. This makes the enforcement of infringements of the CtoP right quite complex. The place where an act of CtoP occurs or has its consequences is another important element to be considered to determine the jurisdiction and applicable law. Summarising, when determining the jurisdiction and applicable law, it is important to consider who is responsible for the potentially liable act of communication and where to locate such an act. This section briefly analyses the conflict of laws in disputes regarding communication to the public of musical works. To proceed with this assessment, the study first categorises potentially liable acts of CtoP as contractual or tortuous and territorial or ubiquitous.

Following the categorisation of acts of communication in three stages, as assessed before, the acts or actions of CtoP or MA can be divided into acts (1) where a user directly displays content to the public, (2) transmissions of broadcasting organisation and streaming services, both non-interactive and on-demand, (3) a user uploads content online and make it available on a platform or a website, (4) a user introduces in their website hyperlinks to other website's content, and (5) an OCSSP gives the public access to uploaded content by its users. All of these categories of communication to the public acts encompass various actions, but they all share the same main features that correspond to one of the five types. Hence, this categorisation helps determine the nature of those actions, their potential liability, and the corresponding path to their enforcement.

As shown in Fig. 5.2, almost all those acts of CtoP occur online except when a subject directly displays musical works to the public. These kinds of acts always occur offline despite the phonogram coming from an online source. Almost all those acts online are multi-territorial or ubiquitous due to the globalness of the Internet.[2] As Professor De Miguel states, country-by-country enforcement in ubiquitous cases may be costly and inefficient.[3] Hence, having a single jurisdiction where individuals can obtain relief in such cases is desirable.

Regarding broadcasting and streaming actions, they have a different nature. Broadcasting is not run through the Internet but through cable or satellite, so it might be considered an offline activity. The Satellite and Cable Directive[4] applies to broadcasting acts of communication to the public, as defined in Article 1. Article 1 (b) determines the country of origin principle or theory of emission[5] to locate where the CtoP act takes place. The provision states that.

> The act of communication to the public by satellite occurs solely in the Member State where, under the control and responsibility of the broadcasting organisation, the programme-carrying signals are introduced into an uninterrupted chain of communication leading to the satellite and down towards the earth.[6]

[2]De Miguel Asensio (2020), p. 221.

[3]*Ibid*, p. 221.

[4]Directive 93/83/EEC of 27 September 1993 on the coordination of certain rules concerning copyright and rights related to copyright applicable to satellite broadcasting and cable retransmission, OJ L 248, 6.10.1993, pp. 15–21. Council of the European Comunities.

[5]For a summary of the different theories of where an act of communication to the public occurs, including the *emission theory*, see the study of Professor Koo (2020).

[6]Cable & Satellite Directive, Article 1(b).

Act of CtoP	Online/ offline	Potentially Liable Action	Contractual nature	Type of Infringement	Infringes CtoP	Potentially liable party	Location of the CtoP infringement	
USER DIRECTLY DISPLAYS CONTENT TO A PUBLIC	offline	CtoP with no authorisation	non contractual	CtoP Infringement	Yes	USER	place of CtoP	territorial
		Breach of licensing agreement	contractual	Breach of contract	No	USER	n/a	n/a
BROADCASTING AND STREAMING	offline online	CtoP or Makes content available with no authorisation	non contractual	CtoP Infringement	Yes	Broadcasting Organisation	place of emision*	territorial
	online					Steaming Service	Internet	ubiquitous
		Breach of licensing agreement	contractual	Breach of contract	No	Broadcaster / Steaming Service	n/a	n/a
USER UPLOADS CONTENT ONLINE	online	Makes content available with no authorisation	non contractual	CtoP Infringement	Yes	Uploader user	Internet	ubiquitous
				Non-commercial acts covered by the OCSSP authorisation	No	Uploader user	Internet	ubiquitous
		Breach of terms and conditions of the platform or website	contractual	Breach of contract	No	Uploader user	n/a	n/a
USER IN THEIR WEBSITE HYPERLINKS TO OTHER WEBSITE'S CONTENT	online	Makes content available with no authorisation	non contractual	CtoP Infringement	Yes	Uploader user	Internet	ubiquitous
OCSSP GIVES THE PUBLIC ACCES TO UPLOADED CONTENTBY USERS	online	CtoP with no authorisation	non contractual	CtoP Infringement	Yes	OCSSP	Internet	ubiquitous
		Breach of licensing agreement	contractual	Breach of contract	No	OCSSP	n/a	n/a

Fig. 5.2 Nature of Acts of CtoP and their potential liability for CtoP infringement. Source: Author's elaboration

Therefore, according to the Satellite and Cable Directive, the location of the act of communication in broadcasting activities is territorial as it occurs in only one Member State. However, nowadays, broadcasting organisations are "increasingly offering, in addition to their broadcasts of television and radio programmes, online services ancillary to such broadcasts, such as simulcasting and catch-up services".[7] The Broadcasting Directive defines 'ancillary online service' as

> an online service consisting in the provision to the public, by or under the control and responsibility of a broadcasting organisation, of television or radio programmes

[7] Directive 789/2019, Broadcasting Directive, Recital 2.

> simultaneously with or for a defined period of time after their broadcast by the broadcasting organisation, as well as of any material which is ancillary to such broadcast.[8]

A clear and spread example of those ancillary online services is podcasts. Podcasts are broadcast programs available online and on demand at a time and place chosen by the listener. The 2019 Broadcasting Directive also applies the country of origin principle to broadcasters' ancillary online services in Article 3. According to that provision, the acts of CtoP of works, and making works available to the public on-demand when providing to the public content like radio or television programmes owned or fully financed own productions of the broadcasting organisation, including news and current affairs programmes in an ancillary online service "by or under the control and responsibility of a broadcasting organisation [...] shall be deemed to occur solely in the Member State in which the broadcasting organisation has its principal establishment".[9]

Streaming can also be simultaneous and non-interactive (e.g. online radios), like broadcast, or interactive and on-demand (e.g. Spotify) like the mentioned broadcasters' ancillary online services. Although broadcasting and streaming services are similar, the main difference is that streaming is essentially online, and broadcasting is always linked to a broadcasting organisation. Because of the essential digital element of streaming services, streaming is considered to be spread on a multi-territorial basis, and consequently, streaming acts are labelled as ubiquitous.

Focusing now on the contractual or tortuous nature, and as Fig. 5.2 shows, most acts can be from any of both natures. Still, only acts non-contractual develop in a CtoP infringement, whereas contractual nature ones require the existence of a contract; this is an authorisation or license. In those contractual relations where an act infringes the CtoP right, it is because such an act is supposed to be out of the scope of the agreement, either by exceeding its terms or because the act is not authorised in any agreement. In the first case, the issue is not about the existence of a CtoP infringement but rather a breach of contract. Hence, the contract's interpretation, scope or validity are the object of the legal action, but not the infringement on CtoP. In cases where a licensing agreement does not authorise an act, it should be considered non-contractual due to the lack of an agreement covering said act. Professor Torremans states that the defence "based on a licence would be characterised as contractual".[10]

However, not all non-contractual acts of CtoP with no authorisation must be considered as potentially liable acts. As examined in the previous section, all those acts of uploading content by users in online sharing-content platforms without commercial purpose or profit intention are covered by the licences obtained by OCSSPs, pursuant to Article 17 CDSMD.

---

[8] Broadcasting Directive, Article 2(1).

[9] Broadcasting Directive, Article 3(1).

[10] Stamatoudi and Torremans (2014), p. 1046

After clarifying the nature of potentially infringing actions by CtoP, this study examines jurisdiction and applicable law in cases of musical works' communication to the public infringement in the following sub-sections.

5.1 Determining Jurisdiction

The previous pages have drafted different types of acts that potentially infringe CtoP rights and their main features. Based on that categorisation, the following lines explore the determination of the jurisdiction in such cases of CtoP infringement.

No one of the international copyright conventions covers conflict of laws. Having no international rules to determine the jurisdiction, especially in disputes on online infringements, makes enforcing copyright and related rights more difficult. CtoP is one of the economic exclusive rights that has become more digital in the last years. The lack of an international rule to determine the jurisdiction led some scholars to develop projects of principles and guidelines of International Private Law on intellectual property matters. The Max Planck Group has elaborated some of these proposals for Conflict of Laws in Intellectual Property ('CLIP'), the American Law Institute, and the International Law Association (ILA). The ILA Committee on Intellectual Property developed in 2021 the 'Guidelines on Intellectual Property in Private International Law' (Kyoto Guidelines). The ILA Committee, based on previous academic projects, developed the Kyoto Guidelines as a solution for the challenges posed by the cross-border exploitation of intellectual property rights, especially on the Internet. Although no binding instrument determines the jurisdiction and applicable law in copyright disputes, those guidelines act as a "soft law" instrument. As Professors Toshiyuki Kono, Axel Metzger and Pedro de Miguel Asensio state in the Editorial of the Commented edition of the Guidelines[11]:

> The Kyoto Guidelines provide soft-law principles on the private international law aspects of intellectual property, which may guide the interpretation and reform of national legislation and international instruments and may be helpful as a source of inspiration for courts, arbitrators and further research in the field.[12]

This lack of regulation at the international level highlights the territoriality of copyright and related rights. However, it does not preclude Member States' courts from hearing cases on foreign copyright and related rights infringements. As Professor De Miguel explains, the territoriality of copyright "refers to the spatial scope of the territory covered by the exclusive rights but not necessarily to the jurisdiction to adjudicate disputes concerning the infringement of those rights, which are regarded as private claims in civil and commercial matters".[13]

---

[11] Kono et al. (2021).

[12] *Ibid*, para 1.

[13] De Miguel Asensio (2020), p. 223.

The European Union provides Regulation (EU) 1215/2012 on jurisdiction and the recognition and enforcement of judgments in civil and commercial matters,[14] also named the Regulation Brussels I recast (RBIr), as a regional instrument to determine the jurisdiction rules within the EU of judgments in civil and commercial matters, which applies to CtoP infringements. This instrument is used to determine the jurisdiction in cases where the defendant has their domicile placed in the EU, except Denmark, because of the specific position of this country in the frame of the European Area of Freedom, Security and Justice. However, Regulation 1215/2012 applies in Denmark under the *Agreement between the European Community and the Kingdom of Denmark on jurisdiction and the recognition and enforcement of judgments in civil and commercial matters.*[15] The necessary legislative amendments[16] in Denmark entered into force on 1 June 2013.[17]

Otherwise, according to Article 6 of the RBIr, the jurisdiction will be determined by the Member State's national law hearing the case unless any other international rule is applicable.[18] Regarding the members of the European Free Trade Association (EFTA, Iceland, Norway and Switzerland), the Lugano II Convention of 2007 is the applicable instrument.[19] Denmark is also a signatory to this convention, which means that it applies to their relations with those three countries. The Lugano II Convention replaced the Lugano I Convention of 1988. It has been in force since January 1, 2010, between the European Union Member States, including Denmark and Norway. The convention became effective in Switzerland on January 1, 2011, while Iceland entered force on May 1, 2011. The Lugano II Convention provisions on jurisdiction[20] adopted the same rules set in the today repealed Brussels I Regulation,[21] which was substituted by Regulation 1215/2012. Lugano II Convention extends to the three EFTA States the regulatory framework in matters of international jurisdiction provided in Brussels I. Although Regulation 1215/2012 was

---

[14] Regulation (EU) No 1215/2012 of the European Parliament and of the Council of 12 December 2012 on jurisdiction and the recognition and enforcement of judgments in civil and commercial matters (recast), OJ L 351, 20.12.2012, pp. 1–32.

[15] Council Decision of 27 April 2006 2006/325/EC: concerning the conclusion of the Agreement between the European Community and the Kingdom of Denmark on jurisdiction and the recognition and enforcement of judgments in civil and commercial matters, OJ L 120, 5.5.2006, pp. 22–22.

[16] According to Article 3(2) of the aforementioned Agreement of 19 October 2005 between the European Community and the Kingdom of Denmark, whenever amendments to Council Regulation (EC) No 44/2001 of 22 December 2000 on jurisdiction and the recognition and enforcement of judgments in civil and commercial matters are adopted, Denmark shall notify the Commission of its decision whether or not to implement the content of such amendments.

[17] 'E-Justice; European Judicial Atlas in civil Matters, Brussels Regulation Recast', available at https://e-justice.europa.eu/content_brussels_i_regulation_recast-350-en.do

[18] Otero García-Carrión (2017), p.10.

[19] Convention on Jurisdiction, Recognition and Enforcement of Judicial Decisions in Civil and Commercial Matters, signed in Lugano in 2007.

[20] See Articles 2–22 of the Lugano Convention.

[21] Council Regulation (EC) No 44/2001 of 22 December 2000 on jurisdiction and the recognition and enforcement of judgments in civil and commercial matters OJ L 12, 16.1.2001, p. 1/23.

adopted after the Lugano II Convention, the application of the 2007 convention is not affected by regulation RBIr according to Article 73 (1). In those situations where the defendant is not a resident of the EU or EFTA,[22] the domestic jurisdiction provisions apply, and those national rules may vary greatly.

The BRIr sets as the general criterion to determine the jurisdiction of the courts of the Member State of the defendant's domicile in Article 4.[23] While Article 4 establishes the jurisdiction for the courts of the MS where the defendant has the domicile, the rules for determining such domicile are referred to in Articles 62 and 63 of the RBIr. Article 62 refers to the national law of the MS, whose courts are seized of a matter to determine whether a party is domiciled in that MS. In case a party is not domiciled in that MS, to determine whether the party is domiciled in another MS, the first court has to apply the national law of that referred MS.[24] Regarding legal persons, companies, and associations; Article 63 sets their domicile at the place where they have their (a) statutory seat; (b) central administration; or (c) principal place of business.[25] The general criterion in Article 4 assigns jurisdiction to the defendant's domicile courts in all disputes referring to any infringing act of CtoP, regardless of the means used or the location in which the act occurred.[26] Unifying all the defendant's claims for online acts, spread around in different countries, into one single forum simplifies and facilitates the plaintiff's legal action. This ensures the possibility to claim for protection of CtoP rights infringed in several Member States before the courts of a single country.

Professors like Paul Torremans and Pedro De Miguel[27] agree that the general jurisdiction in Article 4 is potentially unlimited since even with regard to infringement claims that have no other connection to the forum Member State or allegations of copyright infringement, the courts of the defendant's home are competent.

De Miguel argues that Article 8(1) also allows for an unlimited feature of jurisdiction since the provision permits plaintiffs to file lawsuits in the courts of the Member State where any defendants have their domicile, provided that the claims are closely connected, even when numerous defendants are involved.[28] It is unlikely that there will be multiple defendants in cases of CtoP infringements, as a single individual or organisation usually performs acts of communication to the public at a time. However, the presence of multiple plaintiffs is common in copyright infringements due to the involvement of different rightsholders linked to a musical work, especially in the case of collective works.

---

[22] However, some provisions of both texts apply irrespective of the State where the defendant is domiciled. This is the case of Articles 18.1, 21.2, 24 and 25 (Art. 6.1 of the Regulation) and Articles 22 and 23 of the Convention (Art. 4.2).

[23] Article 4, Brussels I (recast) Regulation.

[24] Article 62(2), Brussels I (recast) Regulation.

[25] Article 63, Brussels I (recast) Regulation.

[26] De Miguel Asensio (2015a), p. 515.

[27] See De Miguel Asensio (2020); Torremans (2014).

[28] De Miguel Asensio (2020), p. 224.

Regarding the cases of infringement of the CtoP right, the general criteria provision is applicable, although Article 24(4) establishes a criteria of exclusive jurisdiction for intellectual property rights.[29] But this exclusive criteria does not apply to copyright as it refers to those issues derived from the registration or validity of intellectual property rights "required to be deposited or registered".[30] Hence, the copyright is not required to be registered in the EU Member States and the rest of the Berne Convention countries. The Berne Convention states in Article 5(2)[31] that the enjoyment and exercise of copyright cannot be subject to any formalities. Hence, registration cannot be constitutive as a condition for these rights' existence, at least in all those States part of the Berne Convention. Consequently, the rules in Article 24(4) do not apply to determining the jurisdiction in disputes of foreign copyright, at least regarding CtoP infringements.

Apart from the rule of defendants' domicile, Article 7 RBIr sets special jurisdiction criteria as an alternative to the general jurisdiction in Article 4. Regarding the CtoP infringements, as assessed above and illustrated in Fig. 5.2, all those infringements are tortious or non-contractual. This is relevant when determining the jurisdiction for those infringements as the alternative to the general rule is fixed in Article 7 RBIr, which makes a difference between contractual and non-contractual situations. Hence, the applicable provision to CtoP infringements is Article 7(2), which refers to delict or quasi-delict matters. Article 7(2) sets the jurisdiction in the courts for where the event occurred or may occur. This provision not only covers the damages that have already taken place but also those that are expected to happen in the future. The purpose of this is to prevent any potential future damages. Moreover, Article 7(2) provision determines international and territorial jurisdiction when it refers to "courts for the place where the harmful event occurred or may occur". This provision does not refer to the 'Member State' but to the location where the damage occurs that the defendant be domiciled in a Member State, but the defendant may be sued in another Member State different from the country of their domicile. In short, Article 7(2 is an "attack forum" allowing the plaintiff to take the defendant out of its domicile.

According to the ubiquity doctrine, the alternative of special jurisdiction in Article 7(2) offers, at the same time, alternative forums, as the CJEU recognised in its judgement in the *Hejduk*[32] case:

> It is clear from the Court's case-law that the expression 'place where the harmful event occurred or may occur' in Article 5(3) of Regulation No 44/2001 is intended to cover both the place where the damage occurred and the place of the event giving rise to it, so that the

[29] For in-depth analysis on exclusive jurisdiction see; Ubertazzi (2012).

[30] Article 24(4), Brussels I (recast) Regulation.

[31] Article 5(2) of the Berne Convention states as follows:

> The enjoyment and the exercise of these rights shall not be subject to any formality; such enjoyment and such exercise shall be independent of the existence of protection in the country of origin of the work.

[32] CJEU Judgement of 22 January 2015, C-441/13, Hejduk, ECLI:EU:C:2015:28.

> defendant may be sued, at the option of the applicant, in the courts for either of those places.[33]

The CJEU refers to the place where the damage occurred or may occur as it may be located either in the place of the event giving rise to the damage or in the place where the act has its damaging consequences. Regarding infringements committed on the Internet, the CJEU determined that the causal "event giving rise to the damage is the activation of the process for the technical display" of the works online (e.g. on a website). Therefore, the CJEU considered that the event giving rise to a possible infringement of copyright lies in the user's actions, like the owner of a site where the works are uploaded.[34] In CtoP infringement cases, such causal events are normally located where the decision and execution of the uploading actions or making content available (like linking or embedding) occur.[35]

The CJEU, regarding infringements over the Internet, to determine where the event gave rise to the damage,e established that it has to be understood as the place of activating the process leading to the infringement.[36] This criterion evokes the theory of the origin of the transmission in the Satellite and Cable Directive as the place of origin where the signals are introduced in the communication chain.

The place of activation of the process leading to the infringement is not a certain place. The uncertainty seems more evident in disputes regarding CtoP online infringement, and especially in cases of making the content available, where the infringing user does not effectively run the activation of the communication but rather the hosting of such content. As the end user, the public activates the uploaded content to be communicated. Upon first glance, one might assume that the location of the harmful event is where the server hosting the infringing content is situated. However, the CJEU, in the judgement of the case *Wintersteiger*, rejected this option:

> The technical display process by the advertiser is indeed activated, ultimately, on a server belonging to the operator of the search engine used by the advertiser. However, given the objective of foreseeability, which the rules on jurisdiction must pursue, the place of establishment of that server cannot, by reason of its uncertain location, be considered to be the location where the event giving rise to the damage occurred.[37]

De Miguel considers that the CJEU approach is consistent with the fact that "those affected by the activity are usually completely unaware of the location of the server whose situation can be altered without influencing the availability of the information stored".[38] Additionally, the author suggests that the location of the server could be

[33] *Ibid*, para. 18. Although the case refers to Regulation 44/2001, the rules are the same in RBIr.

[34] *Ibid*, para. 24.

[35] De Miguel Asensio (2023), p. 333.

[36] The CJEU set this approach in a judgement related to trademark infringement over the Internet, but it is also applicable to copyright infringements as it establishes a criterion valid to determine the jurisdiction in claims for non-contractual damages for the purpose of application of art. 7(2) RBIr. See para. 34 of the CJEU Judgement of 22 January 2015, C-441/13, Hejduk, ECLI:EU:C:2015:28.

[37] CJEU Juclgment of 19 April 2012, *Wintersteiger, C-523/10, EU:C:2012:220*, para. 36.

[38] De Miguel Asensio (2020), p. 229.

Creteira	Forum	Determination of the place of jurisdiction	Determination of the place of jurisdiction in CtoP cases	Number of possible forums	Court rules over	Defendant's domicile MS	International / Territorial jurisdiction rules
General Jurisdiction Article 4 RBIr	Courts of the MS of the defendant's domicile	Place where the subject commiting the infingement is domicilied	Place of the domicile of the User/companiy or domicile of the OCSSP	1 In case of more than one subjects, place any of their domiciles is valid	Damages in any MS	Same MS	International
Special Jurisdiction	Courts for the place where the harmful event occurred or may occur	Place of the event giving rise to' the damage	Place of the origin of technical process to communicate or make the content available: act; emission or upload	1 Where the act of CtoP originates	Damages in any MS	Other MS	International and Territorial
		Place where the damage occurred	Place/s where the communication is delivered or the from where the work is accessible	Multiple: each place where the right is protected and infringed	Only damages in the MS of the jurisdiction	Other MS	International and Territorial

Fig. 5.3 Jurisdiction Criteria and Courts Authority in CtoP cases. Source: Authors' elaboration

relevant in granting interim relief to be complied with in the forum country in accordance with Article 35 RBIr.

In the Hejduk case, the CJEU confirmed that the place of the event causing the damage can be determined by considering where the alleged infringer initiates the infringing process, even in cases of online copyright infringement. The court stated that the causal event is the activation of the process for displaying the content on a website, and it should be located at the place where the owner of the website is based.[39] The location where a company has its seat is determined as the defendant's domicile, following the provisions in Article 4 and Article 63 RBIr. Therefore, the plaintiff rightsholders' alternative to choose between the jurisdiction set in Article 4 or Article 7(2) for CtoP infringement claims makes no difference in the result, as both options are usually coincident. Article 7 can only be applied if it provides an alternative to the general forum. This is if it leads the action to a different Member State of the defendant's domicile. Professor Pedro De Miguel clarifies that in cases using the connection criteria of the place of the event giving rise to the damage, "courts are granted jurisdiction for all the damage sustained. In contrast, the courts of the place where the damage occurs have jurisdiction to rule solely in respect of the harm caused in the Member State of the court seised".[40] The author declares that such an interpretation made in online copyright infringements may be controversial, as it determines an extension of the authority of the competent courts. Figure 5.3 summarises the possible different criteria applicable to determine the jurisdiction in cases of CtoP infringements and the extension of the court's authority, as explained above.

[39] CJEU judgement *Hejduk*, C-441/13, para. 24–25.

[40] De Miguel Asensio (2020), p. 225.

Focusing on determining the place where the damage occurs, the CJEU approach is more simple but also controversial. The damage is considered to occur where the act has direct damaging consequences; hence, the courts of the place where the damage occurs are the ones in the best position to assess the infringement of CtoP rights protected in its territory.[41] A CtoP act must not be actively developed in the forum to determine jurisdiction based on damage location. The simple online availability of protected works in the territory of the claimed court has not been rejected by the CJEU as a criterion to extend the jurisdiction of the courts where the right is protected.[42] De Miguel suggests that at least the verification of the accessibility to the claimed content should be done before determining the competence of the courts through such criterion.[43]

Professor Lydia Lundstedt, in her study *Jurisdiction and Choice of Law in Online Copyright Cases,*[44] analyses the accessibility approach that the CJEU has applied to solve online copyright infringement disputes. The author bases her study on the CJEU leading cases in the subject matter, C-170/12 *Pinckney*[45] and C-441/13 *Hejduk*,[46] and determines that the CJEU approach localises the damage in every Member State where the protected content is or has been accessible. Lundstedt also reminds us that each Member State's jurisdiction is limited to damage occurring within its territory in those cases. The author criticises the mentioned accessibility approach for its inconsistency with BIRr's objectives of foreseeability and proximity as a close connection between the dispute and the court. Lundstedt believes that "the accessibility approach may result in attributing jurisdiction to courts in Member States for a non-existent infringement"[47] and explains that a defendant may be sued in every Member State for each fraction of the damage occurring in each State. According to the CJEU, claims for copyright damages over the internet can only be filed in the Member State that protects the relevant rights of the rightsholders.[48] For Professor De Miguel, "[t]he existence of a particularly close connection between the dispute and the forum is not based on the accessibility of the infringing content in the forum but on the alleged infringement of a right only protected in the forum territory". Despite sound reasoning, the CJEU argument of determining the jurisdiction of a Member State through the criterion of the place where the damage occurs is stuck in the idea that even the mere probability of occurrence of damage regarding the accessibility of the content in that Member State. The availability of Internet content cannot be assumed globally anymore due to advancements in geolocation

[41] De Miguel Asensio, (2023), p. 335.

[42] CEJU Judgment of 3 Oct 2013, para. 33–35 and Case C-170/12, Peter Pinckney v KDG Mediatech AG. ECLI:EU:C:2013:635.

[43] De Miguel Asensio (2015b), p. 20.

[44] Lundstedt (2021), p. 399.

[45] CJEU Judgment of 3 October 2013, Pinckney,C-170/02, ECLI:EU:C:2013:635.

[46] Judgement of 22 January 2015, C-441/13, Hejduk, ECLI:EU:C:2015:28.

[47] Lundstedt (2021), p. 767.

[48] CJEU C-170/02, Pinckney, para. 42.

tools and territorial restrictions.[49] Today, tools like these ensure whether access to content is available in a certain place. The ILA Committee and other soft law projects also rejected the accessibility approach in their Guidelines.[50]

According to Lundstedt, the accessibility approach clearly benefits rightsholders as they might force alleged infringers "to agree to an unfavourable settlement rather than become involved in litigation such a situation in a distant Member State",[51] which is undesirable in any case.[52] Moreover, another advantage for the plaintiff rightsholders is the 'mosaic approach'[53] derived from the possibility of litigating in many different Member States, as per the CJEU approach of the criterion of the place where the damage occurs in Article 7(2). Due to the territorial limitation of the jurisdiction, Member States' courts have no competence to grant protection at the EU level, but only in each country. Consequently, the defendant may be sued in each country where the damage has its consequences, and according to the 'accessibility approach', it may be in each of the 27 Member States.

Addressing this imbalance is not feasible. De Miguel states, "the *forum non-conveniens* doctrine cannot be used by a competent court under the RBIr to decline jurisdiction in favour of another court, on the ground that such other court would be a more appropriate forum".[54] Hence, the forum chosen by the rightsholder cannot be declined by the court determined by the chosen alternative between the general forum or the special forum in Article 7(2). Conversely, a party fearing being accused of copyright infringement could seek a negative declaration from the court of their domicile. This possibility may arise on the ground of jurisdiction of the place where the alleged infringement took place, under Article 7 (2) as long as no other court has been involved yet.[55] Additionally, the case law[56] of the CJEU, aiming to avoid *forum actoris*, rejects Article 7(2) of the RBIr to attribute jurisdiction to the courts of the country where the indirect damages occurred.[57] In any case, the damages claimed in choosing the forum are only direct damages, excluding any indirect damage that may result as an anchor to determine the jurisdiction of where those indirect acts occur or manifest.

In the previous section, a classification the possible infringements of online musical works was exposed. Figure 5.4 in the next page shows the different types

---

49 De Miguel Asensio (2020), p. 237.

50 Kono et al. (2021).

51 Lundstedt (2021).

52 For further information in this matter see Torremans (2017).

53 Professor De Miquel describes the 'mosaic approach as the interpretation of Article 7(2) leading to the fact that "The courts of a multiplicity of Member States may have limited jurisdiction based on the traditional understanding of the place where the damage occurs". See De Miguel Asensio (2020), pp. 238–239.

54 De Miguel Asensio (2020), p. 225.

55 *Ibid.*

56 CEJU Judgment of 19 September 1995.*Marinari, C-364/93, ECLI:EU:C:1995:289.*

57 De Miguel Asensio (2015b), p. 7.

Act of CtoP	Online/ offline	Territorial or ubiquitous action	Jurisdiction Rules	Jurisdiction Criteria	Jurisdiction in CtoP infringements
USER DIRECTLY DISPLAYS CONTENT TO A PUBLIC	offline	Territorial	MS national law	MS national Law	MS where the work is CtoP, displayed
BROADCASTING	Satellite or cable	Ubiquitous	Art. 7.2 RBIr	where the damage occurs	Where the broadcast is available
		Territorial	Art. 7.2 RBIr	where the event giving rise to the damage occurs	Where the signals are introduced in the communication chain Art. 1(b) S&C and Art. 3 Broadcasters
		Territorial	Art. 4 RBIr	Place of the defendant domicile	Domicile of the Streaming Service Provider
STREAMING	online	Ubiquitous	Art. 7.2 RBIr	where the damage occurs	Where the stream is available
		Territorial	Art. 7.2 RBIr	where the event giving rise to the damage occurs	Origin of the Stream
		Territorial	Art. 4 RBIr	Place of the defendant domicile	Domicile of the Streaming Service Provider
USER UPLOADS CONTENT ONLINE	online	Ubiquitous	Art. 7.2 RBIr	where the damage occurs	Where the content is is available
		Territorial	Art. 7.2 RBIr	where the event giving rise to the damage occurs	Where the upload occurs
		Territorial	Art. 4 RBIr	Place of the defendant domicile	Domicile of the uploader user
USER IN THEIR WEBSITE HYPERLINKS TO OTHER WEBSITE'S CONTENT	online	Ubiquitous	Art. 7.2 RBIr	where the damage occurs	Where the content is is available
		Territorial	Art. 7.2 RBIr	where the event giving rise to the damage occurs	Where the sharing website is activated
		Territorial	Art. 4 RBIr	Place of the defendant domicile	Domicile of the uploader user
OCSSP GIVES THE PUBLIC ACCES TO UPLOADED CONTENTBY USERS	online	Ubiquitous	Art. 7.2 RBIr	where the damage occurs	Where the content is is available
		Territorial	Art. 7.2 RBIr	where the event giving rise to the damage occurs	Where the OCSSP has the seat
		Territorial	Art. 4 RBIr	Place of the defendant domicile	Domicile of the OCSSP: place of statutory seat; central administration; or principal place of business

Fig. 5.4 Jurisdiction Alternatives in disputes of CtoP infringements. Source: Auhor's elaboration

of CtoP right infringements, their territoriality or ubiquity, and the various jurisdiction criteria applicable to each infringement. This illustration provides a clear understanding of the complex nature of online music infringement and the legal frameworks that govern it.

International jurisdiction rules do not govern the first actions of direct music displaying to the public, as those actions are by nature territorial and developed offline. Hence, the courts of the place where the musical work is displayed are competent as long as such right is protected in their jurisdiction. Broadcasting actions have their own rules regarding determining the pace at which the event gives rise to the damage that occurs. As mentioned, Article 1(2)(b) of the Satellite and Cable Directive and Article 3 of the Broadcasters Directive determine that the act of CtoP occurs where the signals are introduced in the communication chain. Streaming, uploading content to a website or hyperlinking are actions over the Internet and follow the rules of Articles 4 and 7(2) RBIr, as assessed above.

The figure includes the case of OCCSPs infringing the CtoP right according to Article 17 of the CDSM Directive. In those disputes, as per Article 4 RBIr, the domicile of the OCCSP company is the generally applicable jurisdiction, and as assessed before, it can be set in the place where the OCSSP has its statutory seat, its central administration, or at the principal place of business. Suppose the jurisdiction is determined by the alternative in Article 7(2) of where the damage occurs. In that case, the activation theory may lead the action before the same courts as the domicile of the defendant. However, Article 7 (2) would not apply in this case. Making a broad interpretation of the criteria, the OCSSP neither activates the communication of the infringing content nor decides to activate it, being the uploading user who does it instead. However, the OCSSP decides not to get authorisation from the rightsholders, not to set up any notice-and-takedown mechanism, or not to remove or block the content. In those cases, the jurisdiction should be placed where such decisions were made.

Finally, the figure shows how, in any case, the rightsholders (as plaintiffs), and mainly the 'major masters' in the music industry, have the privilege of choosing between two jurisdiction options: general or special jurisdiction. This is not considered a real *forum actoris*. However, it puts rightsholders in an advantageous position to litigate against OCSSP and users, who sometimes are just individuals who ignore the liable nature of their actions.

5.2 Determining Applicable Law

Regulation 864/2007 on the law applicable to non-contractual obligations,[58] known as Rome II Regulation (RIIR), determines the rules on determining the applicable Law within the EU. As a conflict-of-laws rule, Regulation 864/2007 will be applied only by EU Member States. Still, the law specified by the Regulation shall be applied whether or not it is the law of a Member State, under the "universal application" rule established in Article 3.

Article 8(1) of the RIIR, regarding non-contractual obligations arising from IP infringement, the law of the country where protection is claimed is applicable. This is known as the *lex loci protectionis* criterion.

The rule of *lex loci protectionis* clearly embodies the principle of territoriality because the court approached for protection will assess the infringement based on the jurisdiction's laws where the protection is sought. Thus, it allows each state to determine the level of protection accorded to intellectual property rights within its borders.[59] In most cases, such an approach will lead to the application of the law of the forum, so the competent courts shall apply the law of their own Member State as

[58] Regulation (EC) No 864/2007 of the European Parliament and of the Council of 11 July 2007 on the law applicable to non-contractual obligations (Rome II), OJ L 199, 31.7.2007, pp. 40–49.
[59] Lundstedt (2021), p. 401.

it would be the country where the protection is sought. This is consistent with the idea that the courts of the place where the right is protected are in the best position to assess the dispute as they are also those who better know that law and, at the same time, would be in a particularly good position to evaluate the facts and circumstances of the alleged infringement. However, the law of the country where the protection is claimed is applicable, regardless of how strong the connection with that territory is. According to Lundsted, the EU's approach towards minimum connection applies at the substantive law level rather than the choice of law.[60] Additionally, Article 8 RIIR does not contemplate any escape clause that permits the application of a different law with a more 'manifestly closer connection' to the dispute, in contrast with the rule set in Article 4.3 RIIR. Article 8.3 sets an exception to the 'choice of law rule' in Article 14 by providing that the law applicable under Article 8 "may not be derogated from by an agreement pursuant to Article 14".[61] Applying *lex loci protectionis* seems to be the most appropriate solution, especially when copyright infringement is territorial or clearly located. But, as Kur and Masnubak declare, "copyright is universal and territorial at the same time".[62]

There are two main challenges about acts over the Internet: first, to evaluate how to deal with the fact that several laws may apply to the same act of infringement, and then, to asses if some minimal connection is required for a country's law to be applicable. In CtoP situations, infringing copyright, i.e. when unauthorised content is available online, the disputes result in ubiquitous infringement. In this case, the court must apply the law of all the countries involved in the protection claim in a distributive manner. This leads to the 'mosaic approach' in terms of applicable law determination. Following Lundsted study,[63] there are not only 27 possible national laws at the EU level that may apply, but it is also possible that as many national copyright laws as there are States that are contracting parties to the Berne Convention to be applicable.[64]

Currently, the CJEU has not provided any interpretation of *lex loci protectionis* criteria in the context of copyright nor disputes of online CtoP infringements. However, in 2012, the CJEU made an interpretation of the *lex loci protectionis* referring to the minimum connexons theory in the *Football Dataco* case. In *Football Dataco,* the CJEU interpreted the act of re-utilization under the Article 7(2) (b) Database Directive.[65] According to Lundstedt, that provision has similar

[60] Lundstedt (2021), p. 402.

[61] Article 8.3, Rome II Regulation.

[62] Kur and Maunsbach (2019).

[63] Lundstedt (2021), p. 785.

[64] Pursuant to Art. 5(2)2nd sentence BC, "the extent of protection, as well as the means of redress afforded to the author to protect his rights, shall be governed exclusively by the laws of the country where protection is claimed." As both rules follow the same criteria, the Rome II Regulation would also be applicable to the Berne countries.

[65] Directive 96/9/EC of the European Parliament and of the Council of 11 March 1996 on the legal protection of databases, OJ L 77, 27.3.1996, pp. 20–28.

language[66] to the definition of the act of communication to the public in the InfoSoc Directive.[67] The CJEU, in its judgement, held that for an act of re-utilization to be localised in a Member State's territory, the act takes place, at least where there is evidence that the act "discloses an intention on the part of the person performing the act to target members of the public in [that] Member State".[68]

In the case of a CoP infringement over the internet, the rightsholder can claim protection before the court of the defendant's domicile or before the courts of the place of the event giving rise to the damage. In both cases, the plaintiff can request protection for more than one territory, not only for the forum ones. Under this approach, the infringement claim will not be granted unless the rightsholder can establish a sufficient connection between the infringing act and each different territory for applicable law purposes. That 'targeting' connection, in *Football Dataco's* judgement, seems to be weak. The content may be communicated or distributed via Internet platforms and other services in circumstances where it is made available without territorial access restrictions, which neither have any target. Consequently, there is likely no connection with a State other than the availability of the content. In those cases, this approach linked to the traditional mosaic approach would require OCSSPs and other online services to adapt their global services to many different national laws. Pedro de Miguel asserts that "it may result in excessive territorialisation of the Internet and cause significant costs to such intermediaries[69]".

As the mosaic approach is not a suitable solution for dealing with online copyright infringement, and since most communication and distribution of copyrighted works occur over the Internet, it is clear that legislative action is necessary to establish a single law for addressing online copyright infringement cases, at least at EU level.

The ILA Kyoto Guidelines and other projects provide for a single-law approach in the case of ubiquitous infringements. Guideline 26(1) establishes an exception to territoriality for ubiquitous intellectual property infringements by linking them to a single applicable law, advocating for the criterion of the law with an especially close connection. The Guideline 26 states:

> **26. Law Applicable to Ubiquitous or Multi-state Infringements**
> 1. When the infringement in multiple States is pleaded in connection with the use of ubiquitous or multinational media, the court may apply to the infringement as a whole the

---

[66] Article 7(2)(b) od the Database Directive sates that:

> 're-utilization' shall mean any form of making available to the public all or a substantial part of the contents of a database by the distribution of copies, by renting, by on-line or other forms of transmission. The first sale of a copy of a database within the Community by the rightholder or with his consent shall exhaust the right to control resale of that copy within the Community;

[67] Lundstedt (2021), p. 405.

[68] CJEU Judgment of 18 October 2012 Football Dataco Ltd and Others v Sportradar GmbH and Sportradar AG., C-173/11, ECLI:EU:C:2012:642. para. 47.

[69] De Miguel Asensio (2020), p. 251.

law or laws of the State(s) having an especially close connection with the global infringement. Relevant factors to determine the applicable law (or laws) in these situations include:

- the place where the harm caused by the infringement is substantial in relation to the infringement in its entirety;
- the parties' habitual residences or principal places of business;
- the place where substantial activities in furthering the infringement have been carried out.[70]

This rule would apply in cases of ubiquitous infringements, usually committed over the Internet. Rita Matulionyte in the commented version of the Kyoto Guidelines explains how such infringements are most frequent in relation to copyright, "which is automatically protected in all Berne Union Member States and is easily infringed in all of these States".[71] Matulionyte explains that the "close connection rule has been chosen as a flexible rule that helps to avoid 'forum shopping' and 'race to the bottom' problems that other more specific rules would cause (such as *lex fori* or *lex loci delicti*)".[72] She also points out that the list of factors that should be considered when determining which law has a sufficiently close connection in 26(1) Guideline is a non-exhaustive list providing the courts with different factors to consider. This close connections approach is limited as in case the dispute involves several States with an equally close connection, Matulionyte clarifies that "several laws might apply to different parts of a multistate infringement".[73]

It needs to be mentioned that the Kyoto guidelines introduce conflict rules relating to collective rights management as international disputes with CMOs are gaining relevance, especially in the field of online use of music and multi-territorial licensing. Guideline 27 deals with CMOs' relationship with (1) rightsholders and (2) users. However, aspects related to CtoP infringements are not governed by Guideline 27(2), as is Guideline 25, which deals with infringements. These two Guidelines are ruled by the *lex loci protectionis* principle, applying to both legal and illegal use of rights. Although this study does not cover the multi-territorial licenses issue, it focuses on CtoP rights; the Kyoto Guideline 27 becomes relevant for disputes based on Article 17(4) of the CDSM Directive. Article 17(4) CDMD obliges OCSSP to make their best efforts to obtain an authorisation license. Thus, if any dispute arises regarding whether an OCSSP has made its best efforts to obtain a license for acts of CtoP, it would fall under the Guideline 27(2) scope. Since Guideline 27(2) also proposes the application of *lex loci protectionis* for licencing disputes, there would be no difference in determining the applicable law between cases of infringements and licensing.

Finally, Fig. 5.4 summarises the different jurisdictions and applicable laws for each type of CtoP infringement. In the case of broadcasting acts, the substantive law determines the criteria for the origin of the actions, as happens with jurisdiction

---

[70] Kono et al. (2021), Kyoto Guidelines, at G-26.

[71] Matulionyte (2021), p. 5.

[72] *Ibid.*

[73] *Ibid,* p. 7.

Act of CtoP	Territorial or ubiquitous action	Jurisdiction Criteria under RBIr	Jurisdiction in CtoP infringements	Applicable law under 8(1) RIIR in CtoP infringements *(lex loci protectionis)*
USER DIRECTLY DISPLAYS CONTENT TO A PUBLIC	Territorial	MS national Law	MS where the work is CtoP, displayed	Not applicable - National Law of the MS
BROADCASTING	Ubiquitous	where the damage occurs (Art. 7.2 RBIr)	Where the broadcast is available	Law of each country for which protection is claimed - Multiple laws
	Territorial	where the event giving rise to the damage occurs (Art. 7.2 RBIr)	Where the signals are introduced in the communication chain (Art. 1(b) S&C) or Broadcaster's establishment (art. 3 - Broadcastes Directive)	Law of the MS of origin of the emission (Art. 1(b) S&C) or
	Territorial	Place of the defendant domicile (Art. 4 RBIr)	Domicile of the Streaming Service Provider	Law of each country for which protection is claimed - Multiple laws
STREAMING	Ubiquitous	where the damage occurs (Art. 7.2 RBIr)	Where the stream is available	Law of the country for which protection is claimed
	Territorial	where the event giving rise to the damage occurs (Art. 7.2 RBIr)	Origin of the Stream	Law of each country for which protection is claimed - Multiple laws
	Territorial	Place of the defendant domicile (Art. 4 RBIr)	Domicile of the Streaming Service Provider	
USER UPLOADS CONTENT ONLINE	Ubiquitous	where the damage occurs (Art. 7.2 RBIr)	Where the content is is available	Law of the country for which protection is claimed
	Territorial	where the event giving rise to the damage occurs (Art. 7.2 RBIr)	Where the upload occurs	Law of each country for which protection is claimed - Multiple laws
	Territorial	Place of the defendant domicile (Art. 4 RBIr)	Domicile of the uploader user	
USER IN THEIR WEBSITE HYPERLINKS TO OTHER WEBSITE'S CONTENT	Ubiquitous	where the damage occurs (Art. 7.2 RBIr)	Where the content is is available	Law of the country for which protection is claimed
	Territorial	where the event giving rise to the damage occurs (Art. 7.2 RBIr)	Where the sharing website is activated	Law of each country for which protection is claimed - Multiple laws
	Territorial	Place of the defendant domicile (Art. 4 RBIr)	Domicile of the uploader user	
OCSSP GIVES THE PUBLIC ACCES TO UPLOADED CONTENTBY USERS	Ubiquitous	where the damage occurs (Art. 7.2 RBIr)	Where the content is is available	Law of the country for which protection is claimed
	Territorial	where the event giving rise to the damage occurs (Art. 7.2 RBIr)	Where the OCSSP has the seat	Law of each country for which protection is claimed - Multiple laws
	Territorial	Place of the defendant domicile (Art. 4 RBIr)	Domicile of the OCSSP: place of statutory seat; central administration; or principal place of business	

Fig. 5.5 Summary of the different jurisdictions and applicable laws in CtoP infringements. Source: Author's elaboration

issues. However, it does not apply to the ancillary online service referred to in the Broadcasters Directive. As Pedro de Miguel assesses in Directive 2019/789:

> The country of origin principle applies exclusively to the relationship between rightsholders or entities representing them and solely for the purpose of the provision of, access to or the use of an ancillary online service. It does not apply to any subsequent communication to the public, making it available to the public or reproduction of the works or other protected subject matter contained in the ancillary online service (Recital 9).[74]

As Fig. 5.5 shows, in cases over the Internet where the jurisdiction is determined by the place where the damages occurred, as the possibility of claiming protection over

[74] De Miguel Asensio (2020), p. 267.

the damages that occurred in other territories is not possible, the corresponding applicable law will be just one; the law country for which protection is claimed. In other cases of disputes on infringements over the Internet, where the jurisdiction has been determined by the MS of the defendant's domicile or by the place where the event giving rise to the damage occurs, different laws will be applicable. Since those jurisdiction criteria give competence to the forum court to rule over all the damages that occurred in other places, the mosaic effect of Article 8(1) RIIR allows the application of the law of each country for which the rightsholder claims protection.

Although CtoP is the copyright's exclusive right that provides the most number of exploitation acts of musical works, basically online, the current EU legal framework does not provide suitable instruments for the enforcement of such right. The current private international rules set at the EU level do not facilitate the enforcement of online infringements of the CtoP right, not when determining the jurisdiction nor when multiple laws are applicable for a single action. Such a situation does not provide an ideal balance between the interests of rightsholders, online services, and users.

5.3 Overview: Need for a Renewal of International Enforcement Rules for Online Infringements

There is a lack of international rules determining the jurisdiction and conflict of laws in the International copyright conventions. Regarding regional regulation, the current legal framework in the EU raises some doubts about effectively enforcing the CtoP right for infringements of such rights when exploiting copyright-protected musical works. This is particularly true in the online domain, where private international law rules hinder the enforcement of CtoP violations by making it challenging to determine jurisdiction and eventually having to apply multiple laws to a single action.

The mosaic effect in current legislation's does not account for the widespread nature of digital reality, resulting in an imbalance between rightsholders acting as plaintiffs and online services and users as defendants. This places rightsholders, again, in a favourable position, now when litigating against OCSSP and users. At this point users, may be even unaware of the liability associated with their actions.

The EU aims to create a legal framework that balances the interests of rightsholders, users, and online service providers. To achieve this goal, the legal framework must include rules for enforcement and substantive rules. Due to the lack of international conflict rules on copyright matters and issues arising from the current EU legislation, various academics[75] have developed soft laws or guidelines. These projects aim to address these negative situations by proposing fairer solutions, such

[75] The Max Planck Group elaborated a project with some proposals for Conflict of Laws in Intellectual Property ('CLIP'), the American Law Institute, and the International Law Association

as establishing an exception to territoriality for ubiquitous intellectual property infringements by linking them to a single applicable law. The law would be determined by the criterion of the law with especially close connections.

The EU legislators could follow these guidelines to adapt the legislation to the digital reality adopt new enforcement rules and provide a fair litigation field for all parties in disputes regarding CtoP online infringements.

References

De Miguel Asensio PA (2015a) El lugar del daño como fundamento de la competencia internacional en los litigios sobre derechos de autor. In: Estudos de direito intelectual em homenagem ao Prof. Doutor José de Oliveira Ascensão: 50 anos de vida universitária. Almedina, Coimbra, p 1067

De Miguel Asensio PA (2015b) La litigación sobre derechos de autor en Internet y la sentencia Hejduk. La Ley Unión Eur, pp 19–22

De Miguel Asensio PA (2020) Conflict of Laws and the Internet, 1st edn. Edward Elgar Publishing

De Miguel Asensio PA (2023) Manual de Derecho de las Nuevas Technologias (Derecho Digital), 1st edn. Aranzadi, Cizur Menor

Kono T, Metzger A, de Miguel Asensio P et al (2021) International Law Association's Guidelines on Intellectual Property and Private International Law (Kyoto Guidelines) with extended comments. J Intellect Prop Inf Technol Electron Commer Law 12:97

Koo J (2020) The right of communication to the public in EU Copyright Law. Hart Publishing

Kur A, Maunsbach U (2019) Choice of law and intellectual property rights. Oslo Law Rev 6:43–61. https://doi.org/10.18261/ISSN.2387-3299-2019-01-07

Lundstedt L (2021) Jurisdiction and choice of law in online copyright cases. Routledge Handb EU Copyr Law :396–412. https://doi.org/10.4324/9781003156277-25

Matulionyte R (2021) Comment on Guideline 26 of International Law Association on Intellectual Property and Private International Law ("Kyoto Guidelines"): Applicable Law. J Intellect Prop Inf Technol Electron Commer Law 12:97

Otero García-Carrión C (2017) Retos para la protección transfronteriz a de los Derechos de propiedad intelectual. In: Serrano Gómez E (ed) Cuestiones de derecho de autor en la Unión Europea. Reus, Madrid, p 173

Torremans P (2014) Intellectual property and the eu rules on private international law: Match or mismatch? In: EU Copyright Law: a commentary. Edward Elgar Publishing, pp 1019–1065

Torremans P (2017) Copyright Jurisdiction under EU Private International Law. In: Torremans P (ed) Research handbook on copyright law, 2nd edn. Edwar Elagar Publishing, p 563

Ubertazzi BCA (2012) Exclusive jurisdiction in intellectual property. Mohr Siebeck

---

Committee on Intellectual Property (ILA) developed in 2021 the 'Guidelines on Intellectual Property in Private International Law', known as *Kyoto Guidelines*.

Chapter 6
A Proposal for a "Streaming Levy" for Communication to the Public Acts of Musical Works Online: Striving for a Fair Balance

During the previous chapters some suggestions have been made to improve the EU copyright protection system and more specifically, the communication to the public right. Some of those aforementioned proposals are introducing a single Copyright title in the EU, which would simplify many aspects of copyright. Another suggestion that was mentioned is to reformulate the international private law rules to make the enforcement of online infringement simpler.

However, to introduce these improvements and propose further recommendations, it is essential to have a clear understanding of the concept of Communication to the Public (CtoP). As none of the legislative instruments within the EU copyright acquis provides a clear and comprehensive definition of CtoP, this study draws upon both the fragmented legislative provisions and the interpretative approach developed through CJEU jurisprudence. Based on this combined analysis, the study proposes the following comprehensive definition of Communication to the Public.

> There is an act of Communication to the public when individuals or entities transmit a work or make it available via wire or wireless means to an indeterminate and relatively large group of people who are not present at the place where the communication originated. Such transmission or availability of works must be performed with the active role of those communicating individuals or entities. When considering an act of Communication to the public, it is important to consider whether the communicating individuals or entities have full knowledge of the consequences of their actions and if they have ensured that their acts are legal, especially if the communications lead to a profit-making nature.

As previous chapters in this book shown, with the current EU copyright legislation there is not an equal scenario for the main actors on the scenario of communication to the public of online musical works. So it is important to find ways to strive for a fair balance between rightsholders, online music services and users.

Communication to the public right nowadays is essential for the music business. According to the data presented by the last IFPI's Global Report (Engaging with Music 2022), a significant majority of music consumption, around 81%, is attributed

L. Ballesta Martí, *The Communication to the Public of Musical Works Online in the European Union's Legislation*, Law, Governance and Technology Series 75,
https://doi.org/10.1007/978-3-031-94132-0_6

to the communication of music to the public. Furthermore, it is significant that more than 80% of this communication occurs online.

These data indicate that the primary source of income for exploiting music works comes from CtoP right. Such income is mainly the licence fees paid by the parties that perform the communication acts, mainly broadcasters, streaming music services, social media, and OCSSPs. All those services are led to private users, who cannot use such streaming services for commercial purposes.

According to a 2018 study conducted by Nielsen, most small business owners worldwide illegally streamed music in their shops without obtaining a business streaming license. The study found that only 17% of the surveyed small business owners had a license to stream music on their premises, while the remaining 83% did not follow copyright laws and instead used personal streaming services to play music in their businesses.[1]

Using a personal music account to display background music in an establishment open to the public constitutes an infringement of the CtoP right in two stages. In the first stage, music service providers can offer services on a business-to-business or business-to-consumer basis. The music service obtains from rightsholders a different license depending on the type of service they offer. Hence, music creators should receive fair compensation when their work is intended to be used for commercial purposes. When the music work is going to be communicated to the public, music service providers pay a higher fee for a licence to run their service. Most personal streaming services prohibit commercial use of their content in their Terms of Use. Such services are designed solely for personal use and not for business establishments. This is because using personal music services in commercial settings results in lower earnings for the rightsholders. However, these terms are often ignored or not carefully read by users.

In the second stage, small business owners must obtain appropriate licenses to use music as background music in their commercial establishments. Hence, they communicate music to the public, despite the music being displayed directly from a CD, the radio or by personal or commercial streaming services. It is irrelevant that the establishment owner is paying for the streaming services because the payment is for the services received but not for the CtoP license. Such a license is independent of the one paid by the music service.

In their study, Nielsen found that by 2018, about 21.3 million businesses were using personal streaming services globally. They estimated that rightsholders could forfeit a total of $2.65 billion annually. That results in an average of $11.96/month. This is lost for every business that uses a free personal music service, and an average of $8.33/month. This is lost for every business that pays for a personal music service. The enforcement of copyright infringements is difficult for rightsholders to control and enforce, and for small users who cannot afford the consequences of such infringement.

[1] Nielsen Music (2018)

However, the Study also shows that the majority of business proprietors hold the incorrect belief that a personal music account confers upon them the right to use it as background music within their commercial establishment, but that is not the case. Most believe that paying services includes all the fees for communicating with the public. What is not indicated in the report is the cost for small businesses of using background music. In many cases, background music does not significantly impact the core business. This is because music does not generate significant profit for the owner. The question is if those small businesses must bear the payment for CtoP right. To answer this question, there are two relevant criteria the CJEU developed to determine the existence of an act of CtoP: the profit-making nature of the act and the notion of "public."

Regarding the profit-making nature of an act of communication to the public, the court stated that "it may be a relevant but not a necessary criterion".[2] In the Premier League judgement, the Court referred to acts of CtoP with indirect profit-making as those in which the "transmission in question has an effect upon the number of people going to [an] establishment and, ultimately, on its financial results[3]". In the Reha Training case, the Court explained that the act of communication carries a profit-making nature when the communication is a supply of additional services, different from the main activity of the communicating user, and it has an impact on the establishment's standing and attractiveness, thereby giving it a competitive advantage.[4] That means that the act of communication needs to have an attractive effect on the people when choosing one establishment or another, which is that the background music is an added value for the customers.

The CJEU ruling in the del Corso case clarified the criteria for determining what constitutes "public" in music broadcasting. According to the ruling, if the listeners are a specific group of people who form a definite circle of potential recipients, then broadcasting the music cannot be considered an act of communication to the public.[5] The Court, in the SGAE judgement, defined the term 'public' as "an indeterminate number of potential listeners " and "a fairly large number of persons".[6] Additionally, the Court defines the public, which is the subject of the communication in these establishments, as not merely 'caught' by chance but is targeted by their operators.[7] That means the CJEU requires that persons with 'accidental' access' to the Works may not be considered 'public'. However, the court states that it has to be considered "the cumulative effect of making works available to the potential audience" as it is relevant to know how many persons have access to the same work at the same time but also to know how many of them have access to it in succession.

[2]CJUE Judgement of 15 March 2012, SCF v Del Corso, C-135/10, ECLI:EU:C:2012:140.

[3]CJEU Judgment of 4 October 2011.Premier League, C-403/08, ECLI:EU:C:2011:631.

[4]CJEU Judgment of 31 May 2016, Reha Training, C-117/15, ECLI:EU:C:2016:379.

[5]CJUE Judgement of 15 March 2012 SCF v Del Corso, C-135/10, ECLI:EU:C:2012:140.

[6]CJUE Judgement SGAE v Rafael Hotels, C-306/05, ECLI:EU:C:2006:764, para. 37 and 38.

[7]CJUE Judgement Reha Training, C-117/15, ECLI:EU:C:2016:379., and SCF v Del Corso, C-135/10, ECLI:EU:C:2012:140. para. 48.

Article 17(2) CDSM Directive establishes that for users who upload content to online content-sharing platforms, their act of making available to the public is covered by the authorisation obtained by the OCSSP, as long as those users "are not acting on a commercial basis or where their activity does not generate significant revenues". This provision puts the burden of the rightsholders' authorisation on the service provider, liberating the user of the hassle of obtaining a license and consequently balancing the interests of users, services and rightsholders.

Reflecting on such a solution for users of content-sharing services and considering the criteria of the CJEU on concepts of "public and making profit", this study proposes different solutions for balancing the interest of small establishments as users of musical works.

This possible solution requires that the establishment using background music should have a low-medium capacity, and its business shouldn't be related to music nor getting significant revenues from it, which means that such music does not represent an added value to the business other than avoiding a silent environment,

The first solution is that in such cases, small establishments should not be considered as performing an act of communication to the public, or at least such an act should not be liable because they do not fulfil the jurisprudential criteria of making profit and public. This is a risky situation for those small businesses under the current legislation. To grant them a safeguard, the EU should set up a new mandatory legal exception to the CtoP right. This situation is similar to the provision discussed in the WTO Dispute DS160. In that case, Section 110(5) of the US Copyright Act permits, under certain conditions, the playing of radio and television music in public places (bars, shops, restaurants, etc.) without paying a royalty fee. This study proposes the same exception for small establishments that fulfil specific requirements.

The second proposed solution mirrors Article 17(2) and adapts to offline music communication. In this case, when those small establishments use streaming on-demand or other online music services, the licence that those services must obtain for running their business covers the communication to the public acts as if they were individual private users. It is true that this would not redress the aforementioned economic loss for rightsholders and may result in a rise in the price of streaming services or even that some free-of-payment or add-on services would become subscriber-based. To address this possible economic obstacle, this study proposes to create a "streaming leavy" system similar to the existing levy systems regarding reproduction rights. In this case, all streaming services' users should indirectly pay a nearly insignificant amount for the "streaming leavy" for small acts of communication to the public. Streaming services should add this amount to the regular fee paid for their services and then relocate the amount collected to the CMO's. CMO's then share the among the music creators to compensate for the loss of excluding the aforementioned small establishments to pay for acts of communication to the public. This system of indirect levies is not intended to be a tax to be paid by the streaming services but by all the end users. The role of streamlining services is to collect the money from users and pay CMO's as an added rate to their corresponding royalty settlement. This indirect system of levies excludes any taxation on the streaming services revenue, avoiding that such a taxation rate intended to be paid by the streaming services turns into a disproportionate rise of the fees paid by users. This levy system is intended to be paid by the users collectively. It just takes a small amount from the millions of users to go directly to creators' pockets, to compensate for those small businesses CtoP acts. In other words, the share corresponding to the communication to the public of music works in small establishments is shared by the users of streaming services in solidarity. The amount that should be paid by those small entrepreneurs, which may significant a disproportionate amount of money for them, represents a very small amount for users collectively.

Conversely the term "streaming levy" has been used to refer to the taxation measures that are aimed to target the revenues of music streaming services. Last year 2024, France and Canada introduced those measures, know as "streaming levy", but with a different nature form the proposed on. In fact those measures are indeed a "streaming tax".

At the beginning of 2024 the tax on music streaming services came into effect in France. This tax was initially set at 1.75% of a streaming service's total revenue, but the rate was subsequently reduced to 1.2%. Payers of the tax are legal persons, whether based in France or not, who engage in the rental of, and collect revenues from, recorded music or music videos owned by legal persons based in France. This tax applies to major platforms such as Spotify, Deezer, Apple Music, and YouTube Music, encompassing both subscription-based and advertisement-generated revenues. The primary objective of this measure is to provide financial support to the *Centre National de la Musique (CNM)*,[8] a quasi-governmental organization that administers various programs aimed at fostering music creation in France. Although a portion of the funds generated by this tax is to be allocated to independent music retailers, the policy is predominantly framed as a strategic investment in national music culture.

Unlike France's taxation policy, Canada has taken a significantly more aggressive approach. On June 4, 2024, as part of the broader implementation of Canada's Online Streaming Act, the Canadian Radio-television and Telecommunications Commission (CRTC) declared its decision to require online music streaming platforms unaffiliated with a Canadian broadcaster and generating at least 25 million Canadian dollars in annual revenue to pay 5% of their earnings as a "base contribution." The funds collected through this measure are designated to promote Canadian and Indigenous content. Big streaming platforms, Spotify, Apple and Amazon, took legal action against Canada's new 5% streaming tax before Canada's Federal Court of Appeal. The platforms argue it's "unsustainable" for them and it will force them to

---

[8] See https://cnm.fr/ or https://cnm.fr/wp-content/uploads/2024/09/taxe-streaming-presentation-version-UK.pdf

raise their prices, affecting users pockets, who would ultimately bear the cost of the tax.

This Canadian measure has been reported under the name "streaming levy" to the European Commission's Directorate-General for Trade, for potential affection to the EU exports to non-EU countries, for being considered a "Trade Barrier".[9]

According the journal Music Business Worldwide, the taxation of music streaming services presents a complex challenge, given that the industry operates on a low-margin business model and remains largely dependent on digital service providers for content distribution. Music streaming platforms typically allocate more than 60% of their revenue to royalty payments to rights holders while simultaneously adhering to existing value-added tax and sales tax obligations in various jurisdictions.[10]

All this taxation measures are different from the "streaming levy" proposed in this study, since this is not aimed at charging companies, but an indirect system to remunerate creators in fairer way and based on users' solidarity.

6.1 Final Overview: Striving for a Fair Balance

The European Union, through its latest copyright reform, aimed to create a fairer playing field for copyright stakeholders, particularly for creators. Despite the intention of adapting the rules to the new digital and global landscape and protecting the interests of rightsholders, the outcome is not as equitable as it should be for all stakeholders. Instead, it has resulted in an unbalanced system that favors the music industry while placing users and independent music creators in a secondary position.

In practice, the music industry is increasingly reliant on data-driven rights management, which is reshaping how the communication to the public right is enforced, managed, and allocated in the digital economy. With the rise of on-demand streaming platforms, social media music integration, and AI-generated playlists, rightsholders are investing in metadata optimization, machine learning algorithms, and real-time tracking systems to ensure they receive fair compensation.

For example, collective management organizations (CMOs) such as SoundExchange provide enhanced digital tracking, ensuring the identification and monetization of even the smallest revenue-generating uses, such as a song playing in the background of a TikTok video or a DJ mix streamed on SoundCloud. Companies like Spotify and Apple Music offer analytics tools that enable rightsholders to

[9] See the report at The Single Entry Point is of the European Commission's Directorate-General for Trade. https://trade.ec.europa.eu/access-to-markets/en/barriers/details?barrier_id=18262&sps=false

[10] Tencer, Daniel. 2024. «What's behind France and Canada's Music Streaming Taxes, and Where Could They Happen next (Hint: The USA?)». Music Business Worldwide, 13 June 2024. https://www.musicbusinessworldwide.com/whats-behind-france-and-canadas-music-streaming-taxes-and-where-might-they-happen-next-hint-the-usa1/

monitor audience engagement, geographic consumption trends, and playlist placements, helping them negotiate better licensing deals with digital platforms. However, the central competition remains between the music industry and platforms, once again sidelining creators and users.

Despite the industry's movement toward greater automation, transparency, and global licensing efficiencies, the communication to the public right will remain a fundamental pillar of the digital music economy. However, continuous technological advancements do not necessarily resolve the issues of effective enforcement and fair remuneration for authors and artists, particularly independent or emerging creators.

While communication to the public rights management may be shaped by innovations such as data-driven royalty allocation, blockchain-backed transparency mechanisms, and AI-powered content monitoring, stronger cross-border mechanisms are essential. A unified copyright system and legal framework at the European Union level could lead to a more efficient and equitable management of the communication to the public right.

In this evolving landscape, record labels, publishers, and CMOs are the rightsholders actively securing their interests, but they cannot be solely responsible for maintaining a fair and sustainable music ecosystem. Achieving this requires an adequate legal framework that reflects the digital realities of communicating musical works to the public while ensuring a more balanced system. A system designed to equitably address the interests of users, content creators, digital platforms, and the music industry.

References

Nielsen Music (2018) The hidden value in music for business. Nielsen Music

Tencer D (2024) What's behind France and Canada's music streaming taxes, and where could they happen next (Hint: The USA?). Music Business Worldwide, 13 June 2024. https://www.musicbusinessworldwide.com/whats-behind-france-and-canadas-music-streaming-taxes-and-where-might-they-happen-next-hint-the-usa1/

Legislation

International Legislation

Berne Convention for the Protection of Literary and Artistic Works. Done at Berne on 9 September 1886. (Last revised; amended on September 28, 1979), UNTS Volume Number 828 (p. 221).

Brussels Convention Relating to the Distribution of Programme-Carrying Signals Transmitted by Satellite, Done at Brussels on May 21, 1974, UNTS Volume Number 1144 (p. 3).

Buenos Aires Convention on Literary and Artistic Copyright, signed in Buenos Aires on August 11, 1910, A-16.

Convention for the Protection of Producers of Phonograms Against Unauthorized Duplication of Their Phonograms, adopted at Geneva on October 29, 1971, UNTS Volumen Number 866 (p. 67).

Convention on Jurisdiction, Recognition and Enforcement of Judicial Decisions in Civil and Commercial Matters, signed in Lugano in 2007.

Inter-American Convention on the rights of the author in literary, scientific and artistic works. Concluded at Washington on 22 June 1946, B-28.

International Convention for the Protection of Performers, Producers of Phonograms and Broadcasting Organisations. Done at Rome on October 26, 1961, UNTS, Volume Number 496 (p. 43).

Stockholm Act, relating to the revision of the Berne Convention Protocol Regarding Developing Countries, revised at Stockholm on July 14, 1967, UNTS Volume Number 1161 (p. 3).

Universal Copyright Convention. Adopted at Geneva on September 6, 1952. (Last revised at Paris on July 24, 1971), UNTS Volume Number 216 (p. 132).

WIPO Marrakesh Treaty to Facilitate Access to Published Works for Persons Who Are Blind, Visually Impaired or Otherwise Print Disabled (2013)

L. Ballesta Martí, *The Communication to the Public of Musical Works Online in the European Union's Legislation*, Law, Governance and Technology Series 75, https://doi.org/10.1007/978-3-031-94132-0

WIPO Copyright Treaty (WCT), adopted in Geneva on December 20, 1996, UNTS Volume Number 2186 (p. 121).

WIPO Performances and Phonograms Treaty (WPPT), adopted in Geneva on December 20, 1996, UNTS Volume Number 2186 (p. 203).

WTO, Agreement on Trade-Related Aspects of Intellectual Property Rights, Apr. 15, 1994, Marrakesh Agreement Establishing the World Trade Organization, Annex 1C, 1869, (1994), UNTS Volume Number 299 (p. 33) I.L.M. 1197.

WTO, Annex 2 of the WTO Agreement - Dispute Settlement Understanding on rules and procedures governing the settlement of disputes (DSU) (1994)

National Legislation

17 Title U.S.Code, U.S. Copyright Act, (1947)

17 Title U.S.Code, Fairness in Music Licensing Act, Pub. (1998)

Canada's Online Streaming Act (Bill C-11), https://www.parl.ca/legisinfo/en/bill/44-1/c-11

European Union Legislation

Council Directive 92/100/EEC of 19 November 1992 on rental right and lending right and on certain rights related to copyright in the field of intellectual property, OJ L 346, 27.11.1992, pp. 61–66

Council Regulation (EC) No 44/2001 of 22 December 2000 on jurisdiction and the recognition and enforcement of judgments in civil and commercial matters OJ L 12, 16.1.2001, pp. 1–23

Council Regulation (EC) No 6/2002 of 12 December 2001 on Community design, OJ L 3, 5.1.2002, pp. 1–24

Council Decision of 27 April 2006, 2006/325/EC: concerning the conclusion of the Agreement between the European Community and the Kingdom of Denmark on jurisdiction and the recognition and enforcement of judgments in civil and commercial matters, OJ L 120, 5.5.2006, pp. 22–22

Council Regulation (EC) No 207/2009 of 26 February 2009 on the Community trade mark, OJ L 78, 24.3.2009, pp. 1–42

Directive 93/83/EEC of of the European Parliament and of the Council of 27 September 1993 on the coordination of certain rules concerning copyright and rights related to copyright applicable to satellite broadcasting and cable retransmission, OJ L 248, 6.10.1993, pp. 15–21

Directive 96/9/EC of the European Parliament and of the Council of 11 March 1996 on the legal protection of databases, OJ L 77, 27.3.1996, pp. 20–28

Directive 2000/31/EC of the European Parliament and of the Council of 8 June 2000 on certain legal aspects of information society services, in particular electronic commerce, in the Internal Market, OJ L 178, 17.7.2000, pp. 1–16

Directive 2001/29/EC of the European Parliament and of the Council of 22 May 2001 on the harmonisation of certain aspects of copyright and related rights in the information society, OJ L 167, 22.6.2001, pp. 10–19

Directive 2001/84/EC of the European Parliament and of the Council of 27 September 2001 on the resale right for the benefit of the author of an original work of art Select: 1 OJ L 272, 13.10.2001, pp. 32–36

Directive 2006/115/EC of the European Parliament and of the Council of 12 December 2006 on rental right and lending right and on certain rights related to copyright in the field of intellectual property (codified version), OJ L 376, 27.12.2006, pp. 28–35

Directive 2006/116/EC of the European Parliament and of the Council of 12 December 2006 on the term of protection of copyright and certain related rights (codified version), OJ L 372, 27.12.2006, pp. 12–18

Directive 2006/123/EC of the European Parliament and of the Council of 12 December 2006 on services in the internal market, OJ L 376, 27.12.2006, pp. 36–68

Directive 2009/24/EC of the European Parliament and of the Council of 23 April 2009 on the legal protection of computer programs (Codified version) OJ L 111, 5.5.2009, pp. 16–22

Directive 2012/28/EU of the European Parliament and of the Council of 25 October 2012 on certain permitted uses of orphan works, OJ L 299, 27.10.2012, pp. 5–12

Directive 2014/26/EU of the European Parliament and of the Council of 26 February 2014 on collective management of copyright and related rights and multi-territorial licensing of rights in musical works for online use in the internal market. (2018). OJ L 84, 20.3.2014, pp. 72–98

Directive (EU) 2017/1564 of the European Parliament and of the Council of 13 September 2017 on certain permitted uses of certain works and other subject matter protected by copyright and related rights for the benefit of persons who are blind, visually impaired or otherwise print-disabled and amending Directive 2001/29/EC on the harmonisation of certain aspects of copyright and related rights in the information society, OJ L 242, 20.9.2017, pp. 6–13

Directive (EU) 2019/789 of the European Parliament and of the Council of 17 April 2019 laying down rules on the exercise of copyright and related rights applicable to certain online transmissions of broadcasting organisations and retransmissions of television and radio programmes, and amending Council Directive 93/83/EEC, OJ L 130, 17.5.2019, pp. 82–91

Directive (EU) 2019/790 of the European Parliament and of the Council of 17 April 2019 on copyright and related rights in the Digital Single Market and amending Directives 96/9/EC and 2001/29/EC, OJ L 130, 17.5.2019, pp. 92–125

Regulation (EC) No 864/2007 of the European Parliament and of the Council of 11 July 2007 on the law applicable to non-contractual obligations (Rome II), OJ L 199, 31.7.2007, pp. 40–49

Regulation (EU) No 1215/2012 of the European Parliament and of the Council of 12 December 2012 on jurisdiction and the recognition and enforcement of judgments in civil and commercial matters (recast), OJ L 351, 20.12.2012, pp. 1–32

Regulation (EU) 2017/1563 on the cross-border exchange between the Union and third countries of accessible format copies of certain works and other subject matter protected by copyright and related rights for the benefit of persons who are blind, visually impaired or otherwise print-disabled, OJ L 242, 20.9.2017, pp. 1–5

Case Law

CJEU Judgment of 8 June 1971, *Deutsche Gramophon v. Metro SB, C-78/70, ECLI:EU:C:1971:59*

CJEU Judgment of 26 March 1987, *Commission v. Council (Generalised Tariff Preferences), Case C-45/86,, ECLI:EU:C:1987:163*

CJEU Judgment of 24 January 1989, *EMI Electrola GmbH v Patricia Im- und Export and others, C-341/87, ECLI:EU:C:1989:30*

CJEU Judgement of 30 May 1989, *Commission v Council, C-242/87, ECLI: EU:C:1989:217*

CJEU Judgment of 13 December 1989., *Salvatore Grimaldi v Fonds des maladies professionnelles, Case C-322/88, ECLI:EU:C:1989:646*

CJEU Judgment of 11 June 1991, *Commission v Council ('Titanium dioxide'), C-300/89, ECLI:EU:C:1991:244*

CJEU Judgment of 19 Sep 1995, *Marinari, C-364/93, ECLI:EU:C:1995:289*

CJEU Judgement of 12 July 2011, *L'Oreal v eBay, Case C-324/09, ECLI:EU:C:2011:474*

CJEU Judgment of 7 Dec 2006, *SGAE v Rafael Hotels, C-306/05, ECLI:EU:C:2006:764*

CJEU Judgment of 4 Oct 2011, *Premier League, C-403/08, ECLI:EU:C:2011:631*

CJEU Judgment of 24 Nov 2011, *Circul Globus, C-283/10, ECLI:EU:C:2011:772*

CJEU Judgment of 15 March 2012, *SCF v Del Corso, C-135/10, ECLI:EU:C:2012:140*

CJEU Judgment of 15 March 2012, *Phonographic Performance (Ireland), C-162/10, ECLI:EU:C:2012:141*

CJEU Juclgment of 19 April 2012, *Wintersteiger, C-523/10, ECLI:EU:C:2012:220*

CJEU Judgement of 18 October 2012, *Football Dataco Ltd and Others v Sportradar GmbH and Sportradar AG., C-173/11, ECLI:EU:C:2012:642*

CJEU Judgment of 7 Mar 2013, *TVCatchup, C-607/11, ECLI:EU:C:2013:147*

L. Ballesta Martí, *The Communication to the Public of Musical Works Online in the European Union's Legislation*, Law, Governance and Technology Series 75,
https://doi.org/10.1007/978-3-031-94132-0

CJEU Judgment of 3 Oct 2013, *Case C-170/12, Peter Pinckney v KDG Mediatech AG. ECLI:EU:C:2013:635*

CJEU Judgment of 13 Feb 2014, *Svensson, C-466/12, ECLI:EU:C:2014:76*

CJEU, Judgement of 22 January 2015, *C-441/13, Hejduk, ECLI:EU:C:2015:28*

CJEU Judgment of 31 May 2016, *Reha Training, C-117/15, ECLI:EU:C:2016:379*

CJEU Judgment of 8 Sep 2016, *GS Media, C-160/15, ECLI:EU:C:2016:644*

CJEU Judgment of 16 Feb 2017, *Verwertungsgesellschaft Rundfunk, C-641/15, ECLI:EU:C:2017:131*

CJEU Judgment of 26 Apr 2017, *Filmspeler, C-527/15, ECLI:EU:C:2017:300*

CJEU Judgment of 14 Jun 2017, *Ziggo, C-610/15, ECLI:EU:C:2017:456*

CJEU Judgment of 19 Dec 2019, *Tom Kabinet, C-263/18, ECLI:EU:C:2019:1111.*

CJEU Judgment of 2 April 2020, *Stim and SAMI,C-753/18, ECLI:EU:C:2020:268*

CJEU Judgment of 9 Mar 2021, VG Bild-Kunst, C-392/19, ECLI:EU:C:2021:181

CJEU Judgment of 22 Jun 2021, *YouTube/Cyando C-682/18, ECLI:EU:C:2021:503*

CJEU Judgement of 26 April 2022, *Republic of Poland v European Parliament and Council of the European Union, Case C-401/19, ECLI:EU:C:2022:297*

CJEU Judgment of 20 June 2024, GEMA, C-135/23, ECLI:EU:C:2024:526

Opinion of Advocate General Szpunar, *delivered on 10 September 2021 on Case C-392/19 VG Bild-Kunst v Stiftung Preußischer Kulturbesitz, ECLI:EU:C:2020:696*

Opinion of Advocate General Saugmandsgaard Øe, *delivered on 16 July 2020 on Joined Cases C-682/18 and C-683/18. ECLI:EU:C:2020:586*

Institutional Documents

Commission of the European Communities, *Staff Working Document 'Better Regulation Guidelines'*, SWD(2015) 111 final, 19 May 2015.

Commission of the European Communities., *Green Paper on Copyright and the Challenge of Technology: Copyright Issues Requiring Immediate Action, COM (88)172, final, 7 June 1988.*

Committee on Legal Affairs, *Opinion on the Legal Basis of on the Proposal for a Directive on Copyright in Digital Single Market*, 19 December 2018.

Committee on Legal Affairs, *Opinion on the Legal Basis of the Proposal for a Directive of the European Parliament and of the Council Laying down Rules on the Exercise of Copyright and Related Rights Applicable to Certain Online Transmissions of Broadcasting Organisations and Retrans*, 24 January 2019.

Committee on Legal Affairs of the European Parliament, *Report - A8-0245/2018 on the Proposal for a Directive of the European Parliament and of the Council on Copyright in the Digital Single Market* (2018).

Council of the European Union, *Proposal for a Directive of the European Parliament and of the Council on Copyright in the Digital Single Market—Agreed Negotiating Mandate (25.05.2018), Interinstitutional File: 2016/0280 (COD), 9134/18.*

European Commission, Communication, *A Single Market for Intellectual Property Rights Boosting Creativity and Innovation to Provide Economic Growth, High Quality Jobs and First Class Products and Services in Europe*, COM(2011) 287 final, 24 May 2011.

European Commission, *Commission Recommendation 2005/737/EC of 18 May on Collective Cross-Border Management of Copyright and Related Rights for Legitimate Online Music Services*, OJ L 276, 21.10.2005, pp. 54–57

European Commission, *Communication from the Commission to the Council, the European Parliament and the European Economic and Social - Committee The*

L. Ballesta Martí, *The Communication to the Public of Musical Works Online in the European Union's Legislation*, Law, Governance and Technology Series 75,
https://doi.org/10.1007/978-3-031-94132-0

Management of Copyright and Related Rights in the Internal Market, 16 April 2004, COM/2004/0261 final.

European Commission, *Communication from the Commission to the European Parliament, the Council, the European Economic and Social Committee and the Committee of the Regions - A Digital Single Market Strategy for Europe*, COM(2015) 100 final.

European Commission, *Communication from the Commission to the European Parliament and the Council 'Guidance on Article 17 of Directive 2019/790 on Copyright in the Digital Single Market', COM(2021) 288 final.*

European Commission, *Green Paper - Copyright in the Knowledge Economy*, COM (2008) 466 final.

European Commission, *Impact Assessment on the Modernisation of EU Copyright Rules*, SWD(2016) 301 final.

European Commission, *Proposal for a Directive of the European Parliament and of the Council on Copyright in the Digital Single Market. COM/2016/0593 final - 2016/0280 (COD),* 14 September 2016.

European Commission, *Proposal for a Regulation of the European Parliament and of the Council Laying down Rules on the Exercise of Copyright and Related Rights Applicable to Certain Online Transmissions of Broadcasting Organisations and Retransmissions of Television and Radio*, COM (2016) 594 final, 14 September 2016.

The manufacturer's authorised representative in the EU is Springer Nature Customer Service Centre GmbH, Europaplatz 3, 69115 Heidelberg, Germany. If you have any concerns regarding our products, please contact ProductSafety@springernature.com

Printed and bound by CPI Group (UK) Ltd, Croydon, CR0 4YY
30/09/2026
02225572-0002